REBELS AGAINST THE FUTURE

KIRKPATRICK SALE

REBELS AGAINST THE FUTURE

KIRKPATRICK SALE

The Luddites and their War on the Industrial Revolution

LESSONS

FOR

THE

COMPUTER

AGE

Q QUARTET BOOKS

First published in Great Britian by Quartet Books Limited 1996

A member of the Namara Group

27 Goodge Street

London

W1P 2LD

First published in the United States of America by Addison Wesley 1995

A catalogue record for this book is available from the British Library

ISBN 0 7043 8007 2

Printed and bound in Finland by WSOY

I have been reading predictions of the future by those who believe they can predict what the world of tomorrow is going to be like. In all cases, the future of which they speak is merely a grotesque extension of the present—simply more and more loading of our environment with the waste production of an industrial civilization. In my opinion, there is no chance of solving the problem of pollution—or the other threats to human life—if we accept the idea that technology is to rule our future.

—René Dubos,
    New York Times, 1982

Your real enemy—one you can neither fight nor reason with . . . it's not a "who." What you're up against is the Future.

—Daddy Warbucks, to workers
    losing their jobs to automation,
    "Little Orphan Annie," 1982

Contents

Author's Note   xi

Introduction   1

1   "With Hatchet, Pike, and Gun"   7

2   The First Industrial Revolution   25

3   The Luddites: *November–December 1811*   61

4   The Luddites: *January–April 1812*   91

5   The Luddites: *April–May 1812*   125

6   The Luddites: *May 1812–January 1813*   153

7   The Luddites: *1813–...*   187

8   The Second Industrial Revolution   205

9   The Neo-Luddites   237

10   Lessons from the Luddites   261

Timeline   281

Acknowledgments   285

Source Notes   287

Index   311

Author's Note

IT IS APPROPRIATE to declare, as I think will become obvious in the pages that follow, that I share some affinity for the ideas and passions that motivated the subjects of this book, particularly their abiding sense that a world dominated by the technologies of industrial society is fundamentally more detrimental than beneficial to human happiness and survival.

But it is clear I have not etched this argument on clay tablets with a stick; I have used a typewriter to compose it and submitted it to a publisher who has used (among much else) wordprocessing and photocomposition to get it out. That is not a contradiction: the question is not whether one uses or abstains from technology—all societies since the earliest have used tools, and speech itself was one of the first technologies—but whether, taken in the broadest context and longest run, that technology is benign or malevolent, to the user, to the community around, to the culture, to the environment, to the future. Even the Luddites were opposed not to all technology, as is sometimes assumed, but rather, as one of their letters put it, to "Machinery hurtful to Commonality"—and to their future. The book, even if produced by means not entirely neutral and untainted, is on the whole an artifact more benign than not, more helpful to commonality than not, with effects generally well understood over the course of centuries, and I suspect that within its multipaginated embrace lies much of the wisdom that will enable us, if anything will, to survive as a sentient species.

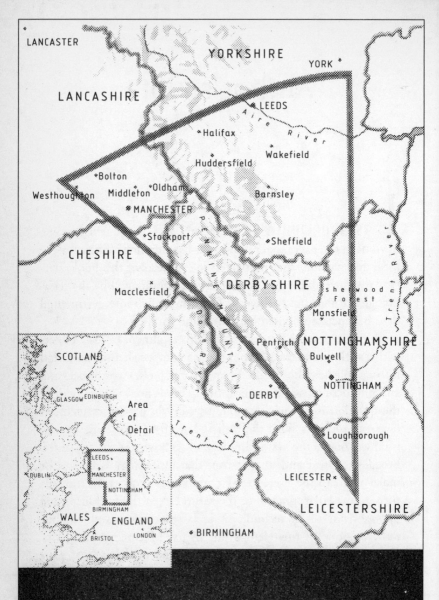

THE LUDDITE TRIANGLE

Introduction

WITHIN THE FIVE counties that form the heart of Britain—Yorkshire, Lancashire, Cheshire, Derbyshire, and Nottinghamshire—lies a triangular area that is haunted to this day by the legend of Robin Hood. Bounded on the north by the Ribble and the Aire, on the south by the Trent, and on the west by the Dove, straddling the lower Pennine Chain that is England's backbone, this triangle embraces all the historic sites associated with the real Robin Hood—or rather the real Robin Hood*s*, since the legend seems to have grown up around at least two (and possibly more) historic figures of the 13th and 14th centuries. Toward the north is the town of Wakefield, on the edge of the Barnsdale Forest in western Yorkshire, where a Robin Hood (or Robert Hode) is thought to have been born, the son of a forester, in the late 13th-century; Clitheroe, in Lancaster to the west, is where he joined with Thomas, Earl of Lancaster, in one of those regular baronial battles against the king; Sherwood Forest, once covering most of the west of Nottinghamshire, is where one of the figures made a spotty living as the head of a band of poachers and highwaymen perhaps early in the 14th century; and Kirklees Priory, not far from Wakefield, is where the supposed burial place of an early 13th-century Robin Hood is marked by a stone, with an inscription dated 1247 but clearly of much later origin.

It is probable that one of the real figures at the center of the legend was the victim of an early industrial policy of the rising English monarchy to encourage a native wool industry by transforming some of the commonly held central forests into private grazing lands for sheep, and his troubles with the Sheriff of Nottingham no doubt stemmed from a clash between his desire to keep on using the woods for food and fuel, as his father and forefathers had before him, and the royal policy (proclaimed in 1217–18) of cutting them down for pasturage. This conflict between old and new, custom and commerce, was dramatic enough to fix itself in the stories of the locals, take life in several early narrative poems (most effectively in the *Lytell Geste of Robyn Hode* of 1495), and eventually be resurrected by several early 19th-century Romantic novelists (notably Scott, in *Ivanhoe*), from where it passes into modern films and fables. And it is commemorated to this day in a dozen tourist sites in the triangle, from "Friar Tuck's Well" outside Mansfield, Nottinghamshire, where Robin fought the duel that began his merry band, to "Robin Hood's Bed" on Blackstone Edge in the Pennines of Lancashire, where the company was said to have lived for years distributing the fruits of the land.

But for all the enduring resonance of this tale, in historical fact it was the royal policy of clear-cutting and wool manufacturing over the forest commons that prevailed. The heartland forests were enclosed and harvested, laid bare for grazing, and within a few centuries nothing much was left of either the great Barnsdale or Sherwood forests but a few scattered clusters of conifers and a few stately oaks in tracts deemed unsuitable for development; wool weaving became the key industry of England and woolen cloth for centuries its most important export, an enterprise nurtured and protected by a succession of kings and parliaments down to the 19th century. Robin Hood's name may have lasted, and a legend about heroic commoners resisting the noble and the powerful may have become burnished by time, but in truth it was not the practice of robbing from the rich, nor the benefaction of the poor, that became the principle means of enterprise in middle England.

It is fitting, and perhaps not accidental, that this triangle of central Britain, seven centuries after it immortalized Robin Hood, was precisely the site of the risings of the Luddites.

The Luddites—many of them weavers and combers and dressers of wool, but many of them artisans in the cotton trades that became increasingly important at the end of the 18th century— were, like Robin's Merry Men, victims of progress, or what was held to be progress. Having for centuries worked out of their cottages and small village shops on machines that, though far from simple, could be managed by a single person, assisted perhaps by children, they suddenly saw new, complex, large-scale machines coming into their settled trades, or threatening to, usually housed in the huge multistory buildings rising in their ancient valleys. Worse still, they saw their ordered society of craft and custom and community begin to give way to an intruding industrial society and its new technologies and systems, new principles of merchandise and markets, new configurations of countryside and city, beyond their ken or control. And when they rose up against this, for fifteen tempestuous months at the start of the second decade of the 19th century, they did so with more ferocity and intensity than anything Robin Hood ever mustered, and were put down with far more force than anything King John ever commanded.

The Luddites took their name from a mythical Ned Ludd— whose origins are still obscure, of which more later—but they were conscious throughout that they were traveling on ground trod by an earlier set of courageous troublemakers; one of the earliest Luddite letters was posted from "Robin Hood's Cave," another was said to have come from "Ned Ludd's office, Sherwood Forest," and a Luddite song that found its way into the Home Office records begins:

Chant no more your old rhymes about bold Robin Hood,
His feats I but little admire,
I will sing the Atchievements of General Ludd
Now the Hero of Nottinghamshire.

Indeed, the Luddites were for a while real heroes in Nottinghamshire—and the other heartland shires, too—and, if measured by their deeds as well as their impact on the psyche of a nation, should be as well remembered today, as celebrated in myth and movie, as the earlier Sherwood heroes: they represented something quite new in English history and, for the economic and political establishments (what William Cobbett, the voluble reformer, was at the time calling "the Thing"), something quite ominous. For one thing, the various Luddite armies that operated in 1811 and 1812 were so carefully organized and disciplined and so effective in their attacks, causing damage to machines and property that amounted to more than £100,000, that they seemed a strong and highly threatening movement of a kind Britain had not known before—of "a character of daring and ferocity," the *Annual Register* for 1812 said, "unprecedented among the lower classes in this country." Then, too, they had enough popular support in the manufacturing districts to be able to carry on their secret, illegal activities for months on end without being betrayed, despite official bribes and threats, nighttime arrests, and interrogations, suggesting to certain minds at least that they were only the most visible part of a very widespread insurrectionary—possibly revolutionary—tendency in the land. Moreover, their threat to the established order, both real and exaggerated, called forth the greatest spasm of repression Britain ever in its history used against domestic dissent, including batteries of spies and special constables, volunteer militias and posses, midnight raids, hanging judges, harsh punishments, and a force of soldiers stationed in the troubled regions greater even than that which had sailed to Portugal with Wellington to fight Napoleon's armies four years before.

Last, and perhaps most important, the Luddites were understood to represent not merely a threat to order, as riotous mobs or revolutionary plotters of the past, but, in some way not always articulated, to industrial progress itself. They were rebels of a unique kind, rebels against the future that was being assigned to them by the new political economy then taking hold in Britain, in which it was argued that those who controlled capital were able to do almost anything they wished, encouraged and protected by government and king, without much in the way of laws or ethics or customs to restrain them. The real challenge of the Luddites was not so much the physical one, against the machines and manufacturers, but a moral one, calling into question on grounds of justice and fairness the underlying assumptions of this political economy and the legitimacy of the principles of unrestrained profit and competition and innovation at its heart. Which is why the architects and beneficiaries of the new industrialism knew that it was imperative to subdue that challenge, to try to deny and expunge its premises of ancient rights and traditional mores, if the labor force were to be made sufficiently malleable, and the new terms of employment sufficiently fixed, to allow what we now call the Industrial Revolution to triumph unimpeded.

That is why, although machine breaking to express on-the-job grievances had been a part of English industrial protest since the late 17th century, this form of it, directed at the machines themselves as symbolic artifacts of a feared technology, was fixed in British consciousness right at the start of the modern transformation. That is why the name Luddite, with all of the symbols and ideas that it calls up, has remained as indelibly a part of the language as the name of another group of English dissenters, the Puritans, in all the long time since.

In a novel called *Ben o' Bill's, the Luddite*—the title refers to Ben Bamforth, son of Bill Bamforth, such appellations being common in an England where the range of boys' names was

unimaginatively small*—two Yorkshire historians of the late
19th century constructed the most intimate tale we have of what a
Luddite might have thought and done, on the basis of records
and conversations with a surviving participant. "It hurts me
sore," says Ben in his old age, "that folk in these days should so
little understand the doings of us Luddites."

It was to remedy this, to try to give them a place alongside
Robin Hood's famous band by showing the flesh of deed and the
bone of purpose that go with the meager word "Luddite"—and
now, when we need it—that this story of the Luddites, in all its
rich detail, has been told.

---

* In the little town of Huddersfield, Yorkshire, with a population of only ten thousand,
out of seventy male baptisms registered between January and June 1812, more than half
used the same three names, Thomas, John, and William.

1

"With Hatchet, Pike, and Gun"

IT WAS ABOUT a half hour after midnight on an April Sunday in 1812 that the band of some six score Yorkshiremen finally made their way down the rutted lane that led to a place called Rawfolds Mill, a looming multistory building, protected by a gated wall, housing the hated woolen machines of the hated manufacturer William Cartwright. Ostensibly organized as a military brigade, though bedraggled somewhat now after their hour-long march on a dark and still winter-cold evening, they stood with kerchiefs and coal-blackened faces readying themselves for their attack: in the front several lines of men armed with rudimentary guns and pistols, behind them rows bearing hatchets and the great "Enoch" hammers that blacksmiths used, and to the rear numbers of men with the kind of assorted weapons—mauls, pikes, bludgeons, even stones—an English village would provide.

"Now men, clear the road!"

The order was issued by George Mellor, 24, a wool-cloth finisher—or "cropper," in Yorkshire parlance—a tall, heavyset man with a short brown beard who worked in the shop of John Woods in Huddersfield, about five miles distant. The croppers in this area, probably five thousand of them at this point, were a proud and independent lot, better paid than average but hurting now with the terrible depression in trade that had taken away work from half of them and the wartime inflation that had put everyday foodstuffs out of the reach of all. They knew better than anyone else the significance of the Cartwright mill that was their target this night: behind that gate, behind the whitewashed stone walls of that mill shining in the half-moon's light, were fifty wool-finishing machines, "shearing frames" run effortlessly by the waterpower of the stream alongside, each one of which could do the work of four or five croppers, the whole assemblage capable of doing several hundred Mellors out of their livelihoods forever. Not only that, but there were at least a half dozen similar mills operating at scattered places in this western section of Yorkshire, some even using the new Watt steam engines for power, and more than a thousand shearing frames at work throughout England since government restrictions against them had been lifted three years before. Behind that gate, too, in his little counting-house at the end of the mill, was the odious Mr. Cartwright, an aloof sort of man in his thirties, with dark eyes in a pale face, a stranger to the county and a teetotaler—"more of a foreigner nor an Englishman," they said around—who was known to be so adamant in the defense of his new finishing machines that he had slept in his mill every night for the last six weeks.

But the croppers were not the only ones to understand this Rawfords Mill as a menace: in that angry crowd were wool weavers and combers and blacksmiths, too, fearful not just of their own displacement by machine and mill—nearly three hundred textile factories had arisen in Yorkshire in just the last twenty-odd years, eliminating handcrafting from many trades, and who knew how many were to come?—but also of the displacement of the traditional cottage culture they had known for so long. What loomed before them was not merely the factory but a whole factory system as it was then taking shape on both sides of the Pennines, with its long hours and incessant work and harsh supervision that reduced self-respecting artisans, with long traditions of autonomy and status, to dependent wage slaves. What loomed, in fact, was a world in which the *machine* seemed to be the principal agent of change, overturning what were seen as the customary and proper modes of life and work, erasing old bonds in both household and marketplace, eroding ancient tenets of honest wages, good goods, and just prices, and substituting instead relations built upon power and capital and a morality guided—or so it would appear—by no aim higher than profit.

At Mellor's command, the men armed with hatchets and hammers moved through the ranks and strode up to the wooden outer gate and set to work. Within minutes the bar-lock was broken, the hinges were knocked loose, and the huge doors fell backward "with a fearful crash," as a local chronicler put it, "like the felling of great trees." The men poured through the opening, spirits high.

For many of them this would be their first action, long anticipated, as part of the new movement against the obnoxious machines—a movement that had been given its name some months earlier by machine-breaking weavers down in Nottinghamshire who declared themselves "Luddites" and issued their communiqués in the name of a mythical all-purpose leader, "General Ned Ludd." But they all knew the successes other bands of Luddite workmen had recently had in the area against the hated factories: raiding parties had set on two mills near Leeds, only ten miles away, at the end of March, and just two days ago a crowd of three hundred men or more had wrecked a woolen mill near Wakefield, just a few miles east. There was reason to feel the kind of confident camaraderie that was in that song they had been singing down at the Shear's Inn the other night:

> And night by night when all is still
> And the moon is hid behind the hill,
> We forward march to do our will
> With hatchet, pike, and gun!
> Oh, the cropper lads for me,
> The gallant lads for me,
> Who with lusty stroke

The shear frames broke,
The cropper lads for me!

Before them the huge mill—the main building four stories
tall and sixty feet or more in length, set with rows of large windows all along the side—seemed abandoned but for a watchdog
that could now be heard barking somewhere within. The crowd
moved forward, and then suddenly, as if on signal, stones and
sticks were hurled at the glass, pikes and hatchets attacked the
window frames, and with the clatter of glass a huge yell, triumphant and joyous and perhaps a little feral, came up from the
men, loud enough to be remembered later by villagers for miles
around. Then the gunners approached and let loose a volley of
fire through the gaping holes into the darkened mill.

Suddenly an answering volley, accompanied by flashes that lit
up the interior, gave awful proof that the factory was not abandoned at all. It was occupied, indeed fortified, by ten armed
men—Cartwright himself, four of his workmen, and five soldiers
of the Cumberland militia deputed from the local garrison—
who were stationed behind an ingenious system the owner had
spent some weeks in preparing: the flagstones that formed the
second-story floor were attached to pulleys and could be lifted a
foot or so to allow a gunman to shoot through onto any attackers
while at the same time being generally protected from answering fire. "The assailants," wrote a correspondent from the *Leeds
Mercury* in the week after the attack, "have much reason to rejoice
that they did not succeed in entering the building, for we speak
from our own observation when we say, that had they effected an
entrance, the death of vast numbers of them from a raking fire
which they could neither have returned nor controlled, would
have been inevitable."

Falling back from the windows, many of the men were no
doubt as surprised as angered by this defense of the mill, the first
time that any serious resistance had been offered to the Luddites

in all the weeks of violence since January, and they moved quickly toward the back to find another means of gaining entrance. At the front gates Mellor led a contingent of men trying to batter the factory doors—"Way for Enoch" was the call—but here the wood had been so studded with large-head nails in such a tight pattern that the hatchets could not effectively penetrate to the wood, and after those weapons were turned and blunted the hammer men stepped forward to try their skills. Blow after blow struck the heavy doors with great thundering noise, wielded by men whose daily labors toughened their arms to steeliness, and still the studded planks resisted. Ben Bamforth, six foot two and self-described as "hard as nails," left an account reconstructed thus:

> You could hear the din of my every stroke rolling away into the emptiness of the mill within, and from the great bolt heads that studded the panels the sparks flew fast and thick as I thundered at the door. . . . With every blow that fell quivering shocks ran up my arm . . . and still I pounded at the door, and still the stout timbers yielded not a jot.

Meanwhile a knot of men trying to find a less-protected entrance on the other side of the factory discovered their way blocked by the millpond and its dam, which provided treacherous footing in the darkness. Thomas Brook, 32, a wool weaver, lost his footing and fell into the water, and it was many minutes before his comrades could haul him out—minus, however, his hat, which would eventually be found by the constables and traced, by complicated and fortuitous steps, to its owner, leading to his arrest a few months later.

Over the sounds of yelling men and gunfire and hammer blows could be heard the ringing of an alarm bell on the roof, installed by Cartwright so as to alert the cavalry brigade that had been stationed near Rawfolds ever since machine breaking had started in the area at the beginning of the year. "Damn the bell!" Mellor shouted. "Fire at the bell! Shoot the bell!" Just then the bell went

silent and a cheer went up, but within minutes its clangor was
heard again; what happened was that the rope from the bell down
to the men on the second floor had broken, but Cartwright had
dispatched two men to the roof to keep it ringing: the cavalry
were not far away, they *must* hear the alarm. "Of all the dismal
dins any body ever heard," said James Brook, a cropper, some
days later, "it was the most dismalest."

Some of the men with muskets and pistols kept firing through
the broken windows, but warily now because the defenders' volleys didn't slacken. Only seven men inside were shooting now,
two having gone to the roof and one of the soldiers refusing to
use his gun "because I might hit one of my brothers," but still, as
Cartwright later boasted, "our Fire was given with much Steadi-
ness and rapidity." John Walker, 31, a cropper from Huddersfield
and a friend of Mellor's, stationed himself beside one of the
openings, peering stealthily over the sill and hoping to lift himself
inside if he had a chance. Suddenly he was sighted by one of the
men inside and a ball was shot through the crown of his hat, leaving him unhurt but angrier still. He raised himself onto the window sill, stuck his pistol through the opening, and fired at the
flash from which the shot had come: "I was determined to do it,"
he told his mates afterward, "though my hand had been shot off,
and hand and pistol had gone into the mill." Mellor was heard in
the background crying, "In with you, lads" and "Damn them,
kill them every one," but still none of the attackers felt inclined to
take the chance of going through the windows.

Back at the front door the heavy pounding of the "great Enoch"
hammers finally cracked the heavy wood and a hole about the size
of a man's head opened up at about shoulder height. "The door is
open," someone yelled, but just then one of the men inside fired
through the opening, and John Booth, a young apprentice sad-
dler who was the son of a local clergyman, cried out and pitched
forward to the dirt, holding his leg, which had been nearly shattered by the ball that struck him. Another shot was sent through
the hole, and Jonathan Dean, 30, a blacksmith then wielding his

hammer to try to widen the breach, gave a painful shout and dropped the instrument from his wounded hand.

The men, in confusion now, fell back—their very success at breaching the door proving their undoing—but still another shot was fired through the opportune hole, and Samuel Hartley, 24, a cropper from Halifax who had been let go from this very mill some months before, was hit in his left breast and sent reeling to the ground, vomiting blood. At least three men wounded now, the alarm bell still clanging through the night, the cavalry contingent presumably on its way, the attacking gunmen running out of ammunition after twenty minutes of useless fire, and the garrison inside showing no signs of weakness: "Cease fire!" Mellor called, and the order was passed along the crowd.

It was a somber moment, the first time the Yorkshire Luddites had known failure, and the men backed off sullenly and silently, gradually forming into small groups to make their way home before the troops arrived. Mellor and a few others hung back in the area where Booth and Hartley were writhing in agony in the dust, both bleeding profusely, and debated what to do with their wounded comrades. It was imperative to leave the mill quickly and get to their beds with some speed, since the soldiers and constables would soon be spending the night visiting the homes of suspected workmen to find out who was absent or who showed signs of recent battle; and they had to make their way without confronting any of the constables or local militia in the villages along the way, many of whom must have been aroused by the alarm bell and would be patrolling their territories. It would be foolhardy to try to carry the wounded men in such circumstances, especially as it looked as if they hadn't long to live in any case. Mellor leaned down to the two men and explained that they would have to remain behind—but, he warned, remember the oath you have taken, never to reveal your comrades "to any person or persons under the canopy of heaven."

When Mellor stood, it was later recalled, there were tears in his eyes. He turned to face the mill, said a few words to his friends about keeping their courage high, and, raising a clenched fist, swore that he would have his revenge on the now doubly hated Cartwright. Then with an oath he fired one last pistol shot at the mill and hastened into the night.

When Cartwright eventually ventured out of the mill a few minutes later, he found the two wounded men and "Traces of Blood . . . very heavy in different Directions," he later wrote, and fourteen "large Hammers Hatchets and Mauls" left behind. By this time a number of nearby villagers had gathered at the front of the mill—including the Reverend Hammond Roberson, a fervent Tory and vocal anti-Luddite, with a sword strapped to his thigh—but Cartwright would let no one go to the aid of the dying men until he got from them the names of their associates, an act of particular callousness that set badly with the people around and undoubtedly inflamed the desire for vengeance in the Luddite ranks.

Only when he could get no answers from the men—"For God's sake," cried one, "shoot me, put me out of my misery!"—and sensed the indignation in the bystanders did he let the two bodies be carried inside and send off a messenger to the doctor's. Both men were then roughly bandaged and, when the detachment of soldiers finally arrived around one-thirty, were taken to the Star Inn in nearby Roberttown. There they were certainly interrogated and perhaps tortured, though apparently without revealing anything; Booth died at about six o'clock in the morning while surgeons tried to amputate his leg, Hartley early the following morning. An unknown number of men who were wounded in the fray were taken care of by friends or family until their wounds were healed so as to forestall suspicion; one, James Haigh, not yet 21, who had gone to a doctor to be treated for a musket ball through the shoulder, was tracked down at a relative's by the authorities over a week later, but the doctor wouldn't talk and Haigh was soon released. Jonathan Dean took himself out of town for two months until his hand healed, though he was arrested and interrogated just after he came back and then also released.

Ignored in the newspaper accounts, and thus forgotten to history, at least two other men who were involved in the raid died that night or shortly afterward. We know of them largely because a local minister, the Reverend Patrick Brontë, saw a group of men he recognized as Luddites go into his church graveyard a few nights later, carrying at least two corpses, which they buried quietly with their own crude ceremony, in the southeast corner. Although this was clearly the act of criminals and the churchman had an obligation to tell the authorities forthwith, he said nothing, watching it all in a silence that he kept—for, as he said later, he would not betray his flock over a Christian burial. This kindhearted man, who later changed his accent for a dieresis, was the father of three rather famous daughters, one of whom attended and then taught at a school only a few miles away that overlooked the field where the Luddite army had gathered before the Rawfolds raid. Years later, in *Shirley,* Charlotte Brontë would have this to say about that fateful event:

> Certain inventions in machinery were introduced into the staple manufactures of the north, which, greatly reducing the number of hands necessary to be employed, threw thousands out of work, and left them without legitimate means of sustaining life. A bad harvest supervened. Distress reached its climax. Endurance, over-goaded, stretched the hand of fraternity to sedition; the throes of a sort of moral earthquake were felt heaving under the hills of the northern counties. . . .
>
> As to the sufferers, whose sole inheritance was labour, and who had lost that inheritance—who could not get work, and consequently could not get wages, and consequently could not get bread—they were left to suffer on, perhaps inevitably left; it would not do to stop the progress of invention, to damage science by discouraging its improvements; the war could not be terminated, efficient relief could not be raised; there was no help then, so the unemployed underwent their destiny—ate the bread, and drank the waters of affliction.

Misery generates hate: these sufferers hated the machines which they believed took their bread from them; they hated the buildings which contained those machines; they hated the manufacturers who owned those buildings. In the parish of [Huddersfield] . . . [William Cartwright] was, in his double character of semi-foreigner and thoroughgoing progressist, the man most abominated.

No Luddite, she, nor sympathizer, but she did have it right: there *was* a moral earthquake heaving under the Luddite triangle of middle Britain, and it burst forth as hatred, never more anguishingly obvious than in the Rawfolds raid.

Although the Rawfolds raid went quickly into the literature and folklore of the time—"How gloomy and dark is the day when men have to fight for their bread," went one Yorkshire song— the Luddism of which it was such a striking part might well have become a forgotten phenomenon except that it so clearly expressed a sentiment and represented a perception that stayed very much alive as Britain continued to industrialize through the 19th century and that surfaced in virtually every other society to which the factory system and its industrial culture were subsequently spread. And for nearly two centuries now, Luddism has meant a strain of opposition to the domination of industrial technology and to its values of mechanization, consumption, exploitation, growth, competition, novelty, and progress—a kind of solid, indelible body of beliefs existing subaqueously as it were, refusing to be eroded by the sweeping tides of triumphant modernism. It is a strain of opposition, of naysaying, that has not been dispelled in all these decades by however many elaborate machines or more elaborate visions the technophiles have paraded.

One of the several expressions of this strain, a deep distrust of technology and resistance to its promises, was being gestated even as the Luddite hammers were being swung. Mary Shelley's prescient tale of techno-madness, *Frankenstein*, published in 1818, was so vivid a message of the dangers of mechanization and the problems of scientific invention—"You are my creator," the monster tells the scientists at the end, "but I am your master"—that it has survived to today, unforgettable. Basically the same message, more philosophically put, would continue to be expressed as the century went on by men like Thomas Carlyle, William Morris, John Ruskin, G. K. Chesterton, and Hilaire Belloc, and from time to time, in more literary form, by Charles Dickens. One particularly interesting form of this sensibility was the resistance of Western Europe's officer corps, made up for the most part of landed and agricultural aristocrats rather than scions of industrial magnates, to the introduction of any industrial machines that would replace man or horse: "Machines had brought with them industrialisation and the destruction of the traditional social order," as a modern historian has described the military mind, but "they must not be allowed to undermine the old certainties of the battlefield—the glorious charge and the opportunities for individual heroism." Thus it was that the machine gun, invented in 1862, was not taken up seriously by any European army until World War I and even then was secondary to the cavalry charge as an offensive weapon.

Another expression of a Luddistic kind, also contemporary with the Luddites, was Romanticism, beginning with Blake and Wordsworth and Byron particularly, who like the machine breakers were repulsed by the Satanic mills and the getting-and-spending of the present and like them were mindful of the ruined paradise of the past. (The identity was so immediate for Byron at least that at one point he was even moved to write, "Down with all kings but King Ludd!") This Romanticism, and particularly its attachment to an unspoiled, machine-free nature, was echoed across the Atlantic by Hawthorne, Poe, and Melville, among literary lions, and notably by Emerson and Thoreau and their great heir, John Muir. Muir, one feels, would have been a Luddite given half the chance, and there is in his tirades against the developers of the West—"These Temple destroyers, devotees of ravaging commercialism, seem to have a perfect contempt for Nature, and instead of lifting their eyes to the God of the mountains, lift them to the Almighty Dollar"—the taste of the acrid anger found in the Luddite letters.

A more purely industrial expression of this strain, in which sabotage was used or threatened for one laboring cause or another, followed the factory system wherever it spread in Europe and the United States through the century. Weaving machines introduced into southern France during the Bourbon Restoration were greeted with protests, foiled only because the French authorities had studied the British response to Luddism and put them down unceremoniously; in the United States at least a dozen factories were attacked in the 1820s and '30s, most of the unexplained fires at textile mills in New England were said to be of "incendiary origin," and in several instances machines were destroyed and cloth burned in labor protests; in Silesia and Bavaria artisans in the 1830s and '40s attacked new factories and their machines. In England itself, agricultural laborers protesting the use of threshing machines and the strangulation of their jobs waged what two modern researchers call "a silent, embittered, vengeful campaign of poaching, burning and rural terror" at several points during the 1830–45 period, most notably the "Captain Swing" demonstrations over a score of counties in 1830 when more than four hundred machines were destroyed and over three hundred fires set. Sabotage continued to play a role in industrial disputes down through the century and into the next (as, for example, the Wobblies in 1912 and after) on both sides of the Atlantic, but most of the time it was an adjunct to a strike or a grievance having little or nothing to do with the machine itself, simply a way of demonstrating workers' rage. But there are times, too, particularly in the French guild movement and syndicalism at the end of the century, when machine breaking was more Luddistically seen as a tactic to help bring about some wider social purpose, usually "the revolution."

As industrialism perfected itself into the 20th century the Luddistic strain could be found most often in the works of a remarkably diverse set of critics and intellectuals, beginning with people like Thorstein Veblen and Max Weber and Oswald Spengler, going on to Martin Heidegger, Aldous Huxley, the Frankfurt School, and the towering Lewis Mumford, and then to Jacques Ellul, Herbert Marcuse, and Paul Goodman, to pick only the most prominent of a quite distinguished set. A notable if problematical offshoot of this set was the group of "Southern Agrarians"—Allen Tate, Robert Penn Warren, Stark Young, and John Crowe Ransom among them—who first announced themselves in 1930 as defenders of the agrarian tradition against "industrial progress, or an incessant extension of industrialization," and who were quite explicit in questioning the value of new machines ("A fresh labor-saving device introduced into an industry does not emancipate the laborers in that industry so much as it evicts them"), consumption, advertising, and most of "what may be called the American or prevailing way." The conclusion of the Agrarians' original "Statement of Principles" has a particularly Luddistic ring: "If a community, or a section, or a race, or an age, is groaning under industrialism, and well aware that it is an evil dispensation, it must find the way to throw it off." (Tate, for one, was specific about the way: "political, active, and, in the nature of the case, violent and revolutionary.")

In limning these various facets of the long post-Luddite tradition I don't mean, of course, to suggest that there is any rigid uniformity to these people or their antitechnological biases. The concerns and causes and methods vary, but there is to it all, at bottom, a message that is unmistakably Luddistic: beware the technological juggernaut, reckon the terrible costs, understand the worlds being lost in the world being gained, reflect on the price of the machine and its systems on your life, pay attention to the natural world and its increasing destruction, resist the seductive catastrophe of industrialism.

And that strain, that Luddism—or perhaps neo-Luddism, more appropriately—exists today, at the end of the millennium, indeed with more passion and urgency, I think, than at any time in the past two centuries. For it stems from the now incontestable understanding that, as *Business Week* put it not long ago, "the United States is in the midst of an economic transformation on the order of the Industrial Revolution"—a transformation, like the first one, driven by swift technological and economic change and, like the first one, accompanied by vast social dislocations and environmental destruction. Call it "third-wave" or "post-modern" or "multinational" capitalism, this new order is something paradigmatically different, a high-tech industrialism of ever more complex technologies—computerization, robotics, biotechnology, artificial intelligence, and the like—and served by ever more remote institutions, notably the multinational corporation. And this new industrialism is sped along by the ministrations of the developed nation-states, especially the American one that generated the second Industrial Revolution, nurtured it with Cold War weaponry and space adventurism, and is now with the Clinton Administration prepared to launch it onto an "information superhighway" and an "automated battlefield" with unprecedented technological consequences.

The neo-Luddites who challenge the current Industrial Revolution (treated in detail in a later section) are today more numerous than one might assume, pessimists without the power and access of the optimists but still with a not insignificant voice, shelves of books and documents and reports, and increasing numbers of followers—and the lessons of history perhaps on their side. They are to be found on the radical and direct-action side of environmentalism, particularly in the American West; they are on the dissenting edges of academic economics and ecology departments, generally of the no-growth school; they are everywhere in Indian Country throughout the Americas, representing a traditional biocentrism against the anthropocentric norm; they are activists fighting against nuclear power, irradiated food, clearcutting, animal experiments, toxic wastes, and the killing of whales, among the many aspects of the high-tech onslaught.

They may also number—certainly they speak for—some of those whose experience with modern technology has in one way or another awakened them from what Mumford called "the myth of the machine." These would include those several million people in all the industrial nations whose jobs have simply been automated out from under them—neat equivalents of the Yorkshire croppers—or have been sent overseas as part of the multinationals' global network, itself built on high-tech communications. They would include the many millions who have suffered from some exposure, officially sanctioned, to pollutants and poisons, medicines and chemicals, and live with the terrible results. They include some whose faith in the technological dream has been shattered by the recent evidence of industrial fragility and error—from Bhopal, Chernobyl, and Love Canal to PCBs, *Exxon Valdez,* and ozone holes—that is the stuff of daily headlines. And they may include, too, quite a number of those whose experience with high technology in the home or office has left them confused or demeaned, or frustrated by machines too complex to understand, much less to repair, or assaulted and angered by systems that deftly invade their privacy or deny them credit or turn them into ciphers.

Wherever the neo-Luddites may be found, they are attempting to bear witness to the secret little truth that lies at the heart of the modern experience: whatever its presumed benefits, of speed or ease or power or wealth, industrial technology comes at a price, and in the contemporary world that price is ever rising and ever threatening. Indeed, inasmuch as industrialism is inevitably and inherently disregardful of the collective human fate and of the earth from which it extracts all its wealth—these are, after all, in capitalist theory "externalities"—it seems ever more certain to end in paroxysms of economic inequity and social upheaval, if not in the degradation and exhaustion of the biosphere itself.

If so little general thought is given now to this impending catastrophe of the second Industrial Revolution, it is not merely that the illusion of technological progress, embedded in an abiding faith in science of nearly religious intensity, is so powerful, not merely that for some minority of the world's population greater longevity, comfort, and dominance is so seductive. It is largely because as a society we are so ignorant about the past—particularly the past that engendered the first Industrial Revolution, the human and environmental traumas it caused, and the pain, the tragedy, of its decades of immiseration—that we can believe that the future might be untouched with any of that.

In a rare, valuable analysis of the forces at work in this second revolution, historian David Noble has said it this way:

> The analogy commonly made between the present transformation and that of the early nineteenth century remains only half complete: the catastrophe has been left out. For a fuller analogy would shake the spirit, not stir it, and give thoughtful people pause: What will happen to the dispossessed? What will the consequences be once our world too has been "turned upside down"?

And, one must add, what will happen to the species and ecosystems destroyed, what will be the consequences if the line of ecological peril is crossed?

This is why the original Luddites, though they occupy but a short historical moment, and so long ago, are important for us to understand today. In their story, as we see it now in modern perspective, we find those two essential elements that may help us to avoid being condemned to repeat a history that we did not understand—or, if repeating it, to become armed and armored with the means of resisting it. First, the *catastrophe,* the wrenching consequences of being in a world suddenly transformed—degraded, despiriting, destroying—whose awful record might possibly impel this society to start thinking about the consequences of its heedless embrace of the second Industrial Revolution; and second, the *resistance* to that catastrophe, eventually unsuccessful then but with myriad lessons now, some philosophic, some even strategic, but instructive for those who might wish to disentangle themselves from that embrace before it is too late. Understanding in an intimate way the narrative of the Luddites, we may not only dispel our ignorance of the past, we may find some necessary guidance for the future.

The figures are uncertain, but it seems reasonable to suggest that something like five thousand croppers and apprentices were at work in Yorkshire, mostly in the West Riding* district where Cartwright's mill was located, in 1806 and nearly as many in 1812; by 1817 only 763 of them were thought to be fully employed, and by the 1830s the craft was all but dead. Thanks to the shearing frames and similar gig mills, whose numbers increased twentyfold by 1817, and the power engines, particularly steam, the work that in 1800 required twenty-seven croppers to do in 1828 could be done, according to a Parliamentary inquiry, in a factory by three men of modest skill and two children. In Leeds alone, one of the three major woolen centers, the number of Watt engines increased from 20 or so in 1800 to more than 120 in 1825, while the number of croppers dropped from 1,733 in 1814, working at 36 to 40 shillings a week, to less than a hundred by the 1830s, earning 10 to 14 shillings. The displaced men from here and elsewhere, as one observer reported, "have turned themselves to any thing they can get to do, some acting as bailiffs, water-carriers, scavengers, or selling oranges, cakes, tapes and laces, gingerbread, blacking, &c, &c."

What is not uncertain—for it eventually becomes so pervasive that it forces countless newspaper exposés and government inquiries—is the misery and despoliation that accompanied these shifts. The factory system became notorious for its multiple evils and cruel impositions—"a state of slavery *more horrid* than . . . that hellish system—'Colonial Slavery,'" as one Yorkshireman wrote in 1830—and the factory towns became infamous for their

---

* "West Riding" was a corruption of "West Triding," the name of an old administrative division of Yorkshire, meaning the western third of the county.

foul, blackened air in which it was said to be difficult to see, much less to breathe, and for the noxious rivers "fitted more for garbage than fishes" and the fields beside them turned sere and brown from industrial pollution. It was in 1814, two years after the Rawfolds raid, that Wordsworth wrote:

> *Like you I grieve when on the darker side*
> *Of this great change I look: and there behold*
> *Such outrage done to nature as compels*
> *The indignant power to justify herself,*
> *Yea, to avenge her violated rights,*
> *For England's bane.*

And:

> *In full many a region, once like this*
> *The assured domain of calm simplicity*
> *And pensive quiet, an unnatural light*
> *Prepared for never-resting Labour's eyes*
> *Breaks from a many-windowed fabric huge. . . .*
> *   Men, maidens, youths,*
> *Mothers and little children, boys and girls,*
> *Enter, and each the wonted task resumes*
> *Within this temple, where is offered up*
> *To Gain, the master idol of the realm,*
> *Perpetual Sacrifice.*

"Perpetual sacrifice": that says it pretty well—the sacrifice of men and women, of their settled lives and cherished environments, of the world that had nurtured them. A darker side, indeed.

2

The First
Industrial Revolution

LANCASHIRE, say 1780:

"Their dwellings and small gardens clean and neat—all the family well clad—the men with each a watch in his pocket, and the women dressed to their own fancy—the church crowded to excess every Sunday—every house well furnished with a clock in elegant mahogany or fancy case—handsome tea services in Staffordshire wear. . . .

"The workshop of the weaver was a rural cottage, from which when he was tired of sedentary labour he could sally forth into his little garden, and with the spade or the hoe tend its culinary productions. The cotton wool which was to form his weft was picked clean by the fingers of his younger children, and was carded and spun by the older girls assisted by his wife, and the yarn was woven by himself assisted by his sons. When he could not procure within his family a supply of yarn adequate to the demands of his loom, he had recourse to the spinsters of his neighbourhood. One good weaver could keep three active women at work upon the wheel, spinning weft [although] he was often obliged to treat the females with presents in order to quicken their diligence at the wheel."

Lancashire, say 1814:

"There are hundreds of factories in Manchester which are five or six storeys high. At the side of each factory there is a great

chimney which belches forth black smoke and indicates the presence of the powerful steam engines. The smoke from the chimneys forms a great cloud which can be seen for miles around the
town. The houses have become black on account of the smoke.
The river upon which Manchester stands is so tainted with colour-
ing matter that the water resembles the contents of a dye-vat. . . .

"To save wages mule jennies have actually been built so that no
less than 600 spindles can be operated by one adult and two children. Two mules, each with 300 spindles, face each other. The
carriages of these machines are moved in one direction by steam
and in the other direction by hand. This is done by an adult
worker who stands in between the two mules. Broken threads are
repaired by children (piecers) who stand at either end of the
mules. . . . In the large spinning mills machines of different kinds
stand in rows like regiments in an army."

It was, make no mistake about it, an industrial revolution, an
alteration of such speed and complexity and scale as to dwarf even
the considerable upheavals that had come in the centuries before.
There has been a fashion of late among academics to minimize
the revolutionary nature of British industrialization and to argue
that the process was gradual and cumulative and uneven, no dramatic upheavals or convulsions about it, and didn't really have
anything to do with machinery anyway. That is nonsense. Of
course (like any revolution's) its causes go way back and its effects
far forward, of course it did not touch all regions or industries
equally or simultaneously, and of course it was accompanied by
changes in agriculture and marketing and finance, too. But the
fact is that it was a vast alteration of the nature of British society,
so successful that it would eventually impose itself—its new civilization, it might be said—on Europe, and the world, before
another century was over; it changed not just the face of manufacturing but the places and purposes of production, the compo-
sition of the workforce, the character of the market, the patterns
and sizes of settlements, and the role of families and communities; it happened rapidly, almost within a modest lifetime if we

take the usual dates of 1785 to 1830, from the first successful steam-powered factory, inaugurating the age, to the first intercity railway, inaugurating another, during which the number of people in manufacturing exceeded that in agriculture for the first time in English history; and it was taken at the time for the cataclysm it was, a phenomenon of "wonder and astonishment [whose] rapidity . . . exceeds all credibility" (Patrick Colquhoun, 1815) and "a new and unforeseen creation . . . industrious to destroy" (Wordsworth, 1814), and was called again and again a "revolution" long before the first Arnold Toynbee popularized the phrase "Industrial Revolution" in the 1880s. The changes in British society between 1785 and 1830, and particularly of course in the manufacturing districts, were greater than any forty-five-year period before or since, a transformation, as the historian E. P. Thompson has said, that "made over human nature and human need."

How to isolate the elements of such a phenomenon: out of the great flow of tracts and tomes and texts and treatises, can we possibly discover some few currents that can help us understand it—understand it not merely as the Luddites might have done, though that is important in trying to assess their motives and their goals, but as the perspective of two hundred years allows us now to do in the midst of a similar sea change?

It is surely too schematic, and reductive, but let me suggest six of these currents that might serve in this process, each of them flowing from the large and detailed economic literature available here.

THE IMPOSITION OF TECHNOLOGY

The steam engine, especially as it was perfected by the Watt and Boulton shop in the experimental years after 1776, was the iron heart of the Industrial Revolution. No matter that it was surrounded by thousands of other ingenious machines and inventions, some more immediately practical—294 patents were issued in Britain in the 1770s, 477 in the 1780s, and 647 in the 1790s, almost twice as many as in the preceding hundred years of patenting—it was the first manufacturing technology in human history that was, in a sense, *independent* of nature, of geography and season and weather, of sun or wind or water or human or animal power. It allowed humans for the first time, restricted only by available supplies of coal (and metal), to have a constant, unfailing source of power at their command, capable of producing an almost infinite variety of objects with a minimum of personal effort or time. And thus it permitted the extraordinary shift from what had been an organic economy based on land and labor and local exchange to a mechanical economy based on fuel and factory and foreign trade, an empowerment of the machine in human society such as had never before been attempted.

All technologies have consequences, inevitable and built in, and imperatives, just as inevitable, essentially separate from human dictates and desires. Norbert Wiener, the mathematician who was the founder of modern cybernetics, has written about "technical determinants" dictated by "the very nature" of machines, and of the steam engine he noted that it automatically leads to large and ever larger scales because it can power so many separate machines at once, to ever increasing production because it must pay back its high investment and operating costs, and to centralization and specialization because factors of efficiency and economy supersede those of, say, craftsmanship or esthetic expression. He might have added that it also necessarily leads to a reduction in face-to-face contacts, social discourse, human autonomy, individual choice, and personal skills, none of which is especially important as far as the operation of the machine goes.

There is, then, a kind of technological logic connected to this "iron monster with a pulse of steam"—what Clark Kerr and his team in the 1960s called "the logic of industrialism," which they say is why all industrial societies look pretty much alike—and by extension of course to the other machinery of the Industrial Revolution. It did not take more than a few decades for contemporaries to start observing where it led: large-scale units of production governed by regimentation and control, increasing refinement and complexity of machinery, a division of labor and hence of training and hence of social status, expanding markets, expanding resources, expanding wastes—all phenomena that the Kerr investigators found wherever they followed industrialism a century and a half later. It also led, and leads, though Kerr lays less emphasis here, to social and political consequences: the squeezing of farm populations and the uncontrollable growth of cities, the evisceration of self-reliant communities, the enlargement of central governments, the enthronement of science as ruling ideology, a wide and increasing gap between rich and poor, and ruling values of profit, growth, property, and consumption. It was so in the early 19th century of Britain, the late 19th century of the United States, the 20th century of Japan, and seems indeed to be so in the process of industrialism everywhere.

That may seem like a lot of weight to load on Watt's simple machine—a restatement in metal, by the way, of a device known to the Greeks two thousand years before*—but contemporaries who lived within the sound of its roar had no doubts. "One of the most striking revolutions ever produced in the moral and social conditions of a moiety of a great nation," said Peter Gaskell in his survey of *The Manufacturing Population in England* in 1833, "is that which has been consequent to the application of steam to machinery." By then steam power was doing what Gaskell calculated to be the work of 2.5 million people—and since the 1831 census had identified no more than 3 million people engaged in manufacturing overall, that meant steam machinery was nearly equivalent to the whole manufacturing workforce, just four decades after its introduction. Indeed, Gaskell warned, "vast and incessant improvements in mechanical contrivances, all tending to overmatch and supersede human labour [threaten] ere long to

---

* Hero of Alexandria designed, and probably built, a steam engine in the first century B.C. that used fire-heated cauldrons and tubes. The Mediterranean world of the time, however, had all the labor power it needed in slaves, and Hero's machine was ignored; in an England of the 18th century where slaves were outlawed and cheap labor hard to control and manipulate, great energy was put into creating just such a device.

extirpate the very demand for it," making the English worker, except for those making the machines, obsolete.

Steam made its impact primarily in the textile industries, most of them traditionally located in that Luddite triangle where streams running from the Pennine hills had long provided the water needed to wash and prepare yarn and the weather systems in from the Irish Sea had long provided the damp climate suitable to its processing into cloth. When the first factories appeared they used the Pennine streams for power, but since this source was so uncertain—many mills were idle in the summer months when the streams dwindled to trickles—the attraction of the steam engine and its ceaseless energy was irresistible, especially since by a whim of Albion the region was replete with coalfields to fire the steam. By 1800, a little more than a decade after their introduction into the factory, some 2,191 steam engines were thought to be at work in Britain—those "Stygian forges, with their fire-throats and never-resting sledge-hammers" that Carlyle wrote of—some 460 of them in the textile trades and responsible for as much as a quarter of all cotton production. By 1813 there were an estimated 2,400 textile looms operating by steam, but that burgeoned to 14,150 by 1820 and exploded to more than 100,000 just a decade later, as factory production came to dominate cotton and moved steadily into wool, silk, and other branches. By then, according to a contemporary expert, one man could do the work that two or three hundred men had done at the start of the Industrial Revolution, "the most striking example of the dominion obtained by human science over the powers of nature, of which modern times can boast."

Although large industrial organizations had been known for some time—the famous arsenal in 16th-century Venice was in most respects a factory, right down to division of labor and mass production—it was the Industrial Revolution, driven by the steam engine, that produced the first factory *system,* an operation both immense and intense, in which not only the machine but the entire production process, humans included, was made up of more or less isolated and interchangeable parts. Very shortly it took this shape, as a German visitor wrote from Manchester in 1823:

> The modern miracles, my friend, are to me the machines here and the buildings that house them, called factories. Such a block is eight or nine stories high, sometimes has 40 windows along its frontage and is often four windows deep. Each floor is twelve feet high, and vaulted along its whole length with arches each having a span of nine feet. The pillars are of iron, as is the girder which they support. . . . A hundred of them are now standing unshaken and exactly as they were erected thirty and forty years ago. A number of such blocks stand in very elevated positions which dominate the neighbourhood; and in addition a forest of even taller boiler-house chimneys like needles, so that it is hard to imagine how they remain upright; the whole presents from a distance a wonderful spectacle especially at night, when thousands of windows are brilliantly illuminated by gaslight.

The human appendages to the machines thus housed were leaden drudges. A Leeds doctor said in 1831:

> While the engine works, the people must work. Men, women, and children are thus yoke-fellows with iron and steam; the animal machine—fragile at best, subject to a thousand sources of suffering, and doomed, by nature in its best state, to a short-lived existence, changing every moment, and hastening to decay—is matched with an iron machine insensible to suffering and fatigue.

This is the factory system, these two machines working together in "a vast automaton," in the words of the great apologist for it, Andrew Ure, in 1835, "composed of various mechanical and intellectual organs, acting in an uninterrupted concert for the production of a common object, all of them being subordinated to a self-regulating moving force."

"Subordinated" is the key word here, though Ure seems to feel there is no distinction to be made between the mechanical and intellectual kind. The task for the factory owner was to make sure that workers would be disciplined to serve the needs of the machines—"in training human beings," Ure said, "to renounce their desultory habits of work and to identify with the unvarying regularity of the complex automaton"—and for this the principal strategies were threefold. First, long and inflexible hours, behind locked doors, twelve and fourteen hours a day being the rule for the first several decades, sometimes as many as sixteen or eighteen, and never less than ten; next, a regimen of shop-floor penalties, such as these (out of a list of nineteen) posted in a cotton mill in 1824—

Any spinner found with his window open	1 shilling
Any spinner found dirty at his work	1 shilling
Any spinner heard whistling	1 shilling
Any spinner being five minutes after the last bell rings	2 shillings

—and assessed on wages that averaged no more than 24 shillings a week; and finally by outright physical force, more commonly used against women and children but available to all, typified by the foreman "kept on purpose to strap," whose job was "continually walking up and down with the strap in his hand," as a Parliamentary inquiry was told in 1833, beating children "late at their work" in the morning or falling asleep at their work in the afternoon—"very cruel strapping," too, and "some have been beaten so violently that they have lost their lives in consequence."

But there was another, wider discipline of the labor force as well: by government policy, sanctioned somehow by laissez-faire ideology, the workers of Britain were made effectively powerless to resist the demands of their employers. Laws passed in 1799 and 1800 that consolidated long-standing antiunion statutes made it illegal to organize, or "combine," to try to get higher wages or shorter hours or better conditions, even to raise funds or attend meetings as a unit; and though certain trades in certain towns could evade some of these restrictions, many employers made full use of the laws (or threat of them) whenever they felt resistance mounting among their workers. Government policies also helped expand the labor pool, especially during the first decades of industrialism (largely by facilitating the immigration of Irish laborers and forcing agricultural workers from the countryside), which worked as it always does to undercut any functional bargaining power of the workers. This was compounded by the fact that there were no restrictions on employing women and children, starting at ages as young as 4 and 5, who came to make up roughly four fifths of the textile labor force by 1833, a population both easier to exploit and cheaper to hire than adult men. Taken together, all this served quite well to make the workers, particularly in the large manufacturing towns where numbers were greater and owners more powerful, for the most part effectually "subordinated" to the larger interests of the new industrialism.

Thus did the "logic of industrialism" work, following out the imposition of its technology with a sweep and power that transformed lives and landscapes within just a few decades to a degree never seen, not even imaginable, before. The steam engine *was,* as Andrew Ure boasted, "the controller general and mainspring of British industry, which urges it onwards at a steady rate, and never suffers it to lag or loiter, till its appointed task be done."

THE DESTRUCTION OF THE PAST

That appointed task was, of course, production—restless, relentless production—which must necessarily lie at the heart of industrial logic and from which must inevitably follow consumption— expansive, incessant consumption. But for both sides of that equation to work properly there needed to be not only a disciplined workforce that would produce on schedule but a captive clientele that would consume in quantity, and that in turn required a concerted transformation of English customary life. Not all at once, not everywhere with the same intensity, but in the course of no more than a few generations England saw the effective end of a world based on an enclosed communitarian life, a high degree of nonmarket self-sufficiency, a simple system of local exchange and barter, a heritage of multiple crafts, and interwoven customs and traditions of mutuality lying outside the chaffer of the market-place.

Of the variety of ways in which this was accomplished, none was as important as the enclosure movement, which in effect turned rural life in England upside down in little more than half a century. Enclosures had taken place before, to be sure, going back to the 12th century, but never was there such a concentrated rate of enclosure with such a sweeping effect as in the years from 1770 to 1830, when some 3,280 bills were passed by Parliament, by which more than 6 million acres of commonly held lands, open fields, meadows, wetlands, forests, and unoccupied "waste" lands, until then the domain of the public at large, were put into private hands and subsequently hedged and fenced and farmed and herded and hunted for private gain. Private arrangements without parliamentary approval probably added nearly as many acres during this same period, the total acreage being equivalent to *more than half* of all the land then in cultivation in England, until not a single county had more than 3 percent of its area out-side of private ownership. "Let us not be satisfied with the libera-tion of Egypt, or the subjugation of Malta," trumpeted Sir John Sinclair in 1803 as he led his fellow lords across the battlefields of this movement, "but let us subdue Finchley Common; let us conquer Hounslow Heath; let us compel Epping Forest to sub-mit to the yoke of improvement."

There is no doubt that the enclosures produced a more "eco-nomical" and "efficient" agriculture in England—the production of cereal probably doubled between 1750 and 1840—as the size of farms tripled, farm production became fully commercialized, and land previously providing little more than steady subsistence as public weal was made to turn hefty profits as private fiefs. No doubt also that the landed aristocracy benefited enormously—it controlled the Parliament that passed the enclosure acts, after all—particularly as the price of wheat doubled and more in this

period and the price of its rents went up by 150 percent, a prosperity shared in too by the landed gentry and smaller landowners,
at least as long as prices stayed high. But as for the rest, the cottagers and freeholders and tenants and squatters, they were
simply done out of their centuries-old households, sometimes
compensated and sometimes not, and turned into hired hands, or
beggars, or forced off the land completely. Sustenance from the
commons lands by cutting fuel and furze, by small-scale farming
and pasturing, by gleaning and foraging, by fishing and hunting, was all gone within a lifetime: "Inclosure," as one man told
Arthur Young on his travels in 1804, "was worse than ten wars."

George Sturt, a man who knew village life intimately, wrote:

> To the enclosure of the common more than to any other cause may
> be traced all the changes which have subsequently passed over the
> village. It was like knocking the keystone out of an arch. The key-
> stone is not the arch; but, once it is gone, all sorts of forces, previ-
> ously resisted, begin to operate towards ruin, and gradually the
> whole structure crumbles down. . . . The enclosure . . . left the
> people helpless against influences which have sapped away their
> interests, robbed them of security and peace, rendered their knowl-
> edge and skill of small value, and seriously affected their personal
> pride and their character. . . .
>
> When the cottager was cut off from his resources . . . there was
> little else that he could do in the old way. It was out of the question
> to obtain most of his supplies by his own handiwork: they had to
> be procured, ready-made from some other source. That source, I
> need hardly say, was a shop.

Now it would be a mistake to exaggerate the tranquillity of the
English countryside before enclosure, or to assume it was somehow untouched by capitalism. The fact is that the agricultural
laborer, who worked long hours and often at the whim of the
farmer who paid him, was by virtue of wages a part of the "farm
proletariat" long before the 19th century; true too that the cottage
weaver, of cotton or wool or silk, who also worked long hours

and often in damp and crowded quarters, was supplied with raw materials (and sometimes machines) by a merchant to whom he also delivered finished goods and thus was a part of an "out-worker proletariat" long before the power loom was perfected. Patriarchy was the norm in the countryside cottage, women had conscribed roles and duties (though many would work the same machines and earn an equal social status), children would be put to household chores as early as 4 or 5, and life was usually as bare and simple and functional as the furniture in the parlor.

And yet it had its virtues, of which every member of the community was aware. Time was a medium, not a commodity, and the workers were not its slaves; in dozens of trades the tradition of "St. Monday," as important a day of rest as sainted Sunday, was inviolable—and as like as not Tuesday too (and even Wednesday) if the tasks were not too pressing—and holidays and festivals and wakes figured regularly through the year. Work usually involved some bodily skill and some mental agility, often a craft in which a person would take some pride, usually with the family pitching in and with occasions for songs and stories and gossip the while, and when times were good it was possible to lay by a shilling or two and when work was slack there was always a small garden and a few animals to fall back on. But work was leavened by a variety of other chores during the day—"the cow-keeping, the bread-making, the fattening of pigs and curing of bacon," as Sturt describes it, along with "turf-cutting on the heath and wheat-growing in the gardens"—and sometimes at the end of it time enough "to enjoy those amusements and bodily recreations then in being" (as Peter Gaskell put it, enumerating dancing, hunting, quoits, and cricket) or just to walk through still unfouled groves and meadows with (Gaskell again) "the cheering influence of nature." "Each had a garden," William Felkin said of the Leicester stocking knitters he knew in the early days, "a barrel of home-brewed ale, a weekday suit of clothes and one for Sundays, and plenty of leisure."

Families then were economic units, to be sure, but central social ones as well, usually intact until the children married in their early twenties, and parental authority and discipline in them was as regular as dinner. The extended family was seldom under the same roof but often in the same parish, and consanguine relationships were close, although neighbors might often intermesh as closely, as suggested in this doggerel of 1811:

> If the stock of our bliss is in strangers' hands rested,
> The fund ill secured oft in bankruptcy ends,
> But the heart is given bills which are never protested
> When drawn on the firm of Wife Children and Friends.

The close-knit villages functioned as true communities, even the more scattered ones of the steep Pennine hills, in which (as a 19th-century historian recounted) people "knew intimately everybody in the village, and could say whether they were married or single . . . who they married, how many children they had, and all their names and distinguishing peculiarities"; in which a common culture, in some cases going back intact some three or four hundred years, provided traditional knowledge (and superstition), traditional rites and games and dances, and traditional relationships among masters and journeymen, workers and merchants, cottagers and squires, parishioners and parsons. And central to it all was a moral custom that was the framework upon which all social and economic relations hung, in large measure based on mutual aid and reciprocity over the back fence ("They helped every one his neighbour," Isaiah 41:6, was a popular offertory theme) and on honesty and fairness in workplace and market ("good goods at a fair price" being the standard assumed by all)—and on an abomination of anything that would upset or alter that custom, including innovations and technologies imposed from without. It was in honor of that morality, for example, that the father of Richard Oastler, the labor reform leader of the 1830s, chose to give up his prosperous Yorkshire cloth business rather than install machines and impose a factory system, because he felt that would be "a means of oppression on the part of the rich and of corresponding degradation and misery to the poor."

It was the task of industrial society to destroy all of that. All that "community" implies—self-sufficiency, mutual aid, morality in the marketplace, stubborn tradition, regulation by custom, organic knowledge instead of mechanistic science—had to be steadily and systematically disrupted and displaced. All of the practices that kept the individual from being a consumer had to be done away with so that the cogs and wheels of an unfettered machine called "the economy" could operate without interference, influenced merely by invisible hands and inevitable balances and all the rest of that benevolent free-market system guided by what Cobbett called, his lip curled toward Hume and James Steuart and Adam Smith, "Scotch Feelosophy."

THE MANUFACTURE OF NEEDS

Necessity, it was the genius of the Industrial Revolution to understand, is not so much the mother of invention as of demand, and hence of consumption: establish needs, or merely the felt perception of needs, and you establish a market.

And so it was not enough just to dismantle the world of the past, it was important, too, to create a new world committed "to the necessity of arousing and satisfying new wants," in the words of the inventor and manufacturer Richard Arkwright, where needs were imperatives, multiple in number and range, and were to be satisfied largely by material objects (or "goods," as the highly self-interested term had it) purchased in the marketplace. That project was, as E. P. Thompson has aptly put it, "the remodelling of 'need,'" and its achievement during these few decades was, he says, "the greatest transformation in history," the effective dividing line between the traditional world and the modern.

Take the effects of the enclosure movement, for example: the alteration of the landscape from haphazard common to orderly field was as nothing compared to the alteration of lives. Those left on the land quite suddenly needed jobs, usually as farm laborers or house servants, because they suddenly needed cash for food and other basics: "So the once self-supporting cottager," George Sturt comments, "turned into a spender of money at the baker's, the coal merchant's, the provision dealer's, and, of course needing to spend money he needed first to get it." And those forced off the land were among those who trudged to the crowded cities or took up cotton weaving or agreed to the low-paying jobs at the collieries and foundries, and their needs similarly revolved around the cash nexus in a world where the ways of mutuality had evaporated:

> We call it a Society [as Thomas Carlyle put it in his *Gospel of Mammonism*] and go about professing openly the totalest separation, isolation. Our life is not a mutual helpfulness; but rather, cloaked under due laws-of-war, named "fair competition" and so forth, it is a mutual hostility. . . . We have profoundly forgotten everywhere that *Cash-payment* is not the sole relation of human beings.

At the same time as this disruption of the old order was taking place, a new one, based on a sharp increase in population and a concentration of it in cities, was arising. The population of England (and Wales) *doubled* from 1785 to 1830 (an estimated 7.5 million in 1781, 16.5 million in the 1831 census), quite an amazing demographic feat and probably unprecedented in Europe, and the population of some cities grew at an even faster rate: Manchester went from around 50,000 to 228,000, Bolton from under 10,000 to 42,000, London from 750,000 to 2 million. The reason for increases of such dimensions is the subject of much debate, but the evidence suggests that it was the stimulus of industrialism that encouraged earlier marriages: because of the impoverishment of traditional cottage labor older boys were forced to leave home and set up families earlier, because of the gradual destruction of the apprentice system in crafts young men were able to go out on their own before 21 for the first time, and because of the increasing employment of children younger families could survive if they reproduced. The English birth rate (per 1,000 of the population), if we can trust imperfect figures, seems to have reached a peak of about 25 percent of women in the 20–40 age bracket in the 1780s and stayed around there until the 1830s—exactly the period of the Industrial Revolution—after which it fell sharply to 20 percent or so.

Just the sheer numbers of this increased population would have impelled some increased demand—particularly for foodstuffs, clothing, and building materials—and the fact that people had little recourse to the land and were clustered in cities served only to amplify that. But there was more to it than numbers. A substantial part of the new population, though still a distinct minority, was made modestly affluent, in some places quite wealthy, by privatization of the countryside and the industrialization of the cities, and by the sorts of commercial and other services that this called forth. This new money stimulated the consumer demand—the "getting and spending" Wordsworth deplored in 1807—that allowed a market economy of a scope not known before: "Without a considerable class of persons who have both the will and power to consume more material wealth than they produce," pronounced the dour Thomas Malthus, "the mercantile classes could not continue profitably to produce so much more than they consume."

How much of this consumption was triggered by a general desire to emulate others in a society where there was just enough fluidity to instill that impulse, and how much by the specific force of fashion in those parts of the society where emulation was honed to a fine art, is impossible to say, but all contemporaries thought that both played a significant part. William Green, for example, darkly warned in 1800 of "the rapid increase of vanity and extravagance" in society and complained that the "frugality which once characterized the middling and lower classes of society among us is no more: the little tradesman and mechanic of the present day, fatally though impotently, ape the luxuries and fashionable vices of their superiors." As for fashion, it took no more than a new style to be paraded by Beau Brummel, the dean of London's Regency "dandies," for whole industries to arise and fall: wearing a loose scarf under a starched collar, or "hessian" shoes tassled in the German style, or pantaloons stretching all the way to the ankle instead of britches ending at the knees.* "A hat, a coat, a shoe, deemed fit to be worn only by a great grandsire," wrote a caustic Vicesimus Knox in 1824, "is no sooner put on by a dictator of fashions, than it becomes graceful in the extreme, and is generally adopted from the first lord of the Treasury to the apprentice in Houndsditch."

But Britain's own population was not the only manufactured market: it also possessed a large colonial empire that was dependent on its industrial output and could be generally manipulated to need what Britain could supply. By 1800 the tiny island kingdom owned not only the seas of the world, with at least a quarter of all shipping under its aegis and no serious rivals, but a good portion of the lands as well, in a system of colonies and entrepots that by 1815 girded the world from Canada and the West Indies to South Africa, India, and Australia, and in between such other essentially captive markets as the United States, Argentina, much of Africa, and southeast Asia. It is no doubt wrong to claim that this empire was the masterkey to Britain's industrial expansion, as once was held, but it is certainly true that its harbors, essentially controlled from London, accepted about a third of all the United Kingdom's exports from 1790 to 1840 and half of all its cotton goods (the leading export product by far) in a trade that

---

* A Macclesfield silk weaver was recorded as complaining in the 1820s, "All at once the taste would pass away, and the silks would be upon the shelves. Soom'mut new was always coming up and that made the changes from the busy times to the slack times."

expanded from £6 million in 1800 to £41 million in 1830. India
provides a nice example here of what can be done with imperial
power in the creation of needs. Although it had a cotton-weaving
industry that was centuries old, India under British control was
forced to export raw cotton back to the United Kingdom cheaply
and import finished cloth from the United Kingdom at prices
that undercut the local weavers and eventually drove them out
of business, thus creating a large and well-primed market on
the subcontinent that would be a source of demand for many
decades.

One last instigator of needs during this time was—as it always is,
which is one reason it finds so much favor with governments—
the great maw of warfare. From 1793 to 1815, with only a few
lapses, Britain waged a protracted and enormously costly war
against France on the continent and in the oceans that required
unprecedented expenditures (and an unprecedented income tax),
something on the order of £1.7 billion over twenty-three years,
or roughly £74 million a year, compared to an average yearly
outlay on domestic affairs in these years of but £20 million.
Government orders to support a military force that amounted to
786,000 men in 1809, and enlisted more than a quarter of the
adult male population before it was over, were powerful stokers
of manufacturing fires: each man, after all, required uniforms and
blankets, armaments and ammunition, equipment, food, and
transportation. Moreover, the British government was largely
financing the anti-Napoleon forces of other nations on the continent—which amounted to at least £3.2 million—and encouraging them to acquire most of their material from British sources;
the Russians in particular were so fond of British woolens that
they kept a permanent agent in Leeds. For Britain the war was, as
one contemporary put it, "a period of exertion, of high excite-
ment," and for the British military in particular "a season of
spending, waste, and reckless prodigality."

All in all, the great French historian Fernand Braudel had it
right when he said that "the Industrial Revolution was in the end

a revolution in demand"—or, more exactly, he says, "a transformation of 'desires.'" But how fitting, how necessary, that it should be able to manufacture that demand and those desires as efficiently as it manufactured the means of satisfying them.

THE ORDEAL OF LABOR

But the prosperity among the few who could profit from the new calculus of needs, and the glitter that surrounds them even now in a kind of Regency glow (the likes of Beau Brummel, Lord Byron, Wellington, Castlereagh, Jane Austen, and the Prince Regent himself, "the Prince of Pleasure"), should not blind us to the extent of suffering among the many during these decades. However much we may become inured to the familiar images from Dickens or Disraeli, or Mayhew or Engels, of hollow-eyed urchins and bone-thin laborers, it is well to realize that they did indeed exist, and in profusion, making up indeed at least *a third* of England's population at any time decade after painful decade.

Fernand Braudel has written that the fact of "general impoverishment" in Britain after 1780—"a decline in real wages," "the catastrophic effects of wretched housing, unhealthy and even contaminated food," and "the social upheaval which tore individuals away from their family roots and the resources of the village community"—is one that too many historians "do not wish to face up to." And little wonder, for, as he goes on to show, "it seems abundantly clear that the English people paid very dearly" for becoming the first industrial nation, "even for the advance in agriculture which enriched only a certain class of farmers, and much more heavily for the machines, the technical triumphs, the commanding lead in trade, the pre-eminence of London, the fortunes of the industrialists and the shareholders in the Bank of England."

The people who paid most dearly were those who simply could not work, or find work, the bulk of whom were supported in the thinnest meager fashion by Poor Law relief. Numbers here are hard to come by, but the Poor Law rates are generally recorded: £2 million in 1785, £4.3 million in 1803, £7 million in 1813, and £8 million in 1818 (around which level they were to stay for the next decade), which suggests numbers on the order of 500,000 people receiving relief in 1785, 1.1 million in 1803, 1.8 million in 1813, and 2 million from 1818 on, or roughly as much as 10 to 15 percent of the population. ("Pauperism," said the *Manchester Mercury* in 1819, "is arrived at a most frightful state and the evil is daily increasing.") In addition, something like 180,000 families (330,000 people or so) were regarded as vagrants in 1803 and thus ineligible for relief, a figure that also must have increased with each passing year. In all the total number of indigents at the very bottom of British society around 1810 must have been well over 2 million, out of a population of 10 million.

That is indictment enough, one would think, but when we add in those who did have work of sorts and who still suffered, the picture becomes even bleaker. Again turning to Colquhoun, he estimated there were 340,000 families of laborers (excluding "artisans," mine workers, and seamen) in 1803—this would be about 1.4 million people—making an average of £31 a year, or 12 shillings a week, at a time when even conservative estimates would suggest that the cost just of food of the simplest kind ranged from 12 to 14 shillings a week. The years from 1790 to 1815, moreover, were years of recurrent harvest failures and inflation caused by the Napoleonic war, which ensured that even 12 shillings a week might not go very far and meals beyond bread and porridge and turnips might be very rare.

Among the laborers, the most famously impoverished were the handloom weavers in the cotton industry, probably a hundred thousand of them in Lancashire and neighboring areas at the turn of the century, more than in any other single industrial occupation in Britain. They had known good times in the recent past, especially after the spinning jenny (patented in 1770) magnified the production of yarn so rapidly that manufacturers would pay handsomely to get enough cottagers to turn it into

cloth, on the order of 15 to 20 shillings a week in the 1790s, sometimes more if government orders for the Army or overseas demands
were strong. But it was a trade that almost anyone could enter—
the machines were cheap (around £2), the skill could be learned
in a week, and no apprenticeship regulations applied—and it didn't
take long before the field was crowded and payments shrank. By
1811 the average weaver's wage was down to 10 shillings, by 1818 to
8 shillings, and by the 1820s to 5 shillings and less—when there
was work at all.

It is impossible to read any firsthand accounts of the weavers'
plight, from Parliamentary reports to workers' petitions, without
being struck by the agonies of their days, year after lamentable
year. But to take just one, from the weaver's own mouth, there is
this version of "The Oldham Weaver" from around 1815:

> *Oi'm a poor cotton-weyver, as mony a one knoowas,*
> *Oi've nout for t'yeat, an' oi've word eawt my clooas,*
> *Yo'ad hardly gi' tuppence for aw as oi've on,*
> *My clogs are both brosten, an stuckings oi've none,*
>   *Yu'd think it wur hard,*
>   *To be browt into th' warld,*
> *To be clemmed, an' do th' best as yo' con.*

True enough, the cotton weavers were the classic trade eliminated by the Industrial Revolution, the buggy-whip makers of
the 19th century—but they were not alone, and similar tales of
distress could be told of other callings, too. Wool combers, for
example, once artisans who could almost dictate their wages and
now displaced by machines:

> We are compelled to work from fourteen to sixteen hours per day
> [went testimony from a Yorkshire wool comber in 1840], and with
> all this sweat and toil we are not able to procure sufficient of the
> necessaries of life wherewith to subsist on. When we leave off work
> at night our sensorial power is worn out with fatigue . . . we have
> no time to be wise, no leisure to be good: we are sunken, debili-
> tated, depressed, emasculated, unnerved for effort; incapable of

virtue, unfit for anything which is calculated to be of any benefit to us at present or any future period.

Or agricultural field workers:

> An English agricultural labourer [said a Member of Parliament in 1830] . . . undergoes the pains of unsatisfied hunger almost all the time that he is not asleep. He is half clad, and has not more fire than barely suffices to cook his scanty meal. And so cold and damp are always at home with him, and leave him only in fine weather. . . . He must support his family, though he cannot do so, whence come beggary, deceit of all sorts, ending in fully developed craftiness. . . . He is depraved through and through, too far gone to possess even the strength of despair. His wretched existence is brief. . . .

All that, and we have still not come to the factory workers.

Some of those who worked in the new factories did quite well, at least in comparison to the wretched cottagers: a male fine-spinner in a Manchester mill could make between 24 and 30 shillings a week in 1810–19 and 26 shillings or so in the early 1830s, and male shop overseers maybe a few shillings better than that. But these were a small minority (only 2,200 spinners were employed in 1818, out of a cotton-factory population of perhaps 123,000), their work fluctuated with a continually up-and-down market, they were typically laid off before they were 30, and even then other members of the family would have to work for them to enjoy much in the way of extras. Overall, it is estimated that the average wage in a cotton mill, considering that something like four fifths of the workers were women and children and paid at a third or less of the men's rate, was between 9 and 12 shillings a week during most of the period from 1820 to 1840.

For all these hands the factory was a punishing and degrading abattoir for Wordsworth's "perpetual sacrifice." Conditions ranged from fair to fiendish—temperatures of 80° or more were standard in cotton mills, the noise of the looms was so deafening that workers developed a system of lipreading (called "mee-mawing") to communicate, the air was commonly so filled with cotton dust ("flyings" or "fuz") that they developed a distinctive lifelong cough, and work on the crowded floors among high-speed machines was so dangerous that accidents, many fatal, were almost daily occurrences. ("If they will invent machines to supersede manual labour," said one Lancashire weaver after his son was crushed to death in a cotton mill, "they must find iron boys to mind them.") A medical man who surveyed Manchester in 1831 found what he called "a mournful spectacle" in the factory workers, "a degenerate race—human beings stunted, enfeebled, and depraved."

So difficult, indeed, were factory conditions that the mill owners were generally hard-pressed to find enough people willing to tolerate them. Only reluctantly did adults succumb to the machines when there was no other work to do, and even then it was more common to have transient workers fill the bulk of the jobs, very often those forced off the land or emigrants from Ireland, rather than the local cottagers. Women and children could be coerced and manipulated more easily than men, but still it was the standard practice in the first three decades of the century to dragoon orphans and pauper children into the mills against their will. It took the lure of high wages, which employers were sometimes forced into, to keep such skilled men as the fine-spinners, warpers and winders, and engineers, but, as a modern historian has put it, the fact "that so many handloom weavers and framework knitters in the 1830s and 1840s preferred to starve rather than accept the discipline of the factory shows that many who did accept felt themselves to be driven there as a last resort." That, in fact, may be said to be the defining achievement of the Industrial Revolution: the creation of a society in which people are reduced to a choice between wage labor and starvation.

Living conditions were hardly better than working ones, except occasionally in those few company towns—New Lanark, Turton, Todmorden—where a shrewd mill owner saw the wisdom of providing decent dwellings. Health and housing in the industrial cities, which were already swelling with unprecedented populations by 1801, were bad and became worse as the factory decades went on,* until conditions became so deplorable that even the complacent Victorians were eventually forced to confront the situation and make—but not until the 1840s—the first attempts at melioration. William Cobbett, on his visit to the manufacturing districts in 1830, was surprised at the "wretched hovels . . . little better than pigsties"; Friedrich Engels described "unhappy abodes of filthy misery" and "tottering filth and ruin that pass all description"; Robert Owen reported conditions "terrible almost beyond belief . . . extremes of inhumanity utterly disgraceful, indeed, to a civilised nation." As late as 1842, when the Poor Law Commission issued the first comprehensive report on urban living conditions, its litany in city after city was the same— "the filthy condition of the town," "streets covered with stagnant water," "the atmosphere an active poison," "dunghills of immense size"—and it concluded: "The annual loss of life from filth and bad ventilation are greater than the loss from death or wounds in the wars in which the country has been engaged in modern times."

Death, indeed, was a way of life for industrial Britain. Deadly diseases—typhus, smallpox, measles, cholera, scarlet fever— coursed through the filthy slums, and children, particularly vulnerable, were described by the actuary of a Parliamentary committee in 1839 as "little blossoms which fall to the ground almost as soon as they see light." The statistics, imperfect as usual, were mostly gathered after 1830, but their burden would not have been much different in any of the years after 1800: in Manchester 57 percent died before the age of 5; in Preston (another factory town) 49 percent before 5, and 28 percent between 5 and 40; in Leeds, 53 percent before 5 and 25 percent between 5 and 40. Life expectancy at birth in 1842 averaged about 40 years for all of England and Wales, but for the "gentry" in Manchester and Leeds, two typical

* Manchester, most notably, grew by 22 percent from 1801 to 1811, an astonishing 40 percent in the following decade, and then by nearly 50 percent *again* by 1831 (when the population was 227,808), but nearly similar rates were shown by Ashton, Preston, Bolton, Oldham, Blackburn, Leeds, Huddersfield, Halifax, and other manufacturing cities.

industrial cities, it was 41, whereas for laborers in those two cities it was not more than 18. It can hardly be called a life, if it is to be ended barely after childhood.

In 1843 a physician of the Sheffield General Infirmary in Yorkshire, who was in a position to know, summarized thus the condition of the manufacturing districts of England: "We have no hesitation in asserting, that the sufferings of the working classes, and consequently the rate of mortality, are greater now than in former times. Indeed, in most manufacturing districts the rate of mortality in these classes is appalling to contemplate."

THE SERVICE OF THE STATE

According to the ideology of industrialism, called the doctrine of laissez-faire, the state was to leave the economy to its own devices and refrain from interfering in the free and self-correcting machinery of the marketplace. In reality, the British state worked in myriad ways, by acts of commission and omission, to advance the whole process of industrialization, enrich and protect the manufacturing sector, ensure a compliant labor force, and provide regular and prosperous domestic and foreign markets. "Handmaiden" would be too flimsy a word to describe it, because it was more active and interventionist than that, and "partner" would be too strong, considering all the ways in which the government stumbled into policies that pinched and disrupted the industrial districts over the years (such as the 1806–9 Orders in Council that stifled trade); perhaps Hilaire Belloc had it right in the title of his scathing work, *The Servile State.*

Of course it is assumed that the task of any state is to maintain the order and defend the border. It just happened that in Britain those tasks were understood to be properly carried out for the benefit of the rich and propertied—and for those, like the new industrialists, coming to be so—a charge that grew increasingly complicated as there was increasingly more to protect and defend, and that grew increasingly expensive as well, with taxes to feed the state taking fully a fifth of the nation's income by 1815. Keeping order, for example, meant not only a local militia and some magistrates in every town and shire—there would be no municipal police until the 1830s—but also, from 1801 on, a standing army, for the first time in British history. Protecting borders meant not only the deployment of this army at home, at levels that mounted from 25,000 before the French wars to 100,000 after, but also maintaining garrisons at all the colonial outposts and building a vast navy—160 ships of the line in 1790, 250 in 1815—to protect the routes between. And as the industrial wealth of England burgeoned, sometimes spectacularly so (it was estimated that the total capital value of the mills of Lancashire in 1816 was more than £20 million), and as the colonial empire of Britain did likewise (more than 1 million square miles were added between 1781 and 1815, and thereafter 100,000 square miles a year to midcentury), these tasks necessarily involved state power of increasing and unprecedented strengths.

Then there was the obligation of the state to enforce those basic rules by which commerce functioned, the kind of "interference" by government that even the most rigid laissez-fairist took for granted. The state's legal system was there to enforce contracts, protect manufacturing secrets, and oversee the body of commercial law; the state's patent system was there to assure that inventors and manufacturers reaped special profits from private ownership of knowledge, also backed up by law and by regular grants from Parliament of £5,000 and £10,000 to its favored inventors; the state's financial system, particularly the Bank of England, was there to control currency, act as a deposit and source for all other banks (696 of them in 1815), and in general, as Adam Smith had said with admiration, be "a great engine of State"; the state's postal system, with perhaps 4,000 employees in 1815 and 61 coaches, 4,000 horses and 54 packet boats, was there primarily for business and government functions; the state's tariff system, with some 7,500 excisemen on the domestic side and 9,000 customs officers on the foreign, was there to regulate trade so that it would favor certain goods and commodities, largely in the interests of the industrial sector, including large-scale agriculture.

All in all, then, enough cosseting and encouragement of profit, property, production, and private enterprise to make, one would have thought, an Adam Smith spin in his grave. But no: this was not interference, this was merely intercession, the normal process of an orderly government on behalf of (at least some of) its citizens. What Ricardo said on the subject of machinery was applicable to all else favored by the commercial classes: "The employment of machinery could never be safely discouraged by the State, for if capital is not allowed to get the greatest net revenue that the use of machinery will afford here, it will be carried abroad."

But there was still one more role of the state, as we have seen, that proved to be essential for the triumph of industry: the control, if not the outright subjugation, of labor. Most of the time this was done by omission, as it were, by Parliament's failure to provide workers with any power to countermand their employers or any means of redressing their growing list of grievances. As it was explained to the cotton weavers in 1811 when they asked Parliament for *some* relief from their obvious plight, "No interference of the legislature with the freedom of trade, or with the perfect liberty of every individual to dispose of his time and his labour in the way and on the terms he may judge most conducive to his own interests, can take place without violating general principles of the first importance to prosperity and happiness of the community." No matter that this freedom of trade had reduced 100,000 men and their families to near paupery, or that this "perfect liberty" somehow did not enable the weaver to find a job more ennobling than breaking stones for twopence a day; it was widely agreed, among sincere and thoughtful men, that the greatest good for the greatest number would somehow arise from manufacturers' ability to hire or not hire, raise wages or lower, at their individual and collective choice.

Nonetheless, these same Parliamentary solons could find reasons to achieve the control of labor by commission when they
saw fit. The acts of 1799 and 1800, for example, preventing "combinations" of workers in effect sanctioned any effort by employers
to lower wages without fear of significant resistance, which those
in the textile trades were not long in taking advantage of. Then
between 1806 and 1815 Parliament effectively disposed of a series
of provisions that had grown up since Elizabethan times by
which workers had been given various protections by the state,
including a required use of apprentices in some trades, prohibi-
tions against certain labor-displacing machinery, and the establishment of a minimum wage for some industries; as one manufacturer gloated about the elimination of apprenticeship, it "broke
the neck" of all labor organizing because protesting workers
could be "so overwhelmed by new men that we could do without
them." Altogether, the effect of Parliamentary action in the early
19th century was not merely, in J. L. and Barbara Hammond's
phrase, a "war on trade unions," but such a tilting of the scales in
favor of the new industrialism that it made the working population almost totally powerless, save for violence and its threat, for
the next half century.

But then, the laissez-faire system never was impartial, nor was
it meant to be, despite the cool recitation of its tenets as "natural law," inevitable and impersonal, by Adam Smith and the "Feelosophers." It was an economy, whatever else might be said about
it, designed to unleash certain human appetites, greed not
insignificant among them, and to enrich certain human endeav-
ors, material amassment being primary. All its talk about a free
market and iron law of wages and invisible hands was basically so
much camouflage for the free working of that system, having the
guise of an impartial economic theory but in fact being little
more than a partisan social blueprint. Take the "free market of
labor," for example: it never existed in Britain because labor was
never free to organize, workers never free to travel, the deskilled
never free to learn new crafts, and the unemployed never free to

enter trades already overstuffed with excess hands, or at least not in any meaningful sense. Parliament again and again used this free-market theory in resisting demands for a minimum wage or regulation of wages or boards to oversee wage settlements, all of which workers proposed in these years; but the theory was always an excuse for Parliament to do nothing so employers could do as they liked. The inequity of this excuse, not to mention its fraudulence, was apparent enough to most of the workers and their spokesmen—"Capital and property are protected and their labour is left to chance," as Richard Oastler complained to a Parliamentary committee in 1835—but they never made any headway with a close-minded government. To Oastler's appeal that "Government ought to establish a board . . . to settle the question of how wages shall be regulated," the committee chairman replied, and we may imagine the feigned horror in his voice, "You would put an end to the freedom of labour?" That is how a servile state operates.

THE CONQUEST OF NATURE

"Our fields are cultivated with a skill unknown elsewhere," Thomas Macauley boasted in full Whiggery in the 1830s, "with a skill which has extracted rich harvests from moors and morasses. . . . Our bridges, our canals, our roads, our modes of communication fill every stranger with wonder. Nowhere are manufactures carried to such perfection. Nowhere does man exercise such a dominion over matter."

The Industrial Revolution was the first spectacular triumph of the human species over the patterned, ancient limitations of the natural world. As Macauley was not alone in exulting, it was such an emphatic carrying out of the biblical order of "dominion over" that it not only changed the face of Britain, and subsequently most of the occupied world, but inaugurated an attitude, a deep-seated conviction, that regardless of the inevitable environmental costs, the powers of industrialization could and should be used to control and exploit the forces, species, and resources of nature. "We war with Nature," Carlyle said from up close, "and, by our resistless engines, come off always victorious, and loaded with spoils."

The transformation of the British countryside, first by enclosure and then by factory, was rapid, dramatic, and catastrophic, so stark that writers of the time could hardly fail to chronicle it. Early on Oliver Goldsmith saw the Midlands commoners driven off the lands—"Ill fares the land, to hastening ills a prey / Where wealth accumulates, and men decay"—and John Clare saw the effect on scenes of his childhood:

> To the axe of the spoiler & self interest fell a prey
>   & crossberry way & old round oaks narrow lane
> With its hollow trees like pulpits I shall never see again
> Inclosure like a buonoparte let not a thing remain
> It levelled every bush & tree & levelled every hill—

And Wordsworth saw his Hill Country become victim to progress:

> The foot-path faintly marked, the horsetrack wild,
> And formidable length of plash lane . . .
> Have vanished—swallowed up by stately roads . . .
> And, wheresoe'er the traveller turns his steps,
> He sees the barren wilderness erased,
> Or disappearing.

The history of England can in a sense be read as the history of its deforestation, which had eliminated maybe 95 percent of the original woodlands by 1700, but it was left to enclosure to privatize and largely destroy the last 4 million acres or so: Enfield Chase in 1777, Exmoor Forest in 1815, Windsor Forest in 1817, Hainault Forest in 1851, turning each such "nest and conservatory of sloth" (as the agriculturist Charles Vancouver put it in 1813) into "productive" acreage. By 1815, even after some prodigious tree-planting efforts, England and Wales were reduced to less than 2 million acres of woods, becoming probably the least-wooded place in all of Europe. All, even the very trees of the ancients, was subjected to human use—a "world with nothing left to the spontaneous activity of Nature," John Stuart Mill was to say, "with every foot of land brought into cultivation . . . and scarcely a place left where a wild shrub or flower could grow."

It is almost never reckoned what the cost to the nonhuman species of the sweeping enclosure movement must have been. Except for a few Romantics, contemporaries did not pay it much mind: there was a certain botanical vogue in England early in the 19th century, but was entirely preoccupied with foreign species—wisteria, dahlias, petunias, tulips—from all the exotic new lands British colonialism was pushing into or with creating elegant variations on the rose, whose varieties increased from less than a hundred in 1800 to 1,393 by 1826. So, although the farming and grazing of the moors, the deforestation of the woods, and the draining of vast wetlands (with steam engines for water pumps, of course) must have eliminated many plant species and decimated others, there seems to have been no specialist to record their passing. About the animal species we know somewhat more, since some hunters at least remarked that animals once available for slaughter in profusion were disappearing along with their habitat—martens, polecats, kits and ravens, eagles, goshawks, larks—but even here we have only occasional anecdotal evidence, nothing of a true measurement. Probably the best we can do is say, with modern historian Keith Thomas, that "the overall effect of human action, whether deliberate or inadvertent, was to bring about a dramatic reduction in the wild life with which England had once teemed."

What enclosure left undone industrialization completed. Cities exploded beyond their ancient boundaries, as grid systems imposed themselves regardless of topography into the fields and up the hillsides, and what there had been of open space or greenery within them was very quickly eaten up with new and usually ugly jerry-built housing for the onrushing populations: "It is

impossible not to notice the total absence of public gardens,
parks, and walks at Manchester," a local doctor testified in 1833.
"It is scarcely in the power of the factory workman to taste the
breath of nature or to look upon its verdure." In Birmingham the
last acres of the ancient heath were enclosed in 1799 and immediately became the site of industrial housing; in Oldham and
Bolton, as elsewhere in Lancashire, the city commons was bought
and built upon before 1800; public parks and large gardens and
orchards all quickly succumbed to the dreary factories and drear-
ier housing blocks, "built back to back; without ventilation or
drainage; and, like a honeycomb, every particle of space is occupied" (according to a Parliamentary report of 1840). Crossroads
villages, especially those near the canals that had now become
vital for coal deliveries and bulk exports, grew into bustling
towns and then small cities, without a shred of planning or regard
for site, guided only by the factory owner's decision as to where
most efficiently to build the plant and, when housing was necessary, where most cheaply to put up the quarters. "Environmental
impact" of course was not thought of at the time, except by a few
sentimental poets, but neither was elementary sanitation, avail-
ability of water, sewage flow, or anything remotely concerned
with the effects on nature or the health of those occupying it.
"Did I not pay them, to the last sixpence, the sum covenanted
for," Carlyle imagines the "rich mill-owner" saying: "What have I
to do with them more?"

The factories themselves in the center of these agglomerations
quickly became notorious for their extraordinary assaults upon
air and water. Coal was the pervasive fuel of the steam engine, 16
million tons were burned up in 1815 and 30 million in 1835, and
coal smoke was the pervasive air of the industrial towns:

> Coketown lay shrouded in a haze of its own [runs Dickens' famous
> depiction of Manchester in *Hard Times*], which appeared impervi-
> ous to the sun's rays. You only know the town was there, because
> you know there could have been no such sulky blotch upon the pros-

pect without a town. A blur of soot and smoke, now confusedly
tending this way, now that way, now aspiring to the vault of heaven,
now murkily creeping along the earth, as the wind rose and fell. . . .
It was a town of red brick, or of brick that would have been red if
the smoke and ashes had allowed it . . . a town of machinery and
tall chimneys, out of which interminable serpents of smoke trailed
themselves for ever and ever, and never got uncoiled.

But we have more than a novelist's word. As early as 1814, just
moments into the Steam Age, a German traveler reported that
"in Manchester there is no sun and no dust. Here there is always
a dense cloud of smoke to cover the sun while the light rain—
which seldom lasts all day—turns the dust into a paste which
makes it unnecessary to polish one's shoes." Or, as an official report
in 1842 put it succinctly, "The rainwater is frequently like ink."

The rivers, too, barely deserved the name. "The Aire," wrote a
correspondent to the *Artisan* in the 1830s, "like all other rivers in
the service of manufacture, flows into the city at one end clear
and transparent, and flows out at the other thick, black, and foul,
smelling of all possible refuse." Engels described the main river of
Manchester thus:

> At the bottom flows, or rather stagnates, the Irk, a narrow, coal-
> black, foul-smelling stream, full of *débris* and refuse, which it
> deposits on the shallower right bank. In dry weather, a long string
> of the most disgusting, blackish-green, slime pools are left standing
> on this bank, from the depths of which bubbles of miasmatic gas
> constantly arise and give forth a stench unendurable even on the
> bridge forty or fifty feet above the surface of the stream. . . . Above
> the bridge are tanneries, bonemills, and gasworks, from which all
> drains and refuse find their way into the Irk, which receives further
> the contents of all the neighboring sewers and privies.

So, too, throughout the Pennines, through the Midlands, down
to the Thames: industrial poisons—chlorine, coal tar, mercury,
lead, sulphuric acid, copper sulfate, tannic acid—joined with

offal and garbage to make a country of gray-black ribbons in which only algae and slime could grow. Fish were driven from the water—trout and bream and dace that once were plentiful in freshwater streams, salmon and flounder that had swum in the Thames for centuries—and only humans remained to drink the stuff. "Behold such outrage done to nature," indeed.

In every industrial town the toll upon life, all forms of life, was enormous, if largely ignored. Nothing could long stay healthy, or alive—save only the indomitable spirit of avarice that seemed to flourish in this atmosphere. Engels tells the story of remarking to a Manchester manufacturer that he had never seen so ill-built and filthy a city: "The man listened quietly to the end, and said at the corner where we parted: 'And yet there is a great deal of money made here; good morning, sir.'"

If we think of the mental and moral as well as the material transformations that took place in these decades around the hinge of the 18th and 19th centuries, it seems clear that industrial capitalism was revolutionary in so many ways that surely it is not an exaggeration to say that it was a whole new *culture*. Because that is the culture we have inherited today, it is sometimes difficult to understand how completely new and different it was, how drastically it changed the ideological as well as the natural landscape.

Perhaps there was no change more profound than the process by which the industrial culture came to believe that there were really *no limits* to what humans could do in the name of industry, or progress—or rather that any such limits could be transgressed, in time if not now. Braudel, in his intricate three-volume analysis of world history from the 15th to the 19th centuries, remarks, as he approaches the end of his survey:

> Until the industrial revolution, every burst of growth came up against what I called in the first volume of this book, "the limits of the possible," a ceiling imposed by agricultural output, by the available means of transport, sources of power or market demand.

Modern growth begins when that ceiling or limit recedes indefinitely into the distance.

Or, rather, when it seems to so recede.

Imagine what happens to a culture when it becomes based on the idea of transcending limits—which is as much as to say, of doing the impossible—and enshrines that as the purpose of its near-global civilization. Predictably it will live in the grip of the technological imperative, devoted unceasingly to providing machinery to attack the possible, encapsulated in modern times by John von Neumann, the mathematician who pioneered the high-speed computer and helped build the atomic bomb: "Technological possibilities are irresistible to man. If man *can* go to the moon, he *will*. If he can control the climate, he will." There can be no exterior authority here, no morality, or none that is not defined by the imperative itself, by which the doable is good and the undone bad, and no way of factoring in the other range of principles and ethics with which human societies have operated.

Imagine then what happens to a culture when it actually develops the means to transcend limits, making it possible and therefore right to destroy custom and community, to create new rules of employment and obligation, to magnify production and consumption, to impose new means and ways of work, and to control or ignore the central forces of nature. It would no doubt exist for quite a long time, powerful and expansionary and prideful, before it had to face up to the truths that it was founded upon an illusion and that there are real limits in an ordered world, social and economic as well as natural, that ought not be transgressed, limits more important than their conquest.

But it would be the obligation of some members of that culture to remind the rest of those truths and of the real dangers that come about when they are ignored. Such were the Luddites in the England of 1811, men and women who needed to call attention, sometimes with hammer and pike, to the consequences of a transcendence of limits that leaves injury and misery in its wake.

3

The Luddites

November–December 1811

UNUSUALLY WARM WEATHER prevailed over most of England in the fall of 1811, a surprise after a summer so cold that in some parts of Nottinghamshire the edges of rivers froze and "ice of considerable thickness" was reported on several nights in late June. Down in Tunbridge Wells, the fashionable resort in Kent just thirty miles southeast of London, it was so warm that society painter Joseph Farrington noted in his diary that no fires were needed until late October. And around Yarmouth, the port in easternmost England, the catch of herrings from the North Sea could not be sent on to the metropolitan market for fear of spoilage, because it would take over a day at peak speed to travel the hundred miles to London.

The warm weather after the freakish summer, however, had done very little to help the year's harvest, down again for the third year in a row both in Britain and on the continent, and the government was taking an increasing share of it to feed the troops of its growing army, including the thirty thousand men it had sent to Portugal to fight Napoleon on his southern flank, in a dreary, no longer inspirational war that seemed to go on and on—nearly twenty years now—without prospect of victory. As a result, the price of food stayed at an unusually high level, about twice that of the prewar rates; a four-pound loaf of bread averaged about one shilling and fivepence, and wheat, oat, and bean prices were all at the highest they had been for several years. What little there was to eat, in short, was for many too expensive to buy.

At the same time, the country was feeling a terrible economic pinch. The Continental Blockade begun by Napoleon five years before to cut off markets for British goods and the retaliatory Orders in Council by the British government that had put an end to the lucrative trade with the Americas earlier that year had caused a terrible downturn in the vital international trade: exports had fallen by a third (from £48 million to £32 million) from the year before, the U.S. market had totally dried up, and bankruptcies, particularly in the export-dependent textile trades, were rising to record levels. Cotton weavers were earning little more than five to ten shillings a week, wool workers about the same, and half of them had no work at all for months on end; Poor Law relief payments to the destitute were at a record high £6.6 million, but even so, most men out of work could not qualify. Three petitions from nearly eighty thousand cotton weavers of Lancashire and Scotland had been sent to Parliament that spring describing "the most dreadful situation, beyond all precedent and example" of "that valuable part of the people the COTTON WEAVERS" and asking for redress; as of November, no such had been forthcoming, the Parliamentary committee devoted to the matter having determined that despite "the great distress of numbers of persons engaged in the cotton manufacture," it would be an improper intrusion of government to provide "grants of pecuniary aid, to any particular class of persons suffering temporary distress," since that would destroy what it liked to call "the equilibrium of labour and of employment." And so the "distress" deepened month by month; even the elder Sir Robert Peel, a Tory not notoriously given to sentiment, remarked that English workers "had never known such misery."

Social London, by contrast, had never known such luxury. With the fashion plates known as the dandies setting the pace—

chief among them Beau Brummel, who estimated about then that "with the strictest economy" a man in London might dress himself for £1,000 a year—London's upper sets swirled from opera to circus to gaming house to theater to billiard hall, from London social club to country estate to seaside resort, showing no signs that they had any idea that three of the apocalyptic horsemen were riding down upon their tight little island. Just that February old King George had finally and officially been declared insane—it was said around London that summer that he was having regular political conversations with Henry VIII and Cardinal Wolsey, and showing great knowledge of English history the while—and the duties and garlands of his office had necessarily fallen to his eldest son George, the Prince Regent, an event that was celebrated with all manner of fetes and balls and galas but none so magnificent as the great banquet staged more or less in his own honor by the Prince himself that June.

The Prince Regent at this point had lived almost fifty years without a single accomplishment to his name, unless it be the accumulation of debts from gambling, drinking, and general profligacy that amounted to an astonishing £630,000 in 1795— just about half the money Britain was then paying to all the countries of Europe to carry on the war against France—and would continue around that level off and on throughout his life. His career had given a new meaning to the term "dissolute," to which his immensely fat body and pocked face bore testimony, and because "he was continually seen in those pavilions of Pleasure," a contemporary biographer said, "where honour is not known," even those with a sense of loyalty to the Crown were hard put to accept the idea of this corpulent scapegrace in the most honorific position in the land. Not without charm and occasional wit, with some flashes of taste—he admired Jane Austen, whose *Sense and Sensibility* had been published earlier that year, and Walter Scott and the architect John Nash—he was nonetheless totally without any notion of propriety and responsibility commensurate with his position, and was utterly insensitive to the subjects he was to inherit. While starvation and destitution grew across a land choked by depression and wracked by war, he chose to celebrate his accession with a royal fete at Carleton House, his London palace, for two thousand guests and the French royal family in exile, that featured an actual two hundred-foot stream flowing by the main table, with fish swimming in it, and courses of fish soups, fish roasts, and fish fries, platters of peaches and other fruits, puddings and cakes in endless succession, and a special staff whose only task was to serve uninterrupted champagne. It cost, according to young Percy Shelley, who hated the event and its luminary, not less than £150,000, which was about how much five thousand laboring families would earn in a year.

Five months later, on November 3, a Sunday, a National Society for Promoting the Education of the Poor in the Principles of the Established Church was launched, with the Archbishop of Canterbury as its president. Its royal patron was the Prince Regent.

That fall in Nottingham—a city exactly in the middle of England's north-south axis, in the area hence called the Midlands—a considerable gloom hung over the city as a result of what its Common Council called "the very depressed state of the Manufacturers for the last twelve months," which hit hard at the hose- and lace-weaving industries that the area depended heavily upon. Taxes to pay for the continental war were high, the Orders in Council had dried up cotton and silk exports, and warehouses were now filled with the goods—plain and fancy stockings, laces and nets, gloves and mittens, cravats and handkerchiefs and other incidentals of fashion—that once had made the city famous. In the face of that the few bright moments of recent weeks, such as the visit by Sir Sidney Smith, whose naval heroics had forced Napoleon to retreat from Acre to Cairo in 1798, when the war was still popular, and the opening of the new lunatic asylum in October, had not done much to alter the mood of darkness and foreboding, and even the mild weather provided only illusory relief.

Census results from the May count had been announced over the summer, giving Nottingham a total of 34,358 people, up from the 1801 census of 28,801, the kind of growth that was bound to cause housing and sanitation problems, especially in a city like this that was effectively cut off at the northern end by high ground difficult to build on. In all there were 6,538 inhabited houses counted but 7,245 families, suggesting that already people were packed into the jerry-built "back-to-backs" that would shortly give Nottingham the reputation as the place where "the poor live on each other's backs"—typically on unpaved and undrained dirtpaths that were catchments for rain, dung, ashes, and refuse. Females outnumbered men 18,824 to 15,534, probably because so many of the latter were in uniform elsewhere; 6,793 families were listed as involved in trade and manufacturing, 110 as being in agriculture of unspecified kinds, and 298 as "other," at both ends of the income spectrum.

The weavers who were the heart of the Nottinghamshire textile trade—usually doing cotton work, sometimes silk, with most of the wool work done some miles south in Leicester—were known as *frame-work knitters,* from the frames, or looms, they worked on, or as *stockingers* or *lace-workers,* from the products they made. They generally worked at home, particularly in the outlying villages, where the bulk of the work was done, or in shops of four or five in the larger towns, renting their frames from and doing piecework for hosiers who would usually be responsible for supplying the raw yarn and marketing the finished product. They had known a number of good years in the decades following the outbreak of war with France, in part because of military orders from the government, in part because rich and poor alike wore knee-stockings with their britches, and the rich demanded fancy hose in multiple patterns. But with the overseas trade cut off, where half the hosiery and three quarters of the lace production had previously gone, and with the damnable fashion in London having turned to pantaloons and loose-fitting "trowsers" that made fancy stockings unnecessary, the knitting business was in a serious slump. Probably as many as 9,000 stocking frames had operated in Nottinghamshire in the peak years and another 11,000 in Leicestershire and Derbyshire, plus maybe 1,500 lace machines overall, but by 1811 it was estimated that fully a fifth of them were idle and the others worked mostly sporadically, and at an average of just seven shillings a week. As many as four thousand families in Nottingham were reduced to Poor Law charity, more than half of all the families of the city:

> How many thousands of times [wrote the contemporary Nottingham historian William Felkin, a knitter himself], was that cry repeated—"Give us work at any price; half a loaf is better than no bread!" It was a heavy cry uttered too often ever to be forgotten. . . . The misery of the poor . . . readily drew towards the point that passes endurance.

That misery had many components. In addition to the high food prices and depressed wages common throughout the industrial counties, grievances particular to the frame-workers rankled: being at the mercy of the hosiers, the merchant capitalists of Nottingham, for how much work was given out, how much would be paid for it, how much rent would be charged for their frames, what kinds of articles would be produced; having no way to stop new workers entering a trade already overpopulated, because certain hosiers would always accept new hands without adequate apprenticeships who would work at cheaper rates; becoming trapped in a "truck" system of payment in goods (whatever goods were found to be convenient and cheap) instead of cash, whenever the hosier was short of funds. "This is a state of misery," went a knitters' petition of these years to the Duke of Newcastle, "wretchedness itself cannot depict."

And the new machinery. Factories as such were not that common in Nottinghamshire, but more than a hundred cotton-

spinning mills were operating in nearby Derbyshire, some of
immense size, and at least eleven wool factories and four calico
mills, all of which unmistakably suggested an ominous future for
anyone in the textile trades. For the lace-makers the future was
already present: a new wide-frame machine had been patented in
1809 by John Heathcoat that significantly increased output and
decreased the need for labor (some five hundred of the old
machines had already been put out of business), and his proto-
type lace-making factory in Loughborough, some fifteen miles
south of Nottingham, which opened in 1810, was about to convert to steam and was being copied even now by other manufacturers. For the stockingers the prospect of the factory lay still
ahead—though in some respects the total control by the hosiers
of frames, materials, and remuneration was nothing less than
a kind of extended factory system—but the impact of new
machines could already be painfully felt. Or rather of an old
machine newly adapted: a wide frame that previously had been
used only for pantaloons had in recent years been given over to
shoddy hosiery products called "cut-ups," because men hard-
pressed, or unscrupulous, would knit a large cloth and then proceed to cut up the faces of the stockings with scissors and sew
them together instead of knitting them in a single piece on a normal narrow frame. Using these machines one man, it was said,
could turn out the work of six, and a Parliamentary inquiry the
next year estimated that five hundred knitters had already been
done out of jobs because of it, and here, too, the future was clear.
Worse than that, though, these cut-ups were so inferior in quality
that they would usually fall apart after one wearing, discrediting
the entire Nottingham hosiery business and quickly drying up
the market for legitimate products; the "goods being wrought"
on wide machines, the *Nottingham Review* said that November,
"are deceptive to the eye, are disruptive to the trade, and therefore pregnant with the seeds of its own destruction." Yet there
were hosiers who insisted on manufacturing cut-ups, and men
reduced to supplying them for want of any other work, and

knitters in any Nottinghamshire village could tell when they were being made, the sound of a wide frame making cut-up cloths being so distinctive an experienced hand could hear it from the street.*

But at bottom the workers' grievance was not just about the machinery—it *never* was just the machinery throughout all these years—but what that machinery stood for: the palpable, daily evidence of their having to succumb to forces beyond their control, beyond their power even to influence much, that were taking away their livelihoods and transforming their lives. They might concentrate on the hosier and demand from him a higher wage, or more work, or an end to cut-ups, or less frame rent, but they understood that the hosier was part of an infinitely wider net that stretched beyond the shop, beyond the city, beyond the nation even. They knew there were hosiers who would take their side and refuse at first to manufacture cut-ups or offer lower

---

* It is somewhat curious that the impression was widespread at the time that opposition to some kind of new knitting machine had caused the initial Luddite uprising in Nottinghamshire. The Duke of Newcastle, for example, who lived in Nottingham and knew something about the hosiery trade, reported to the Home Office on November 16 that "a new machine had been invented which enabled the manufacturers to employ women in many instances in which men had hitherto been employed." After being briefed by the Home Secretary in early 1812, a select committee of the House of Lords also reported in July that Luddism "was supposed to have been excited or called into action by the use of a new machine, which enabled manufacturers to employ women, in work in which men had been before employed." And Lord Byron, who also knew Nottingham well, referred in his House of Lords speech in March 1812 to "men sacrificed to improvements in mechanisms" and no one contradicted him then or after.

Among modern historians, however, I can find only A. Aspinall in his documents of early trade unions in 1949 who claims that "a new kind of frame had been introduced, which required less manual labour, and women were employed instead of men, at a reduced rate of wages," and he provides no specifics. Many other historians argue that it was not new machinery that drove Nottingham Luddism: "If workmen disliked certain machines," as Malcolm Thomis has said, "it was because of the use to which they were being put, not because they were machines or because they were new."

But the consistent contemporary impression could not have been totally without foundation. There is no doubt that the wide frames newly used for cut-ups and the new lace machines (which in some cases *were* run by women) were generally detested, and that they were the targets of many of the Luddite attacks (especially at the start: see the 1811 *Annual Register*), and it is this that may have led to the contemporary idea that it was always new machinery that was the target of the workers' ire.

wages, but who eventually would complain that they couldn't stay in business, as part of this wider world, with rising expenses and dwindling sales and therefore had to submit to Gresham's Law of the market, that cheap goods drive out dear.* This was the morality of the society of industrial capital, and it apparently had no place in it for the morality of a society where the well-being of workers and their work, the salubrity of family and community, mattered most.

The practice of machine breaking as a tactic in industrial disputes was more than a century old, there having been at least thirty-five instances (as I calculate it from imperfect records) of sufficient severity to attract some public notice. In many instances, though, it seems that the workers' grievances had nothing to do with the particular technology itself, and their destruction of machines was simply a way to wring one on-the-job concession or another from their employers—what historian Eric Hobsbawm has called "collective bargaining by riot," or, more accurately, by sabotage. As recently as 1779, for example, knitters from the Nottingham area had descended on the city to protest the defeat of a Parliamentary bill aimed at establishing a minimum wage, during which they destroyed several hundred stocking frames and burned down the house of a hated hosiery middleman; the tactic succeeded in getting the hosiers to raise wages throughout the trade "up to a fair price, not the highest rate, but the best generally given." At times, however, machine breaking was also an end in itself—Hobsbawm cites a 1675 attack by Spitalfields weavers against a machine they feared could do the work of twenty men—and with the advent of the Industrial Revolution there began a series of attacks aimed at some specific

---

* As a spokesman for the Manchester weavers said in 1823, "I do not mean to insinuate that all our Manufacturers desire that gain, which cannot be had without keeping us at the starving point.—No, Sir, we believe that the greater number of them would rejoice to pay us well. But however good their wishes be, it is impossible for them ever to be realised, while the whole state of our Wages is determined by a few Competitors, who, to effect speedy sales reduce Weavers' wages."

machine or factory that was either putting workers out of their jobs or severely reducing their wages, disputes that had nothing to do with "collective bargaining" at all but rather with the machines themselves, their unwelcome imposition, and their threat to what the workers felt was customary, or just, or legitimate.* As one Yorkshire cropper wrote in a letter in 1802:

> We know that it have been mentioned to our great men and Ministers in Parliament by them that have Factorys how many poor they employ[,] forgetting at the same time how many more they would employ were they to have it done by hand as they used to do. . . . Our Gentlemens time is so took up with skeming Inventions to take away Poors Labour that if a Vestry is called there is hardly any Person to Attend. . . . The burning of Factorys or setting fire to the property of People we know is not right but Starvation forces Nature to do that which he would not[,] nor would it reach his Thoughts had he sufficient Employ. We have tried every Effort to live by Pawning our Cloaths and Chattles so we are now on the brink for the last struggle.

In the case of the Nottingham weavers in the fall of 1811, never had the conditions been riper for waging that "last struggle," against both the hated machines, the new lace-making machines and the wide frames used for cut-ups, and the hated masters who did people out of work with such machines or cut the wages of those still employed on the old machines. And when it finally

---

* At least seventeen industrial actions from 1767 on were aimed at unwanted machines: in 1767 against gig mills, Warminster; 1768 against new looms and against a sawmill, London; 1769 against the spinning jenny, Lancashire; 1773 against new stocking machines, Leicester; 1776 against gig mills, Shepton Mallet; 1779 against Arkwright's mill and spinning machines, Lancashire (Chorley, Wigan, Bolton, Blackburn, Preston) and against a gig mill, Leeds; 1781 against gig mills, Frome; 1786 against new calico printers, Lancashire; 1788 against wool-spinning machines, Leicester; 1789 against wide frames, Nottingham; 1792, against a power-loom factory, Manchester, and against gig mills, Gloucester; 1797 against a cloth mill, Nottingham, and gig mills and shearing frames, Somerset; 1798 against gig mills and shearing frames, West Country; 1799 against gig mills, Leeds; and 1802 against gig mills, Wiltshire.

burst forth it did so with more tumultuous force than England had ever seen before.

The night of November 4, a Monday, was cloudy but still not winter-cold. In the little village of Bulwell, some four miles north of Nottingham, a small band of men gathered somewhere in the darkness and, as we may assume from later accounts, blackened their faces or pulled up scarves across their faces, counted off in military style, hoisted their various weapons—hammers, axes, pistols, "swords, firelocks, and other offensive weapons" (as one report had it)—and marched in more-or-less soldierly fashion to their destination. Outside the house that was most likely the home of a "master weaver" named Hollingsworth they posted a guard to make sure no neighbors interfered with their work, suddenly forced their way inside through shutters or doors, and destroyed half a dozen frames—presumably the wide lace frames, though the accounts of the day say only that Hollingsworth "had rendered himself obnoxious to the workmen"—before scattering into the darkness. Reassembling at some designated spot, the little band responded in turn to a list of numbers called out by the leader, and when each man had accounted for himself a pistol was fired and they disbanded, heading for home.

A week later, this time on a Sunday night, the workers attacked again: same procedure, same target, only this time Hollingsworth was ready. In preparation for a renewed attack, he had sent some of his frames to Nottingham for storage and had arranged for seven or eight of his workers and neighbors to stand watch with muskets over the seven frames remaining. When the attackers approached the house they demanded that Hollingsworth let them in or surrender his frames, and when he refused a shot rang out and a fusillade of eighteen or twenty shots was exchanged. One young man, a weaver from the nearby village of Arnold named John Westley (or Wesley), was shot—while "tearing down the window-shutters to obtain entrance by force," according to one account, or "when in the act of entering the door of the room in which the frames stood," according to another, which added that before he died he "had just time to exclaim—'Proceed, my brave fellows, I die with a willing heart!'" His comrades bore the body to the edge of a nearby woods and then returned "with a fury irresistible by the force opposed to them" and broke down the door while the family and the guards ("or what should have been so") escaped by the back door. They then smashed the frames and apparently some of the furniture, and set fire to the house, which was a gutted ruin within an hour; the men dispersed into the night, never identified, never caught.

That same night just a few miles away in Kimberley, another group of men raided a shop and destroyed ten or twelve frames, apparently in retaliation for the employment there of "colts," young men not properly apprenticed and hired on at wages below standard.

On Tuesday a cart carrying eight or nine looms to safety from the Maltby and Brewett firm in Sutton, fifteen miles north of Nottingham, was stopped as it was driven through Basford, just north of the city, and men with their faces blackened smashed its cargo with heavy hammers, bent the metal parts to uselessness, and made a bonfire of the wooden pieces in the middle of the street. That evening (or, in one account, the next) a thousand men descended on Sutton from nearby villages, assembling at a milestone on the main road to the north, and marched on the town with their axes and pikes and hammers; about three hundred of them were said to be armed with muskets and pistols. The number of machines they broke is given as somewhere between thirty-seven and seventy, said to be "the frames of the principal weavers" of the town, one of whom, named Betts, whose shop was completely destroyed, was reported to have died soon after, "deranged." That night, or early the next day, the Sutton magistrates—local gentlemen of standing, acting as justices of the peace with initial police and judicial powers—finally decided to call for help from a local militia unit, numbering about thirty, from the neighboring town of Mansfield, and to this were added seven dismounted Dragoons who happened to be passing through as an escort for two French prisoners. (There being no local police forces in Britain, magistrates generally relied on local militia units, a kind of domestic army-in-waiting behind the regular troops, or on local volunteer "yeomen," mostly small farmers on horseback.) The troops arrived in Sutton later that day and arrested nearly a dozen of the frame breakers still in town, five of whom were committed for trial the following March.

On the Thursday of that week, the body of John Westley was carried through Arnold, amid a crowd of nearly a thousand men whose mood was described by a local annalist as "of a really terrific character," with "looks of stern and savage defiance . . . on every countenance," the feeling obviously being strong that murder, even of a man coming to attack your machines, was fundamentally wrong and overstepped the bounds. Expecting trouble, the town authorities had assembled a half dozen armed magistrates, a posse of volunteer constables, a company of mounted Dragoons from a Nottingham garrison, and a detachment of local militia, and this force followed the corpse into the churchyard amid "yells, threats, denunciations, and cries for vengeance" on every side. The Riot Act was then read by one of the magistrates— according to which the assembled throng was supposed to disperse immediately under threat of arrest, but without effect, and

as some of the ringleaders were proceeding to address the multitude [according to the account in the *Annals of Nottinghamshire*], even whilst the funeral service was being read, the regimental drums were beaten, and the spirit of confusion, amounting almost to demoniacal phrensy, seemed to pervade the whole assembled multitude. Directly the coffin was lowered, the magistrates gave orders for the church-yard to be cleared. There was at first some difficulty in carrying this order into execution; but as the authorities at length gave orders for taking every one into custody who disobeyed the command, a clearance was at length effected.

But the anger was seething in the district, and a rebellion had begun that would not be smothered by Dragoons and magistrates. It was now that anonymous letters explaining the causes of the machine breaking and threatening more of it started appearing throughout the district, mailed to or slipped under the doors of hated hosiers, sent to local newspapers, or posted in the night on public boards—"many hundreds" of them by the beginning of December, reported one manufacturer. All announced that a new and concerted movement was afoot; all were signed by, sent to, or invoked the name of Edward (Ned) Ludd, "King," "Captain in Chief," or "General." One letter, perhaps the first, etched on copper plate in a meticulous, flowing hand and dated November 1811, began as follows:

DECLARATION: EXTRAORDINARY

Justice.

Death, or Revenge.

To our well-beloved Brother, and Captain in Chief, Edward Ludd. Whereas, it hath been represented to us, the General Agitators, for the Northern Counties, assembled to redress the Grievances of the Operative Mechanics, That Charles Lacy, of the Town of Nottingham, British Lace Manufacturer, has been guilty of divers fraudulent, and oppressive, Acts—whereby he has reduced to poverty and Misery Seven Hundred of our beloved Breth[r]en; moreover, it hath been represented to us that the said Charles Lacy . . . has obtain'd the Sum of Fifteen Thousand Pounds, whereby he has ruin'd the Cotton Lace Trade, and consequently our worthy and wellbelov'd Brethren . . .

It appeared to us that the said Charles Lacy was actuated by the most diabolical motives, namely to gain riches by the misery of his Fellow Creatures, we therefore willing to make an example of the said Charles Lacy, do adjudge the said Fifteen Thousand Pounds to be forfeited, and we do hereby authorize, impower, and enjoin you,

to command Charles Lacy to disburse the said sum, in equal shares
among the Workmen. . . .

    In default whereof, we do command that you inflict the
Punishment of Death on the said Charles Lacy. . . .*

An extraordinary letter, the clarion of an extraordinary movement, clearly expressing, behind all the flowery flourishes, what
E. P. Thompson has called "a violent eruption of feeling against
unrestrained industrial capitalism."
    Luddism had begun.

It is legitimate to call Luddism a movement, even to label it (as
did contemporaries) an "-ism," but it is well to understand how
much it was also an amorphous pattern of events, an unfolding
development rather than a formal and fixed organization or doctrine.
    When it begins in Nottingham, it displays for the first time
some of those essential heightened elements that will mark
it everywhere: pseudonymous letters, nighttime raids, quasi-
military operations, secrecy and solidarity, and a campaign to
instigate fear, or alarm, or dread in the hearts of those at whom it
is aimed. But when it is taken up in Lancashire and Yorkshire
within months—to what extent the result of emulation or of
instigation is a matter of controversy—it adds on public demonstrations, attacks on factories, arson and burglary as its character
hardens and the raids become more frequent, sometimes fren-
zied, even in the face of growing numbers of troops, and marked
with what could be a sense of desperation or maybe an exultant
feeling of impending victory. In Yorkshire in particular Luddism

---

* Charles Lacy, a prominent lace manufacturer, was never harmed and apparently paid no
money, despite this threat. The crime with which he is charged here was using a cheap
lace-making process akin to the "cut-up" stocking process, but he was also the partner in a
lace factory with John Heathcoat, who in 1809 had invented the bobbin-net machine that
could be worked in a factory (and eventually by steam). At some later point the partner-
ship dissolved, after Lacy lost most of his money (said to be £40,000 to £50,000) in failed
"mechanical experiments" and Heathcoat would not give him any more; in 1816 he owned
a lace-making plant in Loughborough in competition with Heathcoat and may have had a
hand in helping the raid on Heathcoat's factory by a rump contingent of "old Ludds."

rises to its most imposing form, rooted as it is in communities with long heritages and strong allegiances, and here there are clearer signs of an authentic insurrection—arms raids and the hoarding of weapons, the voice of a true rebel raised now and again, and eventually even assassination—and here the wave finally crashes against unyielding breaker rocks and is largely spent, only little more than a year after it begins. Thereafter the movement falters, splinters, fades. Over the next four years there are isolated incidents, largely in Nottinghamshire, but the core of it is gone somehow, and only its shadow—and its reputation—remain.

Luddism is, in sum, an organic phenomenon, best taken as a series of events that only gradually—and sequentially—come to reveal its intrinsics, rather than an artificial entity full-sized and unvarying from the first with screw-off parts that can be analyzed separately, as English historians have typically tried to present it.

But if this makes Luddism difficult to assess in the large, it is equally difficult to grasp in its details, which so often remain elusive and suggestive where we would hope for certainty and clarity. Take, for example, the question of when it really began. Following the thesis of F. O. Darvall in the 1930s, historians have traditionally marked its start with a frame breaking that took place in Arnold on March 11, 1811, following an angry outdoor meeting in the Nottingham market square that was broken up by mounted Dragoons. That night some sixty-three machines were broken at several shops of hosiers who had recently cut wages, and in the next three weeks an additional two hundred or so in various villages in that vicinity, including Sutton, Mansfield, Bulwell, and Kirby in Nottinghamshire and, just over the border in Derbyshire, Ilkeston. Another incident took place in mid-April in Bulwell, and then one more isolated incident, probably in Sutton, in July.

Frame breaking there was, but was it Luddism? There were no threatening letters accompanying these raids, there was no group accepting responsibility, and no mention of Ludd in any of his guises. Newspapers reporting these "outrages" did not distinguish them from the sort of machine breaking that had marked labor disputes in the past nor did they mention any grievances against particular machines. Local authorities were quite baffled as to how to prevent the raids, especially since they could not break the workers' web of silence even after making a few arrests, but they did not then call out the militia or the Dragoons as if this was a new kind of civil disorder. Because the frame breaking occurred in the same area as the November Luddite attacks and only a few months before, it might seem natural to lump them together, and yet that may be more than the evidence warrants. And, considering that true Luddism when it emerged in November struck many observers with the high order of its organization and discipline, it is possible to imagine that men who had begun with isolated and spontaneous actions in the spring—and seen them go largely without effect—had decided to develop a more deliberate confederacy over the summer, with the sort of military trappings some might have learned in the regular army or the militia, so as to initiate a more vigorous and concentrated campaign in the fall. It is in the fall, at any rate, that the personage of General Ludd and evidence of his "armies" first surfaces.

Which raises the next question of the origin of the name. All are agreed that it was used as a pseudonym by any number of people in the 1811–12 period and that there was never such a person as General Ludd (or "King Ludd" or any of the other variants) in command of the Luddite troops; but there is no agreement as to where this anonym arose. Historical consensus has followed, although with random variations, an explanation put out by the *Nottingham Review* on December 20, 1811, that once upon a time a boy named Ned Ludd who had been apprenticed to a knitter near Leicester was so reluctant to work that his master got a magistrate to order him whipped; whereupon the lad took a hammer and demolished his knitting frame, an act that gained such renown that when any machine was damaged people would say that Ned Ludd had been there. (Other versions, some also contemporary, suggest that his name was Edward, or Ned, Ludlum, that he was "not one of the brightest," that he was angry with his father, that he was annoyed at other boys tormenting him, that the date was 1779, and that weavers mad at their frames would frequently say, "I have a good mind to Ned Ludd it." Nothing supports or disproves any of this.) No attention, however, has been paid to other explanations with varying degrees of plausibility.

It is possible that the local Nottingham dialect had an expression similar to one in Cornwall, "sent all of a lud," meaning "struck all of a heap," or ruined. The word might connect to a place name, such as Ludlow or Ludbrook, from the Old English *hlude*, loud one. It could conceivably derive from a King Ludeca, an actual if shadowy personage who in A.D. 825 succeeded Beornwulf as king of Mercia, a territory roughly the same as the Midlands and containing Nottingham. Or it could, with more tenability, be rooted in a King Lud who was a fairly well known historical figure of the first century B.C. (connected in legend with the Celtic god Lludd) and who, as John Milton has it, "enlarg'd, and wall'd about Trinovant, there kept his Court, made it the prime City, and call'd it from his own name Caerlud, or Luds Town, now London . . . [and was] buried by the Gate from thence wee call Ludgate." It seems entirely plausible that this King Lud, whom Milton says "was hardy, and bold in Warr, in Peace a jolly Feaster," might well have been carried on in folktale over the centuries among countryfolk outside of London, particularly those who knew Geoffrey of Monmouth's classic 12th-century English history or Shakespeare's story of Cymbaline, Lud's grandnephew (which refers to "Lud's town with rejoicing fires bright," III.1.32).

In any case, the person of "King Ludd" and "Ned Ludd" or "Ned Lud" was repeatedly invoked in November and December of 1811 as the machine breaking incidents continued and became more frequent, spreading out into Nottinghamshire and farther south. But for all the attention they received—personal, journalistic, official, legal—the basic details of the operations were surprisingly few and not always consistent. Of course, all these activities were criminal—at the time frame breaking was punishable by seven or fourteen years' transportation to Australia, burglary by death, and the writing of threatening letters by death as well (though in fact there were no arrests for letters in 1811 and only five in 1812)—and we can't expect much information from the Luddite side. But the authorities too are skimpy with the sort of material that would help to flesh out such of their references as "the rioters proceed in considerable parties" and "the outrage, which was conducted with extraordinary skill and management." And even the newspapers and annals are very often at the level of "the spirit of tumult spread into the neighbouring counties of Derby and Leicester, in the manufacturing parts of which many frames were destroyed." So we are left with flashes of detail here and there, streaks of lightning that flare through the night of these years by which we must make out the landscape and the figures active in it; at times there is surprisingly clarity, but we must be resigned if at others it is all too dim.

"There is an outrageous spirit of tumult and riot," reported the magistrates of Nottingham to the public in November 1811 with not a little indignation. "Houses are broken into by armed men, many stocking-frames are destroyed, the lives of opposers are threatened, arms are seized, [hay]stacks are fired, and private property destroyed, contributions are levied under the name of charity, but under the real influence of terror."

At least a hundred frames were attacked in the last week of November, another hundred fifty or more in December, over an area of nearly thirty square miles stretching from Pentrich in Derbyshire to Shepshed in Leicestershire, in at least thirty-one villages and many parts of Nottingham city, affecting a swath of nearly fifty thousand people. At the same time Luddites were reported to be going around the countryside soliciting—or, as the authorities would have it, extorting—contributions from

fellow knitters and nonknitters alike. One note posted at a village
hosier's shop went:

> Gentlemen all, Ned Ludd's Compliments and
> hopes you will give a trifle towards supporting
> his Army as he well understands the Art of break-
> ing obnoxious Frames. If you comply with this
> it will be well, if not I shall call upon you myself.
>
> Edward Ludd

The tactic was apparently successful: "They have been in the
Country productive of a sense of terror," reported George
Coldham, the Nottingham town clerk, "which has enabled the
emissaries of the people who conduct them to collect considerable sums of Money of the Farmers, and of such of the
Framework-knitters and Lace Hands as are in employment."
William Felkin adds that "farm houses were plundered of provisions and money" by men who declared "they would not starve
while there was plenty in the land."

Nighttime raids were made with stealth and swiftness. As
many as twenty machines may have been destroyed in Basford
one night "within ten yards of the place where a Magistrate and a
party of Dragoons were stationed," without anyone sounding an
alarm; on one raid in well-patroled Nottingham the raiding party
placed sentinels at the doors of all adjacent houses and side streets
and then "demolished eight valuable frames, in about as many
minutes" and "not the least noise was heard in the street." A certain courage and coolness, too, were shown: William Felkin, a
special constable on duty at the time, reported that one night in
Nottingham a Luddite working alone entered a house undetected
but as he was breaking an upstairs frame he aroused several constables nearby and so was forced to scramble out a window onto
the adjacent roof, and

> passing along others he saw in the dim light that the earth had been
> lately turned up in a garden below, and leaped from the eaves of

a three-story house upon it. The frame-breaker quietly passed through a kitchen where a family were at table, and escaped. In a few minutes the shouts of a sympathising crowd were heard at New Radford, half a-mile from the scene of the adventure.

And where stealth and courage failed, numbers could prevail. A party of eight Luddites early one morning entered the house of a Nottingham weaver named Noble, who was turning out the cheap and shoddy kind of lace, put a guard on his wife, and went upstairs to destroy four of his machines with a sword, nearly cutting the man's head off in the process as he was sitting at his frame.

The screams of his wife [goes the account in the *Annals of Nottingham*], which even a severe blow on the head, from the butt-end of a pistol, by the ruffian left in charge of her, could not stop, brought Noble down to her assistance, and also a neighbour, who contrived to enter the house by the back door. They at once seized the fellow, and tried to disarm him; when, perceiving his danger, he shouted out at the top of his voice, "Ned Ludd!" and his associates rushed down stairs to his rescue. In the strife and confusion a pistol was struck by one of the gang, but happily missed fire. Finding the door fastened upon them from the outside, the desperadoes broke out the panels, and forced their way through a crowd of people, threatening with instant death any one who might attempt to arrest, or follow them; and so escaped.

The success of the Luddites in the area, night after night in defiance of an aroused establishment, very quickly won them a special place in the legendry of the Midlands as it did in the annals of the government. We know neither the author nor the date, but this accolade, the one with the Robin Hood comparison, is one of the earliest exhibits in the Home Office files:

Chant no more your old rhymes about bold Robin Hood
His feats I but little admire
I will sing the Atchievements of General Ludd
Now the Hero of Nottinghamshire

Brave Ludd was to measures of violence unused
Till his sufferings became so severe
That at last to defend his own Interest he rous'd
And for the great work did prepare

Now by force unsubdued, and by threats undismay'd
Death itself can't his ardour repress
The presence of Armies can't make him afraid
Nor impede his career of success
Whilst the news of his conquests is spread far and near
How his Enemies take the alarm
His courage, his fortitude, strikes them with fear
For they dread his Omnipotent Arm!

It goes on in that vein, rather skillfully, and in the course of it sets out with remarkable precision the main grievances of the workers: Ludd's "wrath is entirely confined to wide frames . . . these Engines of mischief" and "to those that old prices abate," but most especially—and it is italicized—to the *"foul Imposition"* of those evils by the "guilty" manufacturers. This is a General Ludd who not only has all the courage and daring of Robin Hood and shares his defense of the poor and the "honest workmen," but is the champion of "Custom and Law" by which they have for centuries conducted their lives as free Englishmen:

> *Let the haughty no longer the humble oppress*
> *Then shall Ludd sheath his conquering sword.*

At the outbreak of the Luddite attacks in November, the Nottingham magistrates announced that "all this tends to insurrection" and that it was their duty "to suppress these evils by civil and even military force, and to cause the due execution of laws which will affect the lives of offenders."

Force was a language in which the legal authorities of Britain were fluent—more than two hundred offenses, including the theft of a five-shilling pair of boots, were punishable by death in

Britain, far more than in any other European nation, and nearly 10 percent of those convicted had been sentenced to death in the year before this—and they were quick to exercise it here. Soon after the tumult of John Westley's funeral, ten troops of the Royal Horse Guards Blue and two regiments of the Berkshire regular militia, a total of some eight or nine hundred cavalry under the command of a General Dyott and a thousand infantrymen, were called to Nottingham—the greatest force, as Home Secretary Richard Ryder told the House of Commons the next year, that had ever been used in England's history to respond to a domestic "disturbance." To this force was added a rotating team of thirty-six special constables to patrol the streets at night, various troops of local reserve militia, a further regiment of five hundred or so regular troops in late December, and two police magistrates sent up from London to coordinate policy with Nottingham town officials; one observer said it looked like "a town in a condition of siege," with "the constant presence of numerous bodies of troops, of almost every variety of arms." The Nottingham City Council offered a reward of £500 for information about the "Authors Writers Publishers or Senders" of letters "under the fictitious name of Ned Lud" and another £2,000 (supported by subscriptions from the Duke of Newcastle, Nottinghamshire's lord-lieutenant, or governor, and a number of local lords and businessmen) for information "needful in suppressing the present illegal & felonious proceedings in the Town"; the national government chipped in with a Royal Proclamation on December 23 in which the Prince Regent offered a £50 reward for the conviction of any Luddite and a free pardon for any guilty party that would turn informant. And, it seems, the town officials were willing to use their powers in foul ways as well as fair: the Duke of Newcastle reported to Home Secretary Ryder that

> Special Constables, whose active services I have often mentioned to you, have entered the houses of the offenders and taken them away out of their beds in the middle of the night, and have several times

been fortunate in securing some of them in their own homes on the
first night of their return there after having slept at different houses
since the first commission of their offenses in order to elude the
search of the constables. This had a very great effect upon them, as
I am informed.

Yet none of it succeeded in checking "the outrages" or appre-
hending the leaders of it.

After two full months of apparently unstoppable Luddism, in
length and intensity unlike anything that Nottingham had ever
seen, what alarmed and perturbed the authorities most was that
they could not break the covert casing of secrecy under which its
agents successfully hid. The sizable rewards produced no information, the promises of amnesty and repeated threats of maximum prosecution prompted no confessions, even the use of paid
spies by the Duke of Newcastle and the Nottingham town clerk
provided no effective leads. "The grand difficulty," as the duke
told Ryder on December 9, "is the almost impossibility of
obtaining information respecting the movements and intentions
of the rioters, everything is so well organised among them, and
their measures are conducted with so much secrecy, added to
which, that no one dares to impeach for fear of his life, that it is
scarcely possible to detect them."* Or, as a Loughborough magistrate wrote a week later,

> We find the class of men to whom we are obliged to look for infor-
> mation, in general very unwilling to give it. The loss of their time,

---

* The "fear of his life" was well founded. This is the text of a December 23 Luddite com-
muniqué, probably posted in Nottingham:

> I do hereby discharge all manner of Persons, who has been
> employed by me in giving any information of breaking
> frames to the Town Clerk or to the Corporation Silley
> Committee, any person found out in so doing or attempt-
> ing to give any information, will be punished with death or
> any Constable found out making inquiries so has to hurt
> the cause of Ned or any of his Army, Death
>   By order of King Ludd.

and the dread they have of the vengeance of the ill-disposed among
their own class, operate together against their speaking the truth.

Even when authorities did make arrests—no more than two
dozen by early 1812, and some of those arrested were never
arraigned—the magistrates were not able to get Luddites to turn
in their colleagues.

> Nothing could penetrate the mystery of 'Luddism,' [reported the
> *Annals of Nottingham*], nor break the bond of union which bound
> its deluded and mischievous devotees together. In spite of all their
> errors, and all their crimes, it is impossible to withhold admiration
> from the stern integrity of purpose which thus led a number of
> poor men to withstand the tempting offer of bribes . . . and thus
> betray the cause in which they had engaged.

Such a bond of purpose led the authorities to assume that
there had to be a tightly knit organization at work with an
efficient hierarchy of command, and that was cause for even
greater alarm. Working from reports by magistrates in the field, a
committee of the House of Lords in the following year spoke of
"the systematic combination . . . with which the outrages were
conducted" and "a degree of caution and organisation" that led it
to believe that "all the societies in the country are directed in
their motions by a Secret Committee" that is "the great mover of
the whole machine," dispatching delegates "continually . . . from
one place to another, for the purpose of concerting their plans."
    But a system so elaborate, though possible, seems quite
unlikely, given the sheer number of isolated hamlets and little villages spread broadly across the terrain and the difficulty of travel
and communication among them, especially in secret. That these
groups had contact among themselves over several square miles
seems certain, and it is probable that they passed along forms of
military drilling and guard-posting and strategies of attack and
escape, along with the rhetoric of King Ludd and his "armies,"
since these elements characterized so many of the Luddite actions

in different parts of the Nottingham area (and indeed end up being imitated in the northern counties within months). But there is no shred of evidence for the existence of some overarching "Secret Committee" or a regular dispatching of delegates with its concerted plans. It is more likely that separate groups of men operated on their own under the effective rubric of Luddism, hatching their plans in the local pub and agreeing to train out on the moor a few nights a week, carrying out local grievances against local targets well known to them rather than following designs from afar. And the "systematic combination" that so alarmed the Lords was probably just the unity and sodality of workmen who shared a common trade and common grievance and could trust with their lives men from their community and the villages nearby. As an American sociologist, Craig Calhoun, has argued, all English popular movements were based on the strength of "traditional communities," and Luddism "grew directly out of local community roots" with men "linked communally to each other, and to the rest of the local population within which they lived."

By the end of December, after a Christmastime that must have been bleak indeed (but at least required no expenditure on gift-giving, a need-manufacturing custom only recently brought to England from Germany by the Prince Regent's sister-in-law, the Duchess of York, and not yet well established), there was a pause in Luddite activity sufficient to induce the Duke of Newcastle to believe that "the public tranquility will now be very soon restored" and "appearances are undoubtedly in favor of the near conclusion of the very disgraceful proceedings." Local accounts at the time reported that between eight hundred and a thousand frames had been destroyed so far, with a value of perhaps £25,000, based on the original cost of the machines (about £30 each). Nottingham had spent perhaps £3,000 on trying to keep public order, London's expenditure for troops billeted in the area may have come to an additional £14,000, and an incalculable amount had gone to private payments for armed guards and other systems of protection both by manufacturers fearful of attack and landowners fearful of a general insurrection on the recent French model. (Lord Middleton, for example, put thirty armed men on guard "night and day" at his estate near Nottingham, "which it is my determination to defend at whatever risk," including the placement of a tub of tar on the roof of his mansion to be lighted as a signal for help if the Luddites ever came.)

The practical effect to this point of the Luddite "Omnipotent Arm" was inevitably mixed. Some of the manufacturers took the threats directed at them seriously, as well they might have—

> You must understand there are more methods of revenge than frame-breaking to be resorted to [ran one Luddite letter from "Robin Hoods Cave"] . . . You may think we shall not be able to fire your houses but the means which will be used will be so effectual that the flame will rise to the highest room in the house in a moment. . . . But there are many other modes of revenge or rather punishment to be inflicted on the obstinate equally injurious to Life which will be used where this is not practicable.

—and fifty firms promised on November 30 to increase payments by six shillings a dozen for silk hose, and another hosier with three thousand frames agreed to a one-shilling-per-dozen increase for cotton goods. Several other hosiers and middlemen agreed to face-to-face negotiations with their workers, which were held several times in Nottingham and Mansfield throughout December, though eventually without agreement. Other manufacturers, however, particularly those with cut-up machines or large colting operations, found it harder to come to terms with the Luddite demands and generally preached defiance, urging London to unleash even greater force; William Nunn, for example, a lace manufacturer in Nottingham and one of the most obdurate, asked the Home Office on December 6 to organize a scheme of marked bank notes, declare martial law, authorize the Post Office to open Luddite mail, and in general make "the most severe examples" of the "infamous Wretches who exist in every manufacturing town in the Kingdom ready and ripe for all Mischief."

But whatever its effect as a bargaining tactic, machine breaking in just two months had made a statement about the Luddites' adversity and their determination to resist it that few could mistake. The Duke of Newcastle, even as he saw their campaign waning, had come by the end of the year to feel that "the most rational and best founded" explanation for their uprising was "*the distress of the workmen* who have unquestionably been most hardly treated by their employers; urged by absolute necessity to require a better treatment from their Masters they endeavoured to obtain better terms for themselves." In a long letter to the Home Office, a staunchly Tory magistrate of Southwell, the Reverend John T. Becher, was similarly sympathetic; after detailing a trail of abuses by the manufacturers and the "irritation & disappointment" of the workmen, he said:

> I ascribe the origin & progress of our present offences solely to internal animosities between the manufacturers themselves, and between the manufacturers & their workmen, acting upon the passions of a necessitous & dissolute class, who had been trained for insubordination by those who are now the objects of their vengeance; and who had been repeatedly told by many of their employers, & by the licentious paper brooded under their patronage, (the Nottingham Review), that the sovereignty resided in the people, and that it was their province as well as their duty to avenge their wrongs & to retaliate upon their oppressors.

Farther afield, too, the Luddites were being heard. George Gordon, Lord Byron of the ancient ancestral estate of Newton Abbey, located less than ten miles north of Nottingham, was in London working on the galleys of a poem called *Childe Harold* to be published the following year. In a letter to a friend on December 15 he wrote, somewhat lightheartedly, "I presume ye papers have told of ye Riots in Notts, breaking of frames &

heads, & outmaneuvering the military," and he added, "All my affairs are going on very badly, & I must rebel too if they don't amend." But Luddism obviously touched him deeper than that: within a few weeks, after a visit home at Christmas and exposure to the "Nightly outrage & daily depredation," he determined that he would make the Luddite cause the subject of his maiden speech to the House of Lords in February.

And on Christmas Day, Percy Shelley, who had just returned from a trip to Scotland and the north country and seen the distress of the industrial districts, wrote to his friend Elizabeth Hitchener:

> I have been led into reasonings which make me *hate* more and more the existing establishment of every kind. . . . have beheld scenes of misery. . . . [The workers] are reduced to starvation. My friend, the military are gone to Nott'm—Curses light on them for their motives if they destroy *one* of its famine[-]wasted inhabitants. . . . The groans of the wretched may pass unheeded till the latest moment of this infamous revelry [of the rich], till the storm burst upon them and the oppressed take furious vengeance on oppressors.

Furious vengeance indeed was at work. In the next months it would grow more furious, more vengeful—and more widespread.

4

The Luddites

January–April 1812

FOR ALL ITS DRAMA and effect, it could not be said that the Luddite campaign in Nottinghamshire had done much to relieve the suffering of the general body of workers as the new year began. According to the *Annals of Nottinghamshire,* the year opened "with an aspect of present wretchedness, and a prospect of future misery and destitution to one portion of its inhabitants, and embarrassment and ruin to the other." The severe national depression continued without any signs of political understanding or economic relief, and food prices continued to rise relentlessly, a loaf of bread now averaging a shilling and a half and going up and "every other article of domestic consumption as tea, sugar, spices, &c., at double and (in some instances) treble" its previous level. Spending on the French war increased—it was to end the year at £4 million over the previous year, nearly £30 million in all—but without benefit to the nonmartial stocking and lace trades, and the overseas markets remained cut off, with the United States threatening to go to war if Britain did not lift its blockade.

Little wonder that, as the *Annals* noted, "universal distrust and gloom pervaded the whole town. . . . Is it then to be wondered at that want and misery prevailed to an appalling degree among the working-classes; or that, in the desperation of their circumstances, they should be led to view almost every man, whose position in society afforded him an opportunity, in any degree, of exercising control over the remuneration for labour, as their enemy?" Or that then, "under the pressure of extreme suffering," they should have recourse "to insane projects" such as the breaking of machines, "for the redress of their grievances?"

Frame breaking indeed reached its furious peak in the first month of the new year. On January 3 nine frames were broken at Basford and two at Bulwell, nine more the next day, four more the day after, and eighteen more the following day, in villages all around Nottingham, from Sutton-in-Ashfield in the north to Ruddington in the south, from Heanor in Derbyshire to Melbourne in Leicestershire, forty in one week, ninety the next and well over three hundred in that one month alone. "In many villages in this country," the *Annual Register* reported in early January, "the terror and alarm of the inhabitants is such, occasioned by the late nocturnal attacks on the property of peaceable individuals, that they are afraid to go to bed at nights." The Duke of Newcastle, no longer optimistic, wrote to the Home Office that the region was "in a state of insurrection, for I can scarcely call it by another name." The correspondent of the *Annual Register* agreed, and suggested why it was so fearsome:

> The spirit of insurrection which has so long disgraced the county of Nottingham has been rendered doubly alarming, from the secrecy with which it has been conducted, and the dispatch with which the objects it embraces have been carried into execution. . . . Such is the regularity with which their plans are laid, and the dexterity with which they are carried into effect, that it has been found impossible to detect them. They assemble, and disperse when their object has been obtained, in a moment. They are marshalled and disciplined like a regular army, and are commanded by one particular leader, under whose banners they swear to conquer or die!

Additional troops were sent into the area. Two regiments of regular infantry from the South Devon militia were ordered to Nottingham and nearby villages at the end of January, another thousand men or so, bringing the total force to between three and four thousand. The effect of all these soldiers in such a densely populated area and in a nation where such deployments were completely unprecedented was frightening for many: "It is impossible to convey a proper idea of the state of the public mind in this town during the last four or five days," wrote a correspondent from Nottingham on January 29, "the constant parading of the military in the night, and their movements in various directions during both night and day, giving us the appearance of a state of warfare."

Warfare it was, though the confrontations were few and the Luddites generally continued to operate with impunity. On January 23, a cart full of frames being taken from Kimberley to be worked in Nottingham with greater protection was attacked at Radford at eleven o'clock in the morning by a man wearing a goatskin mask with a beard down to his waist, who went about smashing the machines and threatened to knock the carter's brains out if he interfered; "he was allowed to proceed with the demolition, when he started off at full speed down the road, towards Radford church, and was very soon out of sight." Two dozen men descended on a Nottingham lace-maker one night and after they had broken five of his new-style frames they decided to retreat because their noise had awakened a female neighbor who was screaming "Murder" repeatedly at the top of her voice; they'd had the foresight, though, to dress up in military topcoats, and as they left the premises the neighbors who had come running to help assumed they were a local band of soldiers making an arrest and let them depart unscathed.

Nor was the military all that successful when they were at the scene. One late January night a detachment of six men and a sergeant from the Berkshire militia, assigned to guard a single knitting machine at Bulwell, confronted a party of Luddites and exchanged fire with them but hit no one and captured nothing but a shoe and a sledgehammer. On another night two soldiers assigned to the house of a William Barnes were suddenly set upon "by about Twenty men, some armed with Pistols and

others with large sticks and their faces disguised with handkerchiefs over their chins" who grabbed their muskets, held them
prisoner, and proceeded to smash the frames belonging to a distant hosier while leaving intact those owned by Barnes himself—
Barnes was naturally then suspected of having Luddite lean-
ings—and finally fired the stolen muskets in triumph when they
were through. And on Saturday night, January 25, a group of
Luddites was so desultory about destroying some three dozen
machines in two little villages across the River Trent from Nottingham that word got dispatched to the city for a troop of
Hussars and a party of yeoman cavalry, which then galloped to
the river and sealed off all the bridges along a four-mile stretch.
The Luddites, however, simply found a small boat moored along
the shore, used it to cross the river quietly, not once but twice,
and made their retreat in perfect safety.

But it would be wrong to suggest that the extraordinary show
of government force did not have an effect. For one thing,
though the Luddites' letters continued to vow defiance ("If we
can't do it just tonight we will break them yet, and if we can't
break them we can break something better, and we will do it too
in spite of the Devil"), it was clear that their operations had to be
severely restricted, concentrating mostly on the smaller outlying
villages, and it is probable that the enthusiasm for raids amid
ranks of armed soldiers was somewhat diminished even in the
most fervent follower of "Brave Ludd." In February the nightly
attacks began to slacken —one frame was broken on the tenth in
the little hamlet of Hucknall Torkard, two on the fourteenth in
the same place, one in Derbyshire on the seventeenth—and after
the twenty-fourth there are only the most sporadic raids.

For another, the authorities now showed themselves eager to
make arrests, even on the most tenuous grounds. True, they most
often got men who were hangers-on or innocent bystanders, one
of whom, described as "a well-known maniac of the name of
Waplington," was arrested by a deputed London magistrate who

didn't realize he'd collared the village idiot and "excited much laughter" bringing him in. But their readiness to arrest and interrogate and jail almost at will showed their zealousness, and the fact that they had strong enough cases against at least ten Luddites to bring them to trial in March showed their determination.

It was also significant to the local population that the reaction of His Majesty's government to the knitters' cry for justice against "that *foul Imposition,*" however much they had crossed the line into illegality, was wholesale military vehemence. Such men as the Duke of Newcastle might express sympathy for "the distress of the workmen," but the signal from the ministers in charge was that there was no place in laissez-faire for the softhearted "paternalism" of 18th-century governments and that London's only response to violence would be violence: "Whatever the causes of the disorders," Prime Minister Spencer Perceval told Parliament, "did anyone deny the necessity of putting them down?"

As if to underscore the purposefulness of this position, the Tory government decided on February 14 to introduce a bill "for the more exemplary punishment of persons destroying or injuring any stocking or lace-frames"—in other words, the death penalty for Luddites. Machine breaking was already a crime, punishable by up to fourteen years' transportation, and burglary to effect such a crime was already punishable by death; but the government in its wisdom, and with considerable prodding from certain magistrates and many manufacturers upcountry, now sought to create an even more powerful deterrent and an even more powerful legal weapon: "The fear of death," as William Lamb (a future prime minister) told the House of Commons, "has a powerful influence over the human mind." The measure received token Whig opposition, with several pointing out (as Nottingham officials would later discover) that juries might be reluctant to find a man guilty if it meant his death, but the Tory argument that "the peculiar danger and extent of the outrages" demanded "some more severe punishment" carried the day, and the bill easily passed its decisive second reading 94–17 just three days later.

On February 27 the bill was read in the House of Lords, where no one expected any but the most conventional opposition. Lord Byron, however—the young poet with the chiseled good looks, the oddly deformed club foot, and an obscure and not very prestigious peerage behind him—asked leave to address the chamber, in what would be (though he had officially taken his seat in 1809) his maiden address.

Byron had been working on his speech since Christmastime, when he concluded that "if *conciliatory* measures are not very soon adopted, the most unhappy consequences may be apprehended." In early February he had written to Nottingham officials asking for documents "to bear me out in the statement of facts," and just before the Lords debate he had written to his political mentor, Lord Holland, warning that he was going to oppose the bill even though "your Lordship does not coincide with me entirely on this subject" and arguing that "from my own observations on ye spot" he felt the Luddite grievances "call rather for pity than punishment."

The speech was eloquent even by Parliamentary standards, though somewhat deficient in organization and quite ineffectual in persuasion. Byron made his sympathies with the knitters clear from the start, contending that "nothing but absolute want" and "the most unparalleled distress" could have driven them to "excesses so hazardous"—"never under the most despotic of infidel governments did I behold such squalid wretchedness as I have seen since my return to the very heart of a Christian country"—and that the "real cause of their misery" was "the destructive warfare of the last eighteen years, which has destroyed their comfort, your comfort, all men's comfort." "These men were willing to dig, but the spade was in other hands; they were not ashamed to beg, but there was none to relieve them; their own means of subsistence were cut off, all other employments preoccupied; and their excesses, however to be deplored and condemned, can hardly be the subject of surprise." As to the use of soldiers to control them, he mocked their ineffectuality:

> Such marchings and countermarchings! From Nottingham to Bulwell, from Bulwell to Banford, from Banford to Mansfield! And when at length detachments arrived at their destination, in all "the pride, pomp, and circumstance of glorious war," they came just in time to witness what had been done, and ascertain the escape of the perpetrators, to collect . . . the fragments of broken frames, and return to their quarters amidst the derision of old women and the hootings of children.

Instead, he said, "I did hope that any measure proposed by His Majesty's government . . . would have had conciliation for its basis," for "had proper meetings been held in the earlier stages of the riots, had the grievances of the men and their masters (for they also had their grievances) been fairly weighed and justly examined, I do think that means might have been devised to restore these workmen to their avocations, and tranquility to the county." But no, "your Dragoons and executioners must be let loose against your fellow citizens," and now the death penalty is to be visited upon them:

> Is there not blood enough upon your penal code, that more must be poured forth to ascend to Heaven, and testify against you? How will you carry the bill into effect? Can you commit a whole country to their own prisons? Will you erect a gibbet in every field and hang up men like scarecrows? Or, will you proceed (as you must to bring this measure into effect) by decimation? Place the county under martial law? Depopulate and lay waste all around you, and restore Sherwood Forest as an acceptable gift to the crown, in the former condition of a royal chase and an asylum for outlaws? Are these the remedies for a starving and desperate populace? Will the famished wretches who have braved your bayonets be appalled by your gibbets? When death is a relief, and the only relief it appears you will afford him, will he be dragooned into tranquility? Will

that which could not be effected by your grenadiers, be accomplished by your executioners?

The reaction of his fellow Lords to this impassioned outpouring is not recorded; its author a week later wrote that "I spoke very violent sentences with a sort of modest impudence, abused every thing & every body, put the Lord Chancellor very much out of humour, & if I may believe what I hear, have not lost any character in the experiment." He did, of course, lose the vote. On March 5, 1812, the bill, amended so as to apply to all the counties of Great Britain, passed both houses and the breaking of machines became a capital crime, a true landmark in the annals of industrialism.

Byron, however, had what might be thought of as the last word. On March 2 this bitterly ironic verse of his appeared anonymously in the London *Morning Chronicle:*

> *Those villains, the Weavers, are all grown refractory,*
> *Asking some succour for Charity's sake—*
> *So hang them in clusters round each Manufactory,*
> *That will at once put an end to mistake.*
>
> *The rascals, perhaps, may betake them to robbing,*
> *The dogs to be sure have got nothing to eat—*
> *So if we can hang them for breaking a bobbin,*
> *'Twill save all the Government's money and meat:*
>
> *Men are more easily made than machinery—*
> *Stockings fetch better prices than lives—*
> *Gibbets on Sherwood will heighten the scenery,*
> *Showing how Commerce, how Liberty thrives!*

It ends with an abrupt shift of voice:

> *Some folks for certain have thought it was shocking,*
> *When Famine appeals, and when Poverty groans,*
> *That life should be valued at less than a stocking,*
> *And breaking of frames lead to breaking of bones.*

If it should prove so, I trust, by this token,
(And who will refuse to partake in the hope?)
That the frames of the fools may be first to be broken,
Who, when asked for a remedy, *send down a* rope. *

The new law was greeted with outrage and anger by the Nottingham Luddites, and there is in their response a sense of betrayal that at first seems odd, though it clearly stems from a deeply held belief that the government was reneging on what they felt were obligations to attend to the welfare of its citizens. "I have waited patiently," went a letter in flowery hand from "Genl. C. [*sic*] Ludd" to Prime Minister Perceval on February 22, "to see if any measure were likely to be adopted by Parliam't. to alleviate distress in any shape whatever; but that hand of conciliation is shut and my poor suffering country is left without a ray of hope." It goes on:

> The Bill for Punish'g with Death, has only to be view.d with contempt & oppos.d by measures equally strong; & the Gentlemen who fram.d it will have to repent the Act: for if one Man's life is Sacrificed, !blood for !blood. Should you be call.d upon you cannot say I have not given you notice of de—— [the word is unclear and ends with a squiggle, but in the context "death" is not unlikely].

This sense of injury is reflected in another letter, issued from "Ned Lud's Office, Sherwood Forest," similarly denouncing the government for making frame breaking illegal and asserting, indignantly almost, that by some charter issued by Charles II in the 17th century "the framework knitters are empowered to break and destroy all frames and engines that fabricate articles in a fraudulent and deceitful manner and to destroy all framework knitters' goods whatsoever that are so made." However quirky

---

* And of course Byron had the last, *last* word. One week later *Childe Harold* was published to near-universal acclaim and, as he said later, "I awoke one morning and found myself famous." Not even English schoolboys remember Prime Minister Perceval.

their reading of history, it is clear that the Luddites in some way felt justified in seeking justice in their own way and were offended that their government should see it differently.

In the event, though, all the threats that greeted the death-penalty act turned out to be empty—indeed, Nottinghamshire Luddism, so virulent at the start, now seemed to be suddenly spent: only a dozen frames were broken in early March and after that attacks on machines in the county are but rare and sporadic. Part of the reason for this retreat—aside from whatever intimidation the death penalty might have had—may have been that most of the likely targets owned by the most obnoxious hosiers had already been taken care of, with at least a fifth of all the stocking frames of all kinds in the county now out of commission. Part may have been due to agreements by many of the hosiers, especially in the smaller towns, to raise their wages; Felkin estimated that, overall, knitters were given two shillings more per dozen during these months (though he admits prices fell later after the threat of Luddism abated), and angry letters to the Home Office from manufacturers who had been forced to capitulate to save their frames tend to support this. Another part was also no doubt the diversion of a new campaign organized by the respected knitter Gravener Henson once again to petition Parliament for a law to protect the lace and stocking trades against "frauds and abuses," another of many attempts to gain by law what could not be won by lawlessness, of which Henson was, at least on the surface, contemptuous ("a glaring outrage on Humanity and Social Order"). Henson's first general meeting was held on Monday, February 17, and by April some ten thousand signatures had been collected, many accompanied by two-and-a-half-shilling subscriptions, indicating some substantial support for this campaign.

And probably a substantial part of the check on Luddism was the result of the first trial of Luddites in March at the regular quarterly court session for the county, called "assizes" (rooted in the Old French *asseoir,* to sit). There ten men were brought before Sir John Bayley and given rather summary trials, of whom three were acquitted and seven convicted of frame breaking. Since the offenses occurred before the death-penalty act was passed, transportation to Australia was the stiffest punishment, and four men, aged 16 to 22, were sent for fourteen years, and three others, 16, 17, and 22, sent for seven. Those were not the harshest sentences Bayley could have set—especially if he had had the men tried for burglary instead of frame breaking, as the most vengeful manufacturers wanted—but they were cruel enough so that, according to the Nottingham town clerk, "the Luddites are certainly very much enraged" but also "very much alarmed."

The trial, incidentally, gives us two nice glimpses into the character of the Luddites and their community. All through the preparations for the assizes the authorities were stymied by the fact that no one would come forth to testify against their prisoners, not even the hosiers who had been attacked, and the men themselves refused to break. Large rewards were offered in the hopes of producing evidence—and London took the extraordinary step of paying the costs of the prosecution itself, relieving the county of a considerable burden—but the officials were embarrassed to discover, as the Nottingham town clerk reported, that men were turning informer just to get the money to pay for their comrades' defense, their testimony afterwards proving to be of no use whatever. (In the end a hosier and his wife who had been victims of a November raid agreed to testify, for £50 each, but were so vilified for it they subsequently had to move "to a distant part of the kingdom" when the trial was over.) Fear of reprisals may have held some witnesses back, but one senses a real operation of community here in which a Judas would fear to be cut off from the web of village life, vilified and ostracized. Even those who agreed to serve as jurors were not immune from the popular wrath; this threatening letter was sent to the foreman of the jury that found the seven Luddites guilty:

> By General Ludds Express Express [*sic*] com-
> mands I am come to Worksop to enquire of
> your character towards our cause and I am sory
> to say we find it to correspond with your con-
> duct latly shewed towards us, Remember the
> time is fast approaching when men of your
> stamp will be brought to Repentance, you may
> be called upon soon. Remember—you are a
> marked man
>
>   Yours for Gen¹ Ludd
>   a trueman

As it happened, the man lived unscathed—but not, it is said, untroubled.

The other glimpse is the first into the kinds of people who became Luddites. The convicted men were all young, with an average age of 19 (compared to an average of 31 in the total of all Luddites eventually transported), and all were caught during the very first weeks of machine breaking, apparently before schemes of stealth and retreat were perfected. The two ringleaders were both 22: William Carnell, who led a raid of thirteen men that smashed seven frames in Basford, and Benjamin Hancock, who was part of the "mob" that set on Sutton and raided the hosier Betts (the one who reportedly thereafter died "deranged") in November. Carnell was described by the judge as having had "the merit of protecting the occupier of the House, an old man of 70 from any personal violence," but that did him no good when he sent up a pitiably contrite note after the sentencing ("God says them that shewes mercy shall find it") asking for an audience with the judge, which, Bayley said, "of course" he did not grant. Two other men, Gervas (or Gervase) Marshall, 17, and George Green, 21, were also described as having "very good characters," and though Bayley said "they were probably drawn into the out-rage without considering the consequences," he nonetheless sent each of them off for seven years. About Green we know something in his subsequent life, which suggests that his character was at any rate adapted to the colonies: he finished his sentence in 1819 and a dozen years later owned five hundred acres of land near Hobart, Tasmania, with seven cows, six horses, and 2,500 sheep, and on his death in 1845 he left his elder brother in Nottingham an estate worth £300 a year.

Whatever the mixture of reasons that led to the cessation of machine breaking in Nottinghamshire—and Judge Bayley was only one saying cautiously by March, "I think the spirit of outrage will not break out again"—it was by no means the end of Luddism. For even as the struggle was subsiding in Sherwood Forest it was beginning to boil on both sides of the Pennines farther north.

The first suggestion that Luddism was spreading from the Midlands was a report to the Home Office that two Nottingham delegates had attended a meeting on December 21, 1811, of disgruntled weavers in Stockport, a town at the northern tip of Cheshire just south of Manchester and very much a part of the cotton world of Lancashire. It would certainly have been fertile ground for the movement there, where the general deprivation of the poor was compounded by the desperation of the handloom weavers at their lowest ebb: "an *honest, industrious fellow*," one manufacturer wrote at the start of 1812, "by *hard labour* cannot get *bread* much less *clothes* for himself and children, and there is a point beyond which human nature cannot bear." As many as 200,000 weavers were crowded into Manchester and the cotton country around, working for less than "the lowest species of day-labourer" when there was any work to do, and every day more people from Ireland and the farm districts poured in to take up the trade, and even the factories that took work from them— thirty mills in Stockport alone by then—were idle in some weeks because of the strangulation of exports. The *Manchester Gazette* began the new year thus: "1812 opens with a gloom altogether so frigid and cheerless, that hope itself is almost lost and frozen in the prospect."

Just two weeks later and forty miles away there were reports of nighttime meetings in the West Riding district of Yorkshire, the last corner of the Luddite triangle, and then on January 12 in Leeds, the wool-country capital, the first overt act of Luddism in the north destroyed a "gig mill" machine used in cloth finishing. Three days later the magistrates in Leeds raided a meeting of men with blackened faces, the familiar disguise of the Nottingham Luddites, and arrested one man they accused of plotting attacks on local finishing factories containing the hated shearing frames and gig mills. Here, too, there was nothing but fertile ground for Luddism: widespread misery and starvation, wages down by half and more, thousands with no work at all and "the remainder have one-third or one-fourth part work" (as one manufacturer put it). Factories of all kinds, wool and worsted mostly, but cotton and flax as well, had sprung up in the preceding twenty years, more than 220 of them by 1812, but they largely used women and children at pittance wages, and those too could not find enough work to keep going regularly. William Thompson, who was forced to cut his workforce from 650 to 450 at the beginning of 1812, reported that he "never knew the poor in such a distressed situation as they are at present"; a fellow clothier added that "I have been a manufacturer for twenty-eight years and I never saw anything equal to it at any time." The poor, according to one contemporary, had to make do with "oatmeal boiled in water" as their main staple food, "and if they can get potatoes or something of that kind for dinner, it is as good as most of them and better than many of them can get."

The introduction of labor-saving machinery into such a desperate society was bound to cause resentment and that resentment to be widespread. When the parson in the novel *Ben o' Bill's* says, about the owners of this machinery, that "my mother died in the belief that the curse of the Scriptures was upon them," he was repeating a belief that was held generally in the northern counties, dating back to the first scribbling mills and cotton factories of the 1790s. But the resentment was not, again, just to the machines or even to their agglomeration in giant impersonal buildings, bad as those were, but also to all that they implied as instruments of a new economic order being thrust upon the workers and their communities unbidden. Adrian Randall, the modern historian who has studied the Yorkshire Luddites most carefully, has summarized the feeling of the weavers and their comrades thus:

> Under the old system custom protected the workers' rights, the workers' dignity. It was an impartial arbiter in disputes, the guardian of community morality. The factory would steamroller custom, turn the workers into slaves under an amoral regime dictated only by the factory master's profits. The factory would thus undermine all the values upon which the workers' culture and communities were predicated, replacing them with the new amoral imperatives of the market economy. What was at risk was not just some workers' jobs. Machinery and the factory threatened the very fabric of existing social organisation.

This is what was stirring under the suffering so widespread in the northern arm of the Luddite triangle; this is what burst into virulent life as the new year began.

On Sunday, January 19, the finishing mill of Oates, Woods, and Smithson, located just to the north of Leeds, was found to be on fire, and before help could arrive serious damage had been done to the gig mills that had only recently been installed inside. It was assumed to be an act of deliberate sabotage, since there was no one at work inside that day and because combustible materials were later found at scattered sites around the building. No one took credit for the attack, but there was no doubt in the minds of the wool manufacturers that Luddism was afoot in Yorkshire.

Exactly three weeks later, February 9, the warehouse of the manufacturing firm of Haigh, Marshal and Company in Manchester was set on fire and the cloth stored inside, which had been made on power looms, was entirely destroyed. In this case warning letters had been sent to several factory owners of the area, with a list of the places selected for destruction; though Haigh, Marshal was first on the list, no special precautions were taken. Again no one took credit for the attack, but there was no doubt in the minds of the cotton manufacturers that Luddism had come to Lancaster as well.

The connections from Nottinghamshire's Luddism to the Luddism of the north are uncertain but suggestive. One of the spies working for a magistrate in Bolton, a dozen miles west of Manchester, reported that Nottingham "delegates" had been sent both to Stockport and Yorkshire in mid-January; a Manchester manufacturer reported on February 11 that "already we have plenty of Nottingham, Carlisle and Glasgow delegates" holding "private meetings *every night* and instigating ours to riot and confusion";* and at the end of February the Duke of Newcastle warned the Home Office that delegates from Nottingham had been sent out to "all the great towns" of the kingdom, an exaggeration that might contain some truth.

But of course it was not necessary for the Nottingham Luddites to make overt contact with other clothworkers in nearby counties in order for the news of Luddism to spread and find eager disciples. Newspapers, though too expensive for most workers to buy, could be found in every pub worth its name and coffeehouses and barbershops as well, and the dramatic stories of the Nottingham machine breakers made good, and suggestive, reading throughout the provinces: a Yorkshire prosecutor later blamed Luddism there on men's acting "in imitation of the framebreakers at Nottingham" whose accounts they "were unfortunately in the habit of reading in the newspapers." Travelers, too, commercial and otherwise, were frequent—the distance

---

* A surviving ticket, presumably created for one such meeting, reads, "ENTER. NO GENERAL BUT LUDD/MEANS THE POOR ANY GOOD."

from Nottingham to Manchester or Leeds was about seventy-five miles by road, which could be done by coach in a day for under half a pound—and it was quite common for men, especially in times of unemployment, to walk great distances in search of work, naturally retailing stories at every stop. Mail service was efficient—in 1812 the Royal Mail averaged just over twenty-eight hours to go 180 miles—and in fact one letter intercepted during this time provides a clear Luddite link: in April, a man writing from Yorkshire to his brother in Nottingham reported that "we have enjoy'd ourselves over a pot or two of Beer" with "the friend from you" who had been visiting, "& he read Mr Luds Song" to them.

Whatever the connections, it is especially interesting that the Luddism of the northern counties is more violent, more disciplined, and (at least at its fringes) more explicitly political, even insurrectionary, in character, than in the Midlands, perhaps because lessons had been learned, perhaps because the threats of factories and displacing machines were clearer. For example, here for the first time is evidence of a Luddite oath by which new recruits were admitted to the ranks—"twisted in" was the expression, probably having some connection with the "twisting" by which thread or yarn was formed of separate strands—and were sworn to strict and uncompromising allegiance. Such oath taking was seen as so subversive an act in England that it had been made punishable by transportation in 1797, no matter what the cause being pledged; its emergence now, as reported to the authorities by spies and infiltrators, was taken as a particularly fearsome, particularly threatening, feature of the new movement. In the version reported most commonly the oath was a rather highfalutin protestation meant to induce loyalty and fear in equal amounts:

I *A.B.* of my own voluntary will, do declare, and solemnly swear, that I never will reveal to any person or persons under the canopy of heaven, the names of the persons who compose this Secret Committee, their proceedings, meeting, places of abode, dress, features, connections [in other versions "complexion," in one version both],

or any thing else that might lead to a discovery of the same, either
by word or deed, or sign, under the penalty of being sent out of the
world by the first brother who shall meet me, and my name and
character blotted out of existence, and never to be remembered but
with contempt and abhorrence; and I further now do swear, that I
will use my best endeavours to punish by death any traitor or trai-
tors, should any rise up amongst us, wherever I can find him or
them, and though he should fly to the verge of nature [a phrase so
strange as to inspire "verge of Statude," perhaps meaning "statute,"
and "verge of existence" in other versions]. I will pursue him with
increasing vengeance. So help me God, and bless me to keep this
my oath inviolable.

Strange as the language is, the oath seems genuine. Some historians have suggested that it may have been manufactured by government spies to lend an air of seriousness and authenticity to
their accounts, but scenes of oath taking are reported so often in
so many different locations, and they have such a clear place in
subsequent oral histories, that this seems far-fetched. Besides,
the business of giving and taking oaths was a familiar part of
Freemasonry and craft-guild ritual—where, as E. P. Thompson
notes, "such oaths had a long ancestry"—as a way of inspiring
awe and ensuring purpose. According to one informer, the Luddites also had a system of intricate recognition signals and pass-
words borrowed from similar sources:

> You must raise your right hand over your right eye if there be
> another Luddite in company he will raise his left hand over his left
> eye—then you must raise the forefinger of your right hand to the
> right side of your mouth—the other will raise the little finger of his
> left hand to the left side of his mouth and will say What are you?
> The answer, Determined—he will say, What for? Your answer,
> Free Liberty—then he will converse with you and tell you any-
> thing he knows.

Moreover, it is possible that the oaths served as necessary reminders of the seriousness of the business afoot. The fact that

they seem to begin only after machine breaking becomes a capital offense—there are no instances of oathing that have come to light in Nottinghamshire—suggests that they may have been seen as a useful tactic, over and above community sanctions, for protecting oneself against betrayal in case of arrests and prosecutions when one's life was on the line.* If that was the intent it was apparently successful: "the secrecy with which the plans of the disaffected are carried on," a Manchester constable wrote, echoing many, "is scarcely credible."

Along with oathing, a greater emphasis on training and marching surfaces in the Lancashire and Yorkshire accounts, suggesting that the intensity was ratcheted higher there. The report of the Committee of the House of Lords that investigated Luddism later that year may be somewhat florid, but the details are mostly corroborated elsewhere:

> They assemble in large numbers, in general by night, upon heaths or commons, which are numerous and extensive in some of the districts where the disturbances have been most serious; so assembled they take the usual military precautions of paroles and countersigns; then muster rolls are called over by numbers, not by names; they are directed by leaders sometimes in disguise; they place sentries to give alarm at the approach of any persons whom they may suspect of meaning to interrupt or give information of their proceedings; and they disperse instantly at the firing of a gun, or other signal agreed upon, and so disperse as to avoid detection.

Whether or not such training was going on in every area of the counties, certainly stories of "midnight drills" and "the measured tramp of feet" and "mysterious shots in the moors" were common enough.

Ratcheted higher, too, was the violence. Although shops with no more than a dozen machines were often targets, to a great

---

* There is one reported instance of oathing before February 14 (the date the capital punishment bill was introduced) in Stockport, Cheshire, on February 3, 1812, but the source for this is a magistrate's spy who is not wholly reliable.

extent the attacks now focused on the large factories—the power-loom mills of Lancashire, the finishing mills of Yorkshire—since they were the source of the most immediate grievances. And as the targets were larger so the forces amassed were greater, the weapons more numerous, and the damage more extensive.

After the January fire in Leeds, attacks in Yorkshire were aimed mostly at Huddersfield, a town of some ten thousand souls located on the River Colne as it came down from the Pennine hills just to the west, where already fourteen wool factories were at work; within a five-mile radius were another fifty, including the Rawfolds Mill of William Cartwright. By March 15, eleven establishments in that area had been attacked by Luddites, raids confined to the breaking of machinery but done with great thoroughness—shearing frames were destroyed, as well as shears, cloths on the machines and off, and sometimes windows and furniture—and with a toll never tabulated but probably amounting to at least a hundred machines in a little more than two weeks. Some suggestion of these raids is given in *Ben o' Bill's*, the novel based on Luddite memoirs, which reports a meeting of about a dozen Luddites one night in March at the Nag's Head pub on a road a few miles southwest of Huddersfield. The men, their resolution fortified by ale, marched to the little village of Marsh and there smashed down the gate of a Mr. Smith, a minor but pugnacious user of the new shearing frames, who appeared at his door with "knees knocking together quite audibly." The Luddites forced him to give them the key to the small mill behind his house, and a team of three went out with their heavy hammers to crush the frames: "Poor Mr. S.—— groaned as if his heart were breaking, and his wife at the stair head gave a shriek every time the hammer fell." The party's leader, George Mellor (the same man who was to lead the attack on Rawfolds), forced Smith to swear on a Bible that he would never report the attack—"Oh, yes, Mr. Ludd, I'll swear. I'll swear anything only go leave us"—and would no longer use the new machinery. Then Mellor took a drink from a pitcher of ale at the foot of the stairs, drank a toast to Mrs. Smith, and said "how sorry he was that business had compelled him to pay his respects to so worthy a lady so late at night." With that the attackers faded into the dark and regrouped at the Nag's Head to drink to their success and hear stories from other parties that had been out raiding that night. Smith subsequently reported the event to the local magistrate at Huddersfield, bragging about how he'd scared off forty Luddites the night before, but in truth he kept his promise and for the rest of that year used the shearing frames no more.

Then the actions grew bolder. On Tuesday, March 24, "a large body" of men, some of them armed with pistols, descended on the factory of William Thompson, one of the principal manufacturers in the Leeds area. "First seizing the watchman at the mill and placing guards at every adjacent cottage," a local account relates, "threatening death of anyone who should attempt to give an alarm, and then forcibly entering the mill, they completely destroyed the machinery" (thirty to forty machines), thirty-six windows, and "three pieces of fine woolen cloth." The next night men broke into the finishing shop of Dickinson, Carr and Company in Leeds and destroyed at least eighteen large pieces of cloth but left the machines unharmed. Two weeks later the large factory of another major clothier, Joseph Foster of Horbury, some ten miles east of Huddersfield, was set upon by a body of three hundred men from all over the area after he refused Luddite demands—and a magistrate's suggestion—to stop using "obnoxious machinery":

A large body of armed men [went the *Annual Register* account written two days later] after securing all the approaches to the premises, proceeded to break into that part of the mill appropriated to the dressing of cloth, where they completely destroyed all the shears and frames; the former were not merely snipped, but absolutely broken in pieces. They then demolished all the windows, and, as if actuated by the most diabolical phrenzy, broke into those parts of the premises, against which these depredators do not pretend to have any ground of complaint,—the scribbling-mill and weaving-shops, and materially injured the machinery, and wantonly damaged a quantity of warp ready for the loom; destroyed not merely the glass of the window[s], but the frames which were of cast-iron, the windows of the dye-houses, the counting house, and even the dwelling-houses contiguous to the work shop shared the same fate. . . .

Having accomplished their object, they assembled in a field, when the leader called over their numbers, to which each answered. Having ascertained that their whole number was there, he said, "the work is done, all is well, disperse," which order was obeyed.*

The Foster's raid, the largest anywhere to that point, was quickly celebrated in a Yorkshire song:

> Come all ye croppers stout and bold,
>   Let your faith grow stronger still,
> Oh, the cropper lads in the county of York
>   Broke the shears at Foster's mill.
>   The wind it blew,
>   The sparks they flew,
> Which alarmed the town full soon,
>   And out of bed poor people did creep
> And ran by the light of the moon;
>   Around and around they all did stand,
> And solemnly did swear
> Neither bucket nor kit nor any such thing
>   Should be of assistance there.

Luddism not just afoot, but on the march.

That night or the next day some papers were found on the road next to the mill and eventually sent on to the Home Office.

---

* It was this raid on Foster's that was remembered by the father of Henry Clarkson, who later wrote a history of Wakefield: "My father, as he lay in bed that night, heard the tramp of the feet of these men, passing over Westgate bridge, on their way to wreck this very mill." His father had also received Luddite warning letters, "sometimes signed in blood," and bowed to the pressure by taking down the offending machines.

Consisting of a pamphlet of two long and frankly seditious speeches beginning "Countrymen" and followed by elaborate Paineite flourishes ("Enrol under the sacred Banners of Liberty" to restore "imprescriptable Rights," etc.), and an "Oath" and "Constitution" that had been used by conspirators associated with Colonel Edmund Despard in his ill-fated attempt to foment a revolution in 1802, they were taken by the Horbury magistrate who forwarded them as evidence that Luddism was an insurrectionary threat greater than had so far been acknowledged. The response of the Home Office does not survive, but from this point on the idea that Luddism represented a political threat deeper than a merely industrial protest was apparently fixed in the minds of the government.

Meanwhile, not more than twenty miles away on the other side of the Pennines, the Luddites of cotton country began their attacks in Stockport and Manchester. Here again the targets were usually the large factories, especially those run by steam engines. There were not so many of these in 1812—the number of power looms in the kingdom was estimated at 2,400 and the number of power spindles at 5 million, about half of them run by steam— but they were blunt and massive evidence of what was coming to the industry, very quickly too, and they were taken by the workers to be the source of all that was forcing them into want and misery. (When one laissez-faire apologist retorted "It is not done yet" to a clothworker who expressed fears about the encroachment of factories, the worker replied quietly, "No, but the clouds seem to rise.") The handloom weavers particularly—great numbers of whom, in a further bitter twist, were getting by, if at all, on their wives' and children's wages from the mills—could not hear the clattering of clogs going to and from the factories, morning and night, could not see the four-story monstrosities and what Dickens called their "melancholy mad elephants" inside, could not taste the acrid black air redolent of offal and garbage, without vivid feelings of anger and frustration toward these new-come invasions.

The first objectives of the Luddites' wrath were carefully selected: the three most prominent power-loom manufacturers, all in Stockport, all using steam engines, and all vowing to use more. On February 9 an attempt was made, but foiled, to burn the establishment of Peter Marsland, known locally as "Peter the Great" for his enormous factory and his equally enormous ambitions for power looms, on which he held three patents for minor improvements. On March 20 a large band of perhaps five hundred or so attempted, but also failed, to torch the factory and warehouse of William Radcliffe, also the holder of several power-loom patents and the instigator of a new club for steam manufacturers, who was regarded (as a Luddite letter put it) as "the original projector of the obnoxious looms." And on the night of April 4 a raid took place on the premises of John Goodair, owner of a "great mill" the size of a city block with eight thousand spindles and two hundred looms, during which eleven shots were fired, windows were freely broken, and an unspecified number of steam-run looms were attacked. Compared to Luddite actions elsewhere these might not be called great successes, even though the size and proximity of the targets did suggest some bravery and determination, but they did alarm the cotton lords into setting up private guards in most of the mills and, as reports increased of midnight training sessions on the moors, putting pressure on the magistrates to call out the troops and swear in the constables.

And then, four days after this last raid, the first full-scale public action—this one probably deserving the label "riot" that authorities so often bandied about—took place in the center of Manchester. How much it had to do directly with Luddism is an open question, since it was a demonstration of an entirely different sort than the nighttime raids; at the very least it sprang from the same wells of discontent and played on the same fears of insurrection, and there were surely Luddites in the angry crowds, including one John Buckley, a weaver and Calvinist preacher, who was wearing both the hats of a respectable Parliamentary reformer still partitioning Parliament and Regent and of a member of a "secret committee" of Luddites in Manchester.

The disturbance began when a group of Tories in town announced that there would be a public meeting in the Manchester Exchange Hall on Wednesday, April 8, to express appreciation for the recent decision of the Prince Regent to retain a government of old Tory regulars instead of installing any of the Whig politicians known to be in his circle of friends before taking office. Within hours so many varied opposition groups— some so-called "radical" Whigs, Parliamentary reformers, and unnamed "inflammatory" factions—had begun to rally the public to pack the meeting and force a vote for reform that the Tories eventually called it off. Too late: that Tuesday people were already "crowding to town in every direction from the country"— weavers mostly, so it was said—and the next day they went to the Exchange Hall anyway, took over the building, and began

> throwing chairs, tables, and benches through the windows above the post office [as a young weaver named Samuel Bamford told it in his memoirs], and the furniture being quickly broken up, the fragments were used in smashing the lamps, and front windows of the building. Another party of the mob were in the large room, breaking and destroying everything that stood in their way, or that excited their spirit of mischief. Fragments of tables and chairs were hurled through the windows into the street, and then back again; the costly chandeliers were shivered to atoms, and at length, a heap of straw was piled up and set on fire.

Fortuitously a party of the Cumberland regular militia finally arrived at that point, extinguishing the fire and arresting several men, while the rest spilled outside to join "some thousands of the mob" in St. Ann's Square. The Cumberland regiment and a contingent of the Scots Greys, notorious for their readiness to violence, moved into the square—"filling the town with soldiers"— and read the Riot Act, emphasizing it with a few slashes of their sabres; the crowd dispersed, though small knots of people continued to march through the streets for hours afterward, some burning the Prince Regent in effigy and one carrying a banner with a somewhat enigmatic NOW OR NEVER! One such party— and it is reasonable to assume there were Luddites among them— attacked the factory of a Mr. Schofield containing "obnoxious machinery" and proceeded to knock out the windows but were forced to flee and leave the machines untouched when soldiers appeared. As late as nine o'clock that night, according to an eye witness, there were still remnants of "the mob" going around in "small bodies" who appeared to be so "refractory" that many townspeople "will not go to bed" for fear of having their houses and shops set on fire. As it happened, nothing more untoward took place that night, though turmoil and confrontation were in the air and not likely to disperse in any hurry.

In the next few weeks, indeed—beginning with the assault just three days later on the Rawfolds Mill, where four men died in service to King Ludd at the hands of a manufacturer and the soldiers of a state determined to protect private property at, it seemed, any cost—the stakes of the game for both sides would be starkly raised.

Some foretaste of the new stakes had already been provided by the Luddites in two remarkable communications put out in Yorkshire in March—another ratcheting upwards—suggesting passions, if not purposes, far more insurrectionary than anything visible before. On March 9 the following leaflet, neatly if crudely printed on a folded sheet, appeared in the streets of Leeds:

> To all Croppers, Weavers &c & Public at large
> Generous Countrymen. You are requested to come forward with Arms and help the Redressers to redress their Wrongs and shake off the hateful Yoke of a Silly Old Man, and his Son more silly and their Rogueish Ministers, all Nobles and Tyrants must be brought down. Come let us follow the Noble Example of the brave

Citizens of Paris who in Sight of 30,000 Tyrant Redcoats brought
A Tyrant to the Ground. by so doing you will be best aiming at
your own Interest. Above 40,000 Heroes are ready to break out, to
crush the old Government & establish a new one.

Apply to General Ludd Commander of the Army of Redressers.

This was an overt call to revolution without mistake: the overthrow of the king, the prince, and the government just as had
been done in France, brought about by the "40,000 Heroes"
ready to rise in revolt.

And on the same day, fifteen miles away, the longest and most
explicit Luddite letter of all, this one handwritten, was sent to a
Mr. Smith of Hill End, near Huddersfield (but presumably not
the one who had been victim of the earlier raid), carrying much
the same message. It began with a conventional kind of threat:

Sir. Information has just been given in that you are a holder of
those detestable Shearing Frames, and I was desired by my Men to
write to you and give you fair warning to pull them down, and for
that purpose I desire you will now understand I am now writing to
you. You will take Notice that if they are not taken down by the
end of next week, I will detach one of my Lieutenants with at least
300 Men to destroy them and furthermore take Notice that if you
give us the Trouble of coming so far we will increase your misfor-
tune by burning your Buildings down to Ashes and if you have
Impudence to fire upon any of my Men, they have orders to murder you, & burn all your Housing. . . .

It then switched to a somewhat grand assessment of the Luddite
armies:

I would have the Merchants, Master Dressers, the Government &
the public to know that the Grievances of Such a Number of Men
are not to be made sport of for by the last Returns there were 2782
Sworn Heroes bound in a Bond of Necessity either to redress their
Grievances or gloriously perish in the Attempt in the Army of
Huddersfield alone, nearly double sworn Men in Leeds.

By the latest letters from our Correspondents we learn that the Manufacturers [which here means not factory owners but the workers who did, literally, the hand-making] in the following Places are going to rise and join us in redressing their Wrongs Viz. Manchester, Wakefield, Halifax, Bradford, Sheffield, Oldham, Rochdale and all the Cotton Country where the brave Mr Hanson* will lead them on to Victory, the Weavers in Glasgow and many parts of Scotland will join us[,] the Papists in Ireland are rising to a Man, so that they are likely to find the Soldiers something else to do than Idle in Huddersfield. . . .

And then it provided a clear if not altogether convincing explanation for why this rebellion would take place:

The immediate Cause of us beginning when we did was that Rascally letter of the Prince Regents to Lords Grey & Grenville [denying the Whig leaders a chance to form a government and leaving the Tories in power], which left us no hopes of any Change for the better, by his falling in with that Damn'd set of Rogues, Percival & C° to whom we attribute all the Miseries of our Country. But we hope for assistance from the French Emperor in shaking off the Yoke of the Rottenest, Wickedest and most Tyranious Government that ever existed, then down come the Hanover Tyrants, and all our Tyrants from the greatest to the smallest, and we will be governed by a just Republic. . . . We will never lay down our Arms . . . [until] The House of Commons passes an Act to put down all Machinery hurtful to Commonality, and repeal that to hang Frame Breakers. But We. We petition no more[,] that won't do fighting must.

Signed by the General of the Army of Redressers

Ned Ludd Clerk

Redressers for ever Amen.

---

* Joseph Hanson was a prominent Lancashire businessman and colonel in the Manchester Volunteers who had been imprisoned in 1809 for speaking supportively to a large demonstration of striking weavers, saying, "Stick to your cause and you will certainly succeed," which they did and did not.

This singular letter is Luddism in a nutshell. It is quite explicit in declaring machines to be its grievances—"those detestable Shearing Frames"—but equally so in explaining why: not that they represent some sort of frightening or unholy invention (they had as a matter of fact been known since the middle of the 18th century), but rather they are disruptive to a settled trade and a settled society, "Machinery hurtful to Commonality," to the common people in general and their particular communities long established and much cherished. Thus it is that their use is patently a wrong that must be redressed (a theme also of the previous letter) and the Luddite heroes must be the redressers, soldiers, that is, in a true and proper cause that seeks to remedy an injury, an injustice, done. And because all peaceful routes to achieving that cause have failed, as evidenced by the continuation of the hated Tory government, it is now time for the "rising" to bring about a "just Republic" with a House of Commons that truly understands the threat of machinery.

Now it is difficult to think that these messages were necessarily taken by many at their face value. No one could have known then (and none know now) the actual number of Luddites in the land, but it would seem that only the most gullible magistrate or manufacturer, susceptible to hearsay and frightened by pub talk, could have imagined that there were 40,000 of them ready for revolution (and all got together in the space of six months, too), although a contingent of 2,700 in Huddersfield out of its 10,000 population or of 5,400 in Leeds out of 60,000 was (if unlikely) not beyond reason. And the idea that Lancashire was ready to rise behind Colonel Hanson (or even someone acknowledged to be more rebellious) or that Scotland and Ireland were on the verge of "rising to a Man" was certainly exaggerated if not preposterous, however desperate the conditions there were agreed to be.

Nonetheless, the fear of revolution was quite real just then, at least in more excitable bosoms. The very fact that the workers were led to the kind of rhetorical excess contained in these letters was foreboding enough on its own, and the writing and sending

of such things was an overt act of sedition and as such punishable
by law. But it was combined with enough other elements of the
moment—the marchings and drillings, the frame breaking and
arson, the factory attacks and riots, the pikes and pistols—to
cause serious worry in many quarters that a real uprising was
indeed fomenting. Among a number of authorities who, unlike
the public, were privy to information about the seditious pam-
phlets found after the attack on Foster's mill in Horbury and
were receiving reports from spies of a widespread "Revolutionne
sistom" (as one Lancashire operative put it), the threat to order
seemed palpable and imminent. That April the *Leeds Mercury*, a
Whiggish paper not normally given to exaggeration, said that this
month had seen the dawn of "the insurrectionary era." A message
from the constabulary of Manchester on April 27 warned of a
Luddite call for workers across the land to join "the army of revolution." The Home Office was besieged with reports from the
countryside foretelling "a general rising" that would spread from
the manufacturing districts right to the heart of London, and
warning that the Luddites "had no other object" than rebellion
(April 20) and had established "a complete revolutionary system
now pervading the whole part of this country" (April 27). And
the investigation by the special committee of the House of Lords
just a few months later found solid evidence not only that the
Luddites had succeeded in imposing "a system of turbulence and
disorder" but that "the views of some of the persons engaged in
these proceedings have extended to revolutionary measures of the
most dangerous description."

Moreover, the recent history of these districts, in which rebel-
liousness, though a distinctly minority strain, had been a virulent
one, provided reason enough to give credence to such reports, if
not to succumb to them entirely. The Jacobinism that grew out
of the first optimism of the French Revolution and the Paineism
that followed (Paine's *The Rights of Man* sold an astonishing
200,000 copies in Britain in 1793) both had had strong fol-
lowings in the northern counties, from Sheffield in the east to

Preston in the west, and political riots (or food riots with political overtones) had broken out in Manchester, Nottingham, and several other cities of the Luddite triangle almost yearly in the 1790s.*

After the passage of the Combination Acts in 1799 and 1800, which hit particularly hard at the textile workers' organizations, there followed another wave of radical protest, with oath taking, midnight meetings, talk of a "general rising," and what E. P. Thompson thinks was a "widespread" secret organization, the Black Lamp, in Yorkshire and Lancashire. That protest culminated in the Despard conspiracy in London, for which Colonel Despard was tried and executed in 1803, and the trial of two like-minded men in Sheffield, found guilty of administering subversive oaths and transported in that same year. Reports of continuing political agitation continued in the following years, in which Nottingham, Huddersfield, Leeds, and a ring of cities around Manchester (Stockport, Ashton, Oldham, Rochdale, Bury, and Bolton) figure prominently. To be sure, much of this is the product of spies and informants and must be taken with the salt of suspicion—you'd think, for example, that Bolton 1810 was a Paris 1789, but it's probably because Colonel Ralph Fletcher, the magistrate there, employed energetic spies and wanted them earning their money by finding revolutionaries—but it seems clear that a fundamental political disaffection was growing, radical at times and among a few, but also at times touching large segments of the working population.

To this must be added the continuing operation by the Parliament against what many in the textile trades regarded as their traditional rights—for example, the repeal of protectionist regulations in wool manufacturing in 1809, and its cold rejection of a succession of petitions, in 1808, 1809, 1811, and several times in

---

* According to a Parliamentary Report of 1799, there were eighty-nine "radical societies" known to the authorities in 1797, at least sixteen in the Luddite triangle (Manchester, Rochdale, Salford, Stockport, Ashton, Bradford, Halifax, Leeds, Wakefield, Warrington, Sheffield, York, Derby, Nottingham, Loughborough, and Leicester).

1812, asking for redress. This was taken on many sides as evidence of the abrogation by the state of its legal and moral responsibility to look after its citizens, and hence as nullification of the citizens' obligations to continue their allegiance to it: "What happens in these years," as a modern student of the cotton country has put it, "is the collapse of mass acquiescence on which the authorities had previously relied." That provides the kind of psychological tinderbox that might be sparked into actual insurrection, and there were enough officials close enough to the ground to realize that the fear of such a conflagration was by no means baseless.

It must be taken as heavily fictional, but this speech offered by the local historian Frank Peel in his 19th-century history of Luddism, based on his work in the Yorkshire oral tradition, is probably some indication of the kind of sentiments flowing in the northern counties around this time. He has the Luddites meeting in early April in a private room over the bar at the St. Crispin Inn in Halifax, a hostelry often used by what the Tories called "Tom Painers," and there addressed by an old hatter named John Baines, a figure who was later to stand trial for giving oaths:

> Oh that the long suffering people of England would rise in their strength and crush their oppressors in the dust! The vampires have fattened too long on our heart's blood. Let the people now rise in their majesty and rid themselves for ever of the vile brood who have flung upon them the sole taxation of the country and reduced them to the condition of galley slaves in the land of their birth. . . .
>
> For thirty years I have struggled to rouse the people against the evil and, as some of you here know, have suffered much for my opinions in body and estate. I am now nearing the end of my pilgrimage, but I will die as I have lived; my last days shall be devoted to the people's cause. I hail your rising against your oppressors and hope it may go on till there is not a tyrant to conquer.

Such talk probably could have been heard in those days in other pubs as well, but by its nature of course we have no good way of knowing how often, how widespread. One man who felt he had his finger on England's pulse just then at any rate gave it full credence. Robert Southey—a hanger-on poet who wrote much high-minded stuff but is remembered today for the lines "But 'twas a famous victory" and "You are old, Father William," and for having first published the story of "The Three Bears" (minus, however, Goldilocks, who is only "a little old woman" in this version)—wrote to his friend Grosvenor Bedford that spring:

> This country is upon the brink of the most dreadful of all conceivable states—an insurrection of the poor against the rich. . . . Things are in that state at this time that nothing but the army preserves us: it is the single plank between us and the red sea of an English Jacquerie . . . prepared by the inevitable tendency of the manufacturing system, and hastened on by the folly of a besotted faction of Parliamentary reformers; and the wickedness of a few individuals. The end of these things is full of evil, even upon the happiest termination.

Such fearful Toryism stood him in good stead: the next year he was named Poet Laureate of Britain. But whether he was right about insurrection remained to be seen.

5

The Luddites

April–May 1812

JOSEPH RADCLIFFE, 48, was the most aggressive and dedicated magistrate in the West Riding, and from his home at Milnsbridge House, a few miles southwest of Huddersfield, he directed the operation of finding and punishing the attackers of the Cartwright mill on April 12 in what the *Leeds Mercury* later called an "indefatigable and intrepid" fashion. A large, no-nonsense man of a certain English country type—his portrait shows him fat and jowly, with short white hair, a long nose between two steely, unyielding eyes, a slightly overlarge mouth, and an air of self-satisfaction that can only be called smug—Radcliffe had been the master of Milnsbridge since 1795, when an uncle, also a justice of the peace, had bestowed it upon him as the only available male in a line of Radcliffes going back many generations on both sides of the Pennines. Radcliffe had invested chiefly in agriculture, on lands made so extensive by enclosure that they were known as the Radcliffe Plantation, but he was nonetheless an energetic champion of the local wool manufacturers and in fact was in charge of assigning poor and orphan children to work, some as young as seven and eight, in the Huddersfield wool factories. Taking the manufacturers' part, he had already complained the month before of the "supineness" of the local military commander at York for failing to send him a hundred soldiers to protect the threatened mills from Luddites—the commander, General Thomas Grey, had replied that there weren't enough men to furnish "separate guards for every individual who may be under apprehensions for the safety of his property"—and now that the attacks had escalated he was determined to avail himself of all the troops, plus all the volunteer militia and constabulary, he could muster.

It was after the raid on Cartwright's Rawfolds Mill that Radcliffe became quite relentless in his efforts at "scouring the district for Luds," as one local account put it. That raid had become famous not merely in the Luddite triangle but throughout much of the kingdom, and was in some ways a watershed event for the movement. For the manufacturers and their allies, it was the first signal that a resolute defense of property might halt the heretofore successful Luddite rebellion and that violence in service to Britain's new industrialism, with the soldiers of the state right alongside the masters of the mills, might well assure the success of the new technology in the long run. Indeed, Cartwright was for a time a hero to magistrate and merchant alike all over Britain, and Charlotte Brontë's *Shirley* suggests that the local manufacturers "received him with a certain distinction" and "hailed him as in some sort their champion," while "the clothiers and blanket-makers vaunted his prowess and rehearsed his deeds—many of them interspersing their flatteries with coarse invectives against the operative [i.e., working] class." For the laborers and their families, the raid became a symbol of the heroism of the Luddites and the treachery of the factory owners, now reduced to murder. Stories were told of young John Booth, and how when dying he called one interrogater to his side, saying, "Can yo' keep a secret, sir?" and when assured, "I can, I can," replied, "An' so can I" just before he expired. Songs were made and passed along:

> *You Heroes of England who wish to have a trade*
> *Be true to each other and be not afraid*
> *Though the Bayonet is fixed they can do no good*
> *As long as we keep up the Rules of General Ludd. . . .*

> *And then they can feel for another's woe*
> *For he that never knew sorrow, sorrow doth not know*
> *But there is Cartwright and Atkinson* also*
> *And to show them justice sorrow they shall know.*

And at the burial of Samuel Hartley a week after the raid, "the people came from far and wide to show their sorrow," a local preacher said, "the largest congregation that ever assembled in Halifax Chapel"; "the friends of the Luds," one working man wrote, "followed them every man in Morning with a silk apron edged with Black" and insisted, over the minister's objection, on Hartley's being buried with "a grand Stone."

For all of Radcliffe's zeal, there was no break to be found in the Luddite ranks. Radcliffe sent out patrols of soldiers "more active than ever" to interview townsfolk and track down suspects, many of whom were paraded before his large desk at Milnsbridge House. A local committee of manufacturers doubled its reward for the Rawfolds raiders to £2,000 (about forty times a cropper's annual wage), and constables and soldiers went around rousting people out of their beds at night and harshly interrogating pub crowds in the days. But all to no avail; no one was talking. The Huddersfield parish was normally a tight-knit society, the village ties strong and binding, family bonds wide and dear, and the Yorkshire soul, traditionally proud and independent, was known to have no great love for authority in the best of times. And now that Cartwright, something of an outsider in any case, had caused the murder of four of the local lads in defense of his hated mill and the machines that were doing people out of jobs—and refused even to help the fallen men, it was said around—the feelings of revulsion and outrage, even among those who had no particular sympathy for the Luddites, kept affections tight and mouths closed:

---

* Law Atkinson was a large clothier of Huddersfield, one of the earliest to use shearing frames and other machinery.

A confidential servant tells me [said a magistrate from Headingly to the Home Office on April 15] that it is surprising how much the opinions and wishes even of the more respectable part of the Inhabitants are in unison with the deluded and ill-disposed of the population with respect to the present object of their resentment[,] Gig Mills and Shearing Frames[,] and this extends also to persons having Mills of a different description employed in the Manufacturing branch, [which] will account for the rioters constantly escaping detection.

According to Frank Peel, the local historian, "great alarm and uneasiness prevailed" in the area at this point, and "numbers of croppers disappeared from the town; some enlisted for soldiers and were never seen again at their old haunts; while others who had gone away, returned after the disturbances were finally over." Enough dedicated Luddites remained, however, to keep talk alive of revenge on Cartwright, now especially hated because he was being treated as a Wellington-sized hero by the mill owners and by the politicians and generals who had been urging the clothiers all along to be aggressive in their defense of property. These feelings of vengeance grew even stronger just after the raid when an inquest returned a verdict of "justifiable homicide" for the Rawfolds deaths, and on the following Thursday, April 16, when it was discovered that the county authorities, fearful of a demonstration, had secretly buried John Booth in the early dawn without waiting for the scheduled funeral at noon: "Vengeance for the Blood of the Innocent" was chalked, according to General Grey, on every door of the area. Peel's dramatic reconstruction of the frustrated croppers returning to their workshops that Thursday afternoon has George Mellor raging around the room "like an imprisoned tiger" and ending with an outburst: "Curse the villain, Cartwright! I will yet have his heart's blood." Before the day was over he and his fellows had planned the assassination of the mill owner on the coming Saturday.

On that day Cartwright had to ride into Huddersfield from

Rawfolds in the afternoon to give testimony to the court martial of the soldier who had refused to fire into the attacking crowd at the mill because he might hurt "one of my brothers." The proceedings were swift, the soldier admitting his act, and it did not take long for the officers to find the guilt of a man they considered an outright traitor and to assign him the punishment of three hundred lashes—a sentence so severe that even Cartwright was moved to ask for mercy, the request curtly denied by the presiding officer with a silent bow. By four o'clock Cartwright was on his horse and heading back up the main road north.

About a mile out of town, where the houses grew few between, the mill owner began to pick up his pace: for weeks he had been the target of threatening Luddite letters and he knew that these days no one among the general populace bore him much favor, so a gallop seemed only appropriate. It was fortunate. Just moments later a shot fired from one side of the road whizzed over the horse's flank, causing it to rear and whirl, and when Cartwright got it under control and pressed it forward again another shot from the other side of the road tore by but also missed its mark. He put his head low to the horse's neck, dug in his spurs, and rode off at top speed, unharmed. Peel describes him as being "sick at heart as he drew the rein at his own door," and no wonder: it was no longer just his mill but his life that was on the line, and this attempt on it, the first direct assault on an individual manufacturer, marked another step up on the Luddites' tactical ladder.

Joseph Radcliffe, who two days later received a letter from a "Solicitor to General Ludd" in Sherwood Forest, where the "Ludds Court at Nottingham" decreed his death, redoubled his efforts when he learned of the assassination attempt. "Justice Radcliffe never rested," said Ben Bamforth, who was one of the magistrate's chief targets, and "the least rumour that reached his ear was sufficient to justify an arrest" and an interrogation at Milnsbridge House.

But still no results; still the silence held.

*   *   *

Starting two days after the Rawfolds attack, on Tuesday, April 14, a series of riots swept across the northern segment of the Luddite triangle for a week, punctuated by the largest and bloodiest demonstrations yet.

On Tuesday, market day in Sheffield, which was a city of some forty thousand in the very south of the West Riding, a band of forty or fifty men came marching into the market, grabbing potatoes to throw "in every direction," as the report to the *Annual Register* put it, "breaking the windows all around the market place [and] proceeded to break open the potatoe-cellars, which were soon emptied of their contents." It had every appearance of the kind of "food riot" that had been a recurring response of the English poor in times of famine for nearly a century, a spontaneous and usually successful community action that was normally motivated not only by hunger but, as E. P. Thompson has shown, by some perception of injury or transgression of customs or rights. This time, however, after a couple of hours of tumult in the market, five or six men and some fifty youths worked to stir up the crowd, urging an attack on the local militia's arms depot, something rather more serious than a potato-cellar raid. The idea, however, caught on immediately, and very soon a crowd reported by some (probably with exaggeration) to be four or five thousand people swept out of the market square.

At the depot the crowd sent up a cry of "All in a mind!" and began pelting the building with stones, heedless of the two armed guards who showed themselves at the entrance. Some of the braver men ran to the doors, overcame the guards without a shot being fired, and poured into the armory, gathering up and destroying weapons inside. Before a troop of Hussars arrived to disperse the mob some time later, 198 weapons had been broken and 78 stolen. Among the dozen arrested were the tailor and well-known radical John Blackwell, who was caught with a musket in his hands and was subsequently identified as "the person foremost in the said Riot," and a woman, Mary Gibbons. There is no firm indication that they or any of those at the arsenal were enrolled Luddites (and as far as is known no women were ever "twisted in"), but Luddites were reported several times later this same month stealing arms in locations only a few miles away, a practice that continued throughout the summer, so this may have been the opening salvo in that campaign.

On the same day twenty-five miles due west in Stockport, two men dressed up as women were cheered by their followers as "General Ludd's wives" as they led a sizable crowd to the mansion of John Goodair, the clothier whose factory of steam-powered looms had been a target ten days earlier. (This is the first and only clear instance of men using this disguise in the Luddite years, though there are suggestions from both Nottingham and Huddersfield that at least some articles of women's clothing had been worn on raids previously; it was so striking that it would go on to be a part of local folklore for generations afterward.)* When the demonstrators were stopped by the large gates of the house they started throwing stones at the windows and calling to the family inside to open up, and when there was no response within they set off to other manufacturers' houses nearby, gathering people on the way.

After they had broken windows at the houses of William Radcliffe and Peter Marsland, who had also been targets ten days before, and of John Bentley and William Bradshaw, who were the leading hard-liners against increasing wages, the crowd, several thousand strong by now, returned to the Goodair mansion around noon-time. Here we have a rare view-from-inside account by Goodair's wife, from a letter to her husband who was then in London:

> On perceiving them from our cottage coming down the road, I
> assembled the children and nurse in the parlour, and fastened the
> windows and doors; the gardener presently rushed into the room,

---

* Natalie Zemon Davis makes an interesting case that such female disguises were "quite popular and widespread" in Europe not only because of the effective camouflage itself but for their suggestion of the "sexual power and energy of the unruly woman" and her role as the one to defend "community interests and standards" and "to tell the truth about unjust rule."

and conjured us to fly at that moment, if we wished to save our lives. It was with difficulty I could speak; but each snatching a child, we escaped at the great gate just in time to avoid the rabble. We proceeded to Mrs. Sykes's; but before we reached our destination we saw our cottage enveloped in flames. Everything, I have since learnt, was consumed by the fire, and nothing left but the shell. The mob next proceeded to the factory, where they broke the windows, destroyed the looms, and cut all the work which was in progress; and having finished this mischief, they repeated the three cheers which they gave on seeing the flames first burst from our dwelling.*

It is now nine o'clock at night, and I learn the mob are more outrageous than ever at Edgeley [the factory site]. . . . Fresh soldiers have been just sent there. Another troop of horse is expected to-night.

The first soldiers were men from the Scots Greys stationed in the area, followed by troops in great numbers both from the Stockport inns where they were billeted and down from Kersal Moor, outside Manchester, where a large garrison was encamped. Two men were arrested on the spot and four more subsequently, five weavers and a spinner—one of whom, Joseph Thompson, made the mistake of being still in possession of the silver he had taken from the Goodairs' house before the fire.

This melee, in midday in midweek, by a crowd variously estimated at two to three thousand in a parish of only fifteen thousand, came as something of a surprise to the local authorities, although it had been preceded by several smaller demonstrations and by a series of threatening letters to local manufacturers. One such letter, delivered to a Stockport employer, gives an idea of the depth of feeling of the workers just then:

---

* Ms. Goodair's great-granddaughter recalled in 1926: "One of the most vivid memories of my childhood is hearing [my grandmother] tell how her mother received the news that the mills had been set on fire and the mob was making for the house. The old coachman hurried the family into the carriage—and as they drove over the brow of the hill, they looked back to see their home in flames."

We think it our Bounin Duty to give you this Notice that is if you
do Not Cause those Dressing Machines [power looms for weaving
and finishing cotton cloth] to be Remov'd Within the Bounds of
Seven Days . . . your factory and all that it Contains Will and
Surely Be Set on fire. . . . it is Not our Desire to Do you the Least
Injury But We are fully Determin'd to Destroy Both Dressing
Machines and Steam Looms Let *Who Will* be the Owners. We
neither regard Those that keeps them nor the Army for we Will
Conquer Both or Die in the Conflict!

Hardly surprising then that another crowd, again said to be
some two thousand strong, assembled the next morning on a
heath at the edge of town and, directed by a committee of
weavers, presumably Luddites, declared themselves a "First Congress" to plan a campaign of attack and elect delegates to a
"Second Congress." Speakers advised against going up against
the military now in town until they had greater numbers, and a
proposed march on one local factory was discouraged because the
site was being well guarded by the soldiers. It was put forth
instead that nighttime raids would be safer and that small bands,
calling themselves "Ludd's men," could move through the area
taking money, food, supplies, and weapons from the rich with
impunity. Such robberies had been tried out a few days before,
originally under the guise of asking for voluntary gifts from the
well-to-do gentry and substantial farmers, as had sometimes been
done during hard times in the past, but quickly turning into outright extortionary raids if any resistance was forthcoming; something like a dozen successful visits had been made. This tactic
seems to have been approved by the "Congress" that morning,
and indeed the meeting dispersed into several small units of
"Ludd's men," who were encouraged to go out demanding contributions right then and there.

One such group of about ten men set on the house of a Major
John Parker, broke all his windows, and was finally given money
just when it was descended on by a small force of local volunteer

militia captained by John Lloyd, an attorney who was the clerk to a Stockport magistrate and an energetic, not to say fanatic, enemy of Luddism then working directly under the guidance of the Home Office in London. Seven men were arrested, all but one a weaver; one man, John Parnell, was later pressured by Lloyd into giving evidence that incriminated another Stockport Luddite for illegal oathing, one of the few such breakthroughs ever. Other bands that day seem to have been more successful, setting on "the houses of gentlemen and farmers, from whom they extorted money and victuals," according to a letter to the *Annual Register*. Sometimes they visibly carried weapons, and at one house, owned by a Dr. Mitchell, they fired "several bullets" at him, which, though none hit him, presumably had the desired extortionary effect.

These raids by what the Stockport magistrate, Charles Prescott, called "associated banditti" continued well into May, mostly at night, but the line between those done for some definable political purpose of a Luddistic kind and those that were mere burglaries provoked by need and desperation remains blurry. Suffice it to say that the local authorities took them all to be evidence of some dangerous larger purpose and that Lloyd in particular was of the opinion that they betokened a "general rising" in the offing.

It was Manchester's turn next. On Saturday morning, April 18, as the *Manchester Mercury* reported, the potato market was "the scene of great disorder and confusion, owing to the much increased price on that indispensible part of the sustenance of the poor," an increase from 7 shillings for a load of 250 pounds or so to 18 shillings, in effect a tripling of the retail price. "A number of ignorant, unthinking people, most of whom were women, failing in their endeavours to purchase the potatoes at the reduced rate [at] which they required them"—and which they felt to be the legitimate, customary rate—"immediately put themselves in possession of most of the produce in the Market," a nice way of phrasing it. Most of the farmers' carts were commandeered and the contents sold at 8 shillings the load, with the money for the most part turned over to the frightened owners when the carts were empty. But one woman, Hannah Smith, 54, was heard to say, "Damn them, we will have them for nothing," and proceeded to shovel potatoes out to her companions free. Minutes later she was reported as saying, "We will not be satisfied with potatoes!" and led a group to seize some carts of butter and milk, which she sold at a reduced rate of a shilling a pound. When the troops arrived, she was among the eight, two women and six men, who were arrested: none was identified as a Luddite, but a spy later reported that members of the Manchester Luddite "secret committee" watched the market fracas with "high glee."

Food riots spread the following Monday, April 20, market day for much of this region: Manchester erupted again, as did the surrounding towns of Bolton, Rochdale, Ashton, and Oldham, and several towns just over the border in the northern corner of Derbyshire, including Tintwhistle, where power looms were also broken. In most places the crowds were content with seizing provision carts and selling the contents, and in some places they broke into shops and stole flour, meal, bacon, potatoes, and bread. An eyewitness reported the scene in the little Cheshire village of Gee Cross:

> I saw a large mob attacking a shop opposite our garden gate, and I saw the meal and flour brought out and distributed to the people, chiefly women, who received it into their aprons, handkerchiefs, caps, old stockings, or anything else in which they could carry it away. One man named [William] Walker, for a frolic, had put a paper round his hat with *General Ludd* written on it, but it cost him dear.

Indeed it did: he was arrested as a ringleader, tried for "inciting a mob to disorder and tumult," and died on the ship transporting him to Australia.

But one of the food riots turned into something far more serious, indeed the bloodiest event in all the history of Luddism, save the execution of the men finally blamed for the Rawfolds attack. It was a two-day assault, quasi-military in some parts and quasi-frenzy in others, on the mill and houses of Daniel Burton and his son Emmanuel in Middleton, a little town ten miles northeast of Manchester, where their manufacturing of fine calico prints by steam-operated power looms had, it was said, put half the weavers of the area out of work in the previous two years.

There is no surviving proof that this attack was planned by twisted-in Luddites—a spy operating in a Luddite cell in Manchester said the leaders there were against it—but the fact that so many people converged on Middleton in the early Monday afternoon of April 20 from so many different directions indicates that there was some sort of organization behind it; and we do know that there was a secret Luddite meeting the night before on a nearby moor and that an effigy of King Ludd himself was carried in the fray. Whoever the leaders were, subsequent accounts suggest that as many as two or three thousand people collected before the Burton factory at about two o'clock that day. Many were women and young men up from Oldham, not more than a mile away, where they had taken part in a food riot that morning; there was a large contingent of men from Saddleworth ("rude uncultivated savages . . . of the most desperate cast," one magistrate's agent reported), and there were some boisterous colliers from Hollinwood and any number of men that "seemed to arrive from all parts at once," in the words of Samuel Bamford, the Middleton weaver who left a description of that first day:

> On the report reaching the factory that the mob was coming, the works were stopped, and all the hands, save those detained for the defence of the mill, were sent home. The mob, after a short delay in the market place, proceeded to the bottom of Wood Street, where the factory was situated, and halted in front of the building, and a score or two of boys who led the mob set up a shout, and began to throw stones and break the windows. A number of discharges from the mill followed, but as no one seemed to have been

hurt another shout was set up, and the cry went round, "Oh! they're nobbu feyerin peawther [they're not but firing powder, i.e., blanks]; they darno shoot bullets," and the stone throwing was recommenced. Other discharges from the mill now took place, and some of the mob who had experience in such matters remarked that the crack was different, and that ball was being fired. A moment only confirmed this opinion, for several were wounded, and three fell dead, on seeing which the mob fled in all directions.

Again accounts vary, but the toll was at least four and more likely five dead that day, and at least eighteen wounded. A week after Rawfolds the message was clear: the factory owners were fighting back and no act was beyond them—and none was likely to receive any greater disapprobation from the government than "justifiable homicide" (which was indeed the verdict of the coroner about Burton's the following week, as it had been about Rawfolds).

Outrage was apparently high: "The loss they had suffered," a correspondent wrote to the *Annual Register,* "only stimulated them to seek revenge," and almost at once it was known that there would be another attack on Burton's the following day. A troop of mounted Scots Greys marched through the town, clearing the streets and shutting up the pubs before returning to their camp in Manchester, and a company of the Cumberland militia was sent out to the mill to stand guard. "Fierce denunciations were uttered against Burton and his shooters," Samuel Bamford noticed, "whilst very little anger was expressed against the men." The next morning a group of men, mostly colliers wielding their pickaxes, attacked the militia's arms depot in Oldham and stole some weapons before heading on to Middleton, where they joined up with a crowd said to be even larger than that of the day before. The *Leeds Mercury* reported (in an account headed, "The New Era: THE INSURRECTIONARY ERA"):

A body of men, consisting of from one to two hundred, some of them armed with muskets with fixed bayonets, and others with colliers'

picks, marched into the village in procession, and joined the rioters. At the head of this armed banditti a *Man of Straw* was carried,
representing the *renowned* General Ludd whose standard-bearer
waved a sort of red flag.

Whatever King Ludd might once have represented, it is clear that
now, at least to this angry assemblage, he was nothing less than a
symbol of revolution, complete with a *drapeau rouge* from 1789.*

The crowd moved on to Burton's mill with determination,
but considering the casualties of the day before and the sight of
the Cumberland militia in the mill yard, there was no taste for
further confrontation. Nevertheless, one party stayed there facing
the fence that guarded the mill, keeping the soldiers occupied,
while several other groups spread out and began attacking the
houses of the mill's favored workmen located nearby, ransacking
the cottages and piling the furniture outside to be set afire. One
large group went on to Emmanuel Burton's stately mansion a few
hills away. There, unopposed, they stormed into the house, raided
the pantry and the cellars, and began smashing the furniture;
when that was done, Bamford relates, one of two "tall, dark-haired,
and handsomely formed daughters of a venerable old weaver"
turned to the other and said: "Come, let's put a finish to this job":

> Taking up a shred [of cloth] which lay on the floor, she lighted it at
> the fire which had been left burning in the grate. In a moment the
> sofa was on fire; the sofa set the curtains in a blaze, and sofa and
> curtains communicated the flames to the floor and window, and at
> the expiration of probably half an hour not a beam nor a board
> remained unconsumed in the whole building.

Even as the flames were taking hold here another segment of
the crowd started off in the direction of Daniel Burton's home

---

* In his imaginative modern account of these events, Glyn Hughes describes this as "a six-
foot-high figure out of sacks stuffed with straw," with "a card saying KING LUDD" pinned to
its chest, a giant turnip for its head, dressed in "white corduroy trousers" and a "blue
liberty cap" from the French Revolution, and, finally, a "large carrot between his legs"
making him "truly a king."

just a few minutes away, determined to reduce it to the same condition.

It was then, however, at about three in the afternoon, that the
cavalry and troops of the Scots Greys finally showed up in force;
one company rode into the crowd as it approached the Burton
mansion, viciously using swords and stanchions to disperse it,
while another went to the mill, where it seems that the armed
attackers stood their ground and fired two volleys at them before
a return of fire and the charge of the horses sent them running.
Two men were shot as they tried to escape and fell on the spot;
two more bodies were found not far away the next day; and much
later that afternoon, when all had returned to quiet, an innocent
old man was shot dead by a sergeant of the militia as he stood
alone in the Middleton graveyard.

In all at least ten people lost their lives in the two days'
action—one as young as 16, another as old as 53, and a baker, a
glazier, and a hatter among them—and the figure may in fact
have been much higher. Reports to the *Annual Register* said that
the toll was "considerably greater than was at first supposed,"
since "a number of dead bodies had been found in the adjoining
woods," and the editors concluded that "from twenty-five to
thirty of the misguided populace became the victims of their own
folly and criminality." Unfortunately no exact figure was ever established, presumably because the authorities would have wanted to
minimize the number to keep the reaction as muted as possible.

Tensions were now particularly taut in the western corner of the
Luddite triangle. The feelings of much of the populace were
expressed in a somewhat overwrought Luddite letter sent to the
local coroner, Nathaniel Milne, after he returned another of
those "justifiable homicide" verdicts for the Middleton murders:

> Had some poor man murder'd two or three rich
> ones in cool blood, Nat. Milnes would then have
> buss'd in their ears[,] a 'Packed Jury' loaded
> with Contagion, these Words: 'Willful Murder',

instead of 'Justifiable Homicide', but know thou
cursed insinuator, if Burton's infamous action
was 'justifiable' the Laws of Tyrants are Reasons
Dictates.

Beware, Beware! A month's bathing in the
Stygian Lake would not wash this sanguinary
deed from our minds, it but augments the heri-
table cause, that stirs us up in indignation. . . .

Ludd finis est.

Newspaper reports that week spoke of "great alarm" and "confusion" and "terror," and the *Leeds Intelligencer* announced that "there
is a dark, subtle and invisible agency at work, seducing the ignorant and the inexperienced." Letters to the Home Office, at least
from the more impressionable informants, were full of the impending "general rising" and tales of "revolutionary Jacobins"; a
colonel of the local Oldham militia sent word from a "reliable
source" who had been told, shortly after the Burton mill attack,
that "the rising would be general in London and all over the kingdom" in "Numbers to overturn and overwhelm every Thing." And a
local businessman wrote just after the affair that "the spirit of turbulence . . . has assumed a new character, since Jacobinism was in-
fused into the lower orders and is now become perfectly infernal."

All such fears were transformed into certainties when on the
Friday afternoon of that week, April 24, in the village of Westhoughton only a dozen miles to the west of Middleton a fierce
attack was launched on the establishment of Wroe and Duncroft,
another cotton factory with more than 170 power looms, much
disliked. This assault, the most destructive Luddite raid ever, also
had the most bizarre preliminaries ever.

It seems that Colonel Ralph Fletcher, the magistrate of Bolton
(about midway between Manchester and Westhoughton) and a
rabid persecutor of "Jacobins" of all stripes wherever he imagined
them to be, had organized a network of spies from around 1801

that were then actively at work not merely infiltrating but actually instigating Luddite operations. Sometime in early March he brought into his service one John Stones, at the rate of £1 a week and expenses of anywhere from £2 to £5 a week, who took his task of organizing a Luddite cell in Bolton with such zeal and ambition that it wasn't long before he became the local "General Ludd," right down to drilling the men in units of ten at night on the empty moors west of town. At a meeting of delegates from various Luddite "secret committees" in Manchester on April 5, Stones first proposed burning down the Westhoughton mill but got no support whatever. He then convened another meeting just for the Bolton initiates two days later and proposed the job again but was similarly frustrated. Nothing daunted, that night he set April 19 as the date for an attack on the mill, urged his followers to be sure to get several hundred men to the meeting place next week, and proceeded to go around administering oaths, making plans for the assault, holding forth (and, as the records show, buying drinks) in the local pubs, and drilling whatever men, probably not more than fifty, would turn out on the chilly spring nights.

On the night of April 19 about twenty men did show up on the moor, soon joined by another dozen or so in blackened faces, brandishing pistols. A long discussion took place (whose details are in a subsequent legal deposition) in which some men without disguises went on about the miseries of the weavers and the need for a minimum wage, finally interrupted by one of the blackfaces saying it was "all damned nonsense to talk of law as no justice would be done except they did it themselves." The argument went on a bit, but in the end it was only the dozen blackfaces and a handful of others who agreed to go through with the Westhoughton raid that night. The meeting then dispersed, the promised raiders having agreed to go by separate routes to a place on the Westhoughton road where, they were assured, they would be met by two hundred more. When these few finally regrouped they found no one there to meet them and the proposed attack a fiasco, so they all voted to go home—spurning the suggestion, probably Stones's, that they break the windows in a nearby church; at the signal of a pistol shot they dispersed into the dark. A militia detachment later that night arrested a number of the blackfaces as they were headed home; it turned out that they and all of the others similarly disguised were not genuine Luddites at all but, to a man, spies of Colonel Fletcher.

For the next several days most of the attention of the area was on Middleton and, as one account put it, the "sanguinary conflict" that so shocked and saddened the countryside. But the talk of a Westhoughton raid was kept up by someone and became widespread enough to convince the local militia there to set a guard at the factory during the first of the week, even to persuade some of the employees of the plant to take over the watch with arms from the militia on Thursday night. But on Friday morning, April 24, with the mill closed for lack of work and rumors of an attack becoming more prevalent, "the Men who worked in the Building," Fletcher reported, "thought it not *prudent* to Protect it as their Families might suffer"—or their homes and furniture might be destroyed, as had happened at Middleton. The owners therefore applied for protection to the Scots Greys stationed in Bolton, five miles away, a party of which rode out from town around noon to survey the scene at the mill. These professional soldiers, and an elite corps at that, little favored the job of sitting around like hired constables protecting property that the owners rightfully should defend—and when they might otherwise be in the Peninsula having a go at Boney—and so when they found no threatening mob gathered there they took themselves back to Bolton and said they wouldn't go out again unless called to do so by the magistrates.

Not long after that, at about one o'clock, a group said to be about fifty strong assembled near the mill. Whether these were in fact Stones's recruits we have no way of knowing, but it seems unlikely: there was no identification of Stones at the scene (nor

does he claim in his reports to have been there), the presence of
women in the crowd suggests that these were not people he had
enlisted and drilled, and the fact that Colonel Fletcher was out of
town that day indicates that he at least had no inkling of the
attack, which would be hard to imagine if Stones really had had a
hand in it. After a few hours of milling around, perhaps expecting
reinforcements that never showed up, this contingent finally
descended on the unprotected mill. They smashed through the
gates and started to break windows in the mill, led by two young
women, Mary Molyneux, 19, and her sister Lydia, 15, who were
seen, according to later court papers, "with Muck Hooks and
Coal Picks in their Hands breaking the Windows of the Building
and swearing and cursing the souls of those that worked in the
Factory" and shouting "Now Lads" to encourage the men on.
With the windows broken, men took straw from the stables and
set a series of fires inside: "The whole of the building," wrote
the *Annual Register* correspondent, "with its valuable machinery,
cambrics, &c, were entirely destroyed. The building being extensive, the conflagration was tremendous. The damage sustained is
immense, the factory alone having cost £6000."

On his return home that night Colonel Fletcher was probably
apoplectic and certainly demonic, sending eighty officers out to
arrest anyone with any information or suggestion of complicity.
The surviving documents leave no doubt about these men's
ferocity: they broke into cottages throughout the district, without warrants and without excuse or apology, hauled people from
their beds and fires, tied or shackled them for the trip to Colonel
Fletcher, and did what they could to get confessions and names
of accomplices from them. Dr. Robert Taylor, a Bolton physician, soon after complained that "the houses and bedchambers of
many innocent and peacable individuals were violently broken
open in the dead of night, their wives and families insulted, and
they themselves dragged into confinement, though not a shadow
of accusation was, either at that time or ever afterwards, brought
against them." Fletcher interviewed a score of men that first night

and many more in the next few days, sending some home uncharged but forcing others to stand bail on the ingenious if illegal indictment of having "to answer any charge which might hereafter be made." Within a week twenty-five people had been arrested, though probably as many as ten of them turned out to be spies for one agency or other, and in the event only thirteen were brought to trial.

Four days after the destruction of the Westhoughton mill, on April 28, Luddism entered a new phase.

If we can rely on the reports, pistols had been used in Nottingham Luddism from the beginning and in the north from at least March, but there seem to have been no serious and concerted armed attacks on individuals anywhere between the raid on Hollingsworth's house in Bulwell on November 10 and the attempted assassination of William Cartwright on April 18 (unless we take as homicidal and not merely intimidatory the "several bullets" fired at the Stockport doctor on April 14). In the wake of the Rawfolds deaths, however, and then after the shootings at Burton's in Middleton, the idea of murder in the Luddite cause was no longer unthinkable, even though it was indeed a serious and fateful step in an England where such crimes were still uncommon.

Shortly after the Cartwright attempt a magistrate named Armitage, near Huddersfield, was fired upon as he stood in his window, the bullet lodging in the ceiling of his bedroom, and a special constable at Leeds was also shot at but unharmed. In Nottinghamshire quiet had generally prevailed, until April 27, when an attack was made on William Trentham, 63, a Nottingham manufacturer who not only had ignored a threatening letter—authorized, it said, by "the Captain" (a demotion for Ludd?)—warning him to raise wages for embroidery work he put out from his shop but also had reportedly docked his hands and "told them to tell Ned Ludd." As he stepped up to his front door that night after "a convivial party, periodically held at the

Crown and Cushion Tavern," he was waylaid by two men, one of whom "placed himself before him," the *Annual Register* reported, "and, presenting a pistol, shot him through the left breast: the assassins then made their escape." Trentham survived the attack despite his age, but the Nottingham authorities took this first overt personal assault seriously enough to offer a reward of £700; still, the Nottingham town clerk reported more than a month later that "we have *No* Intelligence of the Persons who attacked Mr. Trentham nor any hopes of obtaining any"—nor did they ever.

It was the day after this attempt, some fifty miles north in Huddersfield, that George Mellor and three other croppers in John Wood's wool-finishing shop decided upon the murder of a prominent local manufacturer, William Horsfall. "Mellor said the method of breaking up the shears must be given up," later court testimony recorded, "and instead of it the masters must be shot. . . . They said they had lost two men, and must kill the masters." Having failed at killing Cartwright with two attackers, Mellor—presumably one of the two, though the identity of the Cartwright assailants was never discovered—decided to use four for Horsfall: himself, Benjamin Walker, Thomas Smith, and William Thorpe, all friends and fellow workers.

Horsfall was a natural, not to say inevitable, target, in some ways more suitable than Cartwright. A feisty and hot-tempered man of middle age, he was just fitting out his factory at Marsden, about seven miles west of Huddersfield on the road to Manchester, with new machines made for him by Enoch Taylor (the same man who with his brother made the "Enoch" hammers). At his mill, as one oldtimer says in *Ben o' Bill's,* "the owd hands are told they're no use, an' young 'uns is being browt fra' no one knows where, to work th' shearing frames." Horsfall was also an ardent supporter of the Huddersfield volunteer militia—a "Wm. Horsfall" is listed as a captain in the 1812 company roster—and was the guiding spirit behind a "Secret Committee for preventing unlawful depredations on Machinery and Shearing Frames" that had recently been formed among some of the region's manufacturers.

He was, moreover, an outspoken enemy of the Luddites who had been heard in a fit of temper, as Frank Peel reconstructed it, "to express his desire to ride up to the saddle girths in Luddite blood," a statement so well known that "the children to teaze him would run out in front of his horse and cry 'I'm General Ludd!' 'I'm General Ludd!' on which he would immediately fall into a violent passion and pursue the frightened urchins hotly with the horsewhip." As if all that wasn't enough, according to a story handed down by Mellor's cousin in *Ben o' Bill's,* Horsfall had once ridden grandly past Mellor as the cropper was comforting a young mother whose baby had just died at her milkless bosom, and when the young man thrust the lifeless form in the mill-owner's face with an accusatory taunt, Horsfall struck at him with his riding whip, leaving a welt across Mellor's face that was visible for days, and rode off without glancing back.

Horsfall was known to visit Huddersfield every Tuesday, market day, usually stopping at the George Hotel for tea around five before riding on to his home in Marsden, often with a break at the Warren House Inn about halfway home for a rum and water, usually served to him while still in the saddle. This Tuesday, April 28, was no different, except that Mellor and his crew took up posts on the south side of the road to Marsden, on the edge of the Radcliffe Plantation (no doubt chosen with some grim irony), just a little ways down from the Warren House and around a bend where the route was deserted. When Horsfall, riding slowly as was his custom, came abreast of Mellor's men, one shot suddenly rang out, Horsfall's horse whirled and staggered, then two more shots were fired, hitting home. The manufacturer raised his head, crying "Murder!" and collapsed against the neck of his horse, bleeding heavily. A local farmer riding not far behind— close enough to see details of the assailants' clothes that would be incriminating—tended the wounded man until two boys with a cart came by awhile later, and they took him back to the Warren House. There, despite the ministrations of the local physician,

Horsfall died thirty-six hours later in the inn's finest room, saying at the end, "These are awful times, doctor."

On the day that Horsfall died—at the end of a month in which at least fourteen and perhaps as many as forty workingmen had been killed, a dozen factories had been attacked and one destroyed utterly, major food riots had torn through a score of cities from Carlisle to Sheffield, and reports of insurrection and rebellion had been sent to the Home Office from all over the Luddite triangle—the Prince Regent in London decided to attend the formal reception that his mother, Queen Charlotte, was giving at St. James's Palace. He did so at the head of a state procession, the first since he had become Regent, from his home at Carleton House:

> The procession of his royal highness [the *Annual Register* reported] consisted of three carriages, drawn by two horses each; within them, his aides-de-camp, pages of honour, &c. The servants wore their state liveries, and new state hats, adorned with blue feathers. Then followed the state coach of his royal highness, drawn by six bays in superb red morocco harness, decorated with red ribands. On the sides of the carriage walked four state helpers.

That evening the Prince invited four hundred of "the higher ranks" to "a magnificent entertainment" at Carleton House, whose furnishings its master was just then redoing at a cost to the public treasury of £260,000—the equivalent of the annual earnings of some ninety thousand workers, when employed, in the textile regions to the north.

Elsewhere in London, however, the "disturbances" in the industrial districts were being taken very seriously indeed. The government of Spencer Perceval, particularly through Home Secretary Richard Ryder, had moved to unleash the army in full force in these areas and to encourage as much as possible the local sheriffs, magistrates, and county officials to assemble units of their own.

Just three months before, Ryder had acknowledged that the force he had sent to maintain peace in Nottingham was the largest ever used in the history of the country—but as of the first of May, an army *seven times as large* was operating in the Luddite triangle.

To the units of nearly 2,000 men the government sent out in November 1811 were added another regiment in December and two more in February, amounting to some 2,500 infantry and 1,000 cavalry, an extraordinary military collocation. About 2,000 of these men were moved to the northern counties in April in response to the Luddism there, but they were made up for by a new force of 2,000 men sent in to establish a permanent camp of 3,500 in Sherwood Forest ready to be sent as needed to any part of the troubled districts. In addition, considerable forces were dispatched to the northern counties from elsewhere in the king-dom, so that by the first of May General Thomas Grey in the West Riding had command of some 4,000 men, at least 800 of them in mounted Dragoon units, and General Thomas Maitland had a huge force of 6,900 men, 1,400 of them cavalry and two companies of artillery, in his charge in southern Lancashire.

That means that London was willing to dispatch to the Luddite region, an area of about 2,100 square miles (the size of Delaware) with a population of one million or so, some 14,400 soldiers—and four years before it had sent the Duke of Wel-lington to Portugal for a war against sizable French armies with a force of only 8,739 men (though to be fair, he there joined a force of between 11,000 and 13,000 before he had to go up against the French).* In effect you could say that if you were in the area on May 1, 1812, one of every seventy people you saw would have been

---

* One of the most common errors in Luddite scholarship is to get this comparison wrong, as for example when George Rudé says that the troops in the textile districts represented "a greater military force than Wellington had under his command in the Iberian campaign." E. P. Thompson, among others, makes this same error; perhaps it is a misreading of F. O. Darvall's careful statement that the force was "larger than that with which Wellesley [later Wellington] set sail for Portugal in 1808." Actually, Wellington had 20,000 men under him in his 1809 victories and as many as 45,000 in his 1812 campaign.

a soldier: this was a military presence, a true army and a sizable
one, the likes of which was so unprecedented as to strike, as it
undoubtedly was meant to do, terror in the most well-meaning.

This invasion of middle Britain, by men regarded as a rough
lot at best, ill-disciplined, unschooled, and ungentle—whom
Wellington himself about then (in a letter to Lord Bathurst) was
calling "the scum of the earth"—must have been only somewhat
less disruptive than the invasion of the Peninsula. What with the
daily movement of troops of cavalry clapping and clanking along
streets and highways, the nightly patrols of soldiers on foot and
horseback in crowded cities and isolated villages, the continual
sight of redcoats in the shops and pubs and churches and the factories themselves, it must have given the area, as the *Leeds Intelligencer* said, "a most warlike appearance." Because military
barracks were only recently approved and still rare in Britain,
most of the men were billetted in local pubs and inns (usually to
the displeasure of the owners, who complained that the soldiers
ran good customers away and bad debts up), and some towns had
the look of encampments: Huddersfield, for example, a town of
ten thousand, had a thousand men stationed in its thirty-three
pubs and inns, and Marsden, just down the road, had an entire
cavalry troop occupying its major hotel.

But that was not the limit of the "forces of order," as the
phrase had it. The voluntary militia, proto-soldiers trained with
annual outings and intermittent drillings, numbered 215,000
throughout England and probably 20,000 in the affected areas;
Huddersfield had as many as 1,300 men in eleven battalions in
1810, and the whole West Riding had at least 5,000. On top of
that, each magistrate usually had a small staff of constables and
agents—the aggressive Colonel Fletcher, in Bolton, was said to
have seventy-one on his staff in 1812, but that must have been
unusual—and an unlimited capacity to swear in citizens as special constables for emergencies at his sole discretion. By May, it
was said, Bolton had 400 special constables making rounds every
night, usually armed; Salford, a suburb of Manchester, had 1,500

(10 percent of the male population); Manchester itself had 4,000; and Nottingham had around 1,000—"merchants and shopkeepers," as one report goes, "after a day's work done, leaving 'home and the pleasing wife' to steal in the shadows along lanes and byeways and highroads." As if that weren't enough, some towns called out Watch-and-Ward battalions armed from town arsenals. Where that was thought to be too risky, as in most of the West Riding, manufacturers and private law-and-order types were encouraged, as in the recommendation of the Lancashire civil authorities in May 1812, to form "regular associations within the several subdivisions and districts of the county for mutual defense"—in effect, private posses operating with public support.

Amid all these forces, there were few as active as Joseph Radcliffe. He would interview processions of people during the day at Milnsbridge House and on most evenings he would ride through the town stopping croppers and farmers and travelers to see what he could learn from local gossip. He was too high-minded, however, to avail himself of spies, and at one point even wrote the Home Office asking what he should do if his only informer on a criminal case were one of the accomplices: "Shall I send him about his business, saying such persons are not to be attended to, or in what manner am I to act?" (London told him to go ahead and accept any such information, however obtained, adding that of course it would also be nice to get some "corroborative Evidence" as well.) He had handbills printed up announcing that the local Society for Prosecuting Luddites had authorized a reward of £2,000 for information about Horsfall's killers. And as he went about he apparently worked hard at playing on the feeling of many thereabouts that this murder—of a man who, for all his faults, was a long-standing member of the community (unlike Cartwright)—represented a serious transgression of legitimate bounds. Even Ben Bamforth admitted that it was seen as "an act so dastard" that many local people turned away from the croppers, and he mentions one local innkeeper as saying he'd have "neither Luds nor their brass" in his place. But still no results; still the silence held.

As if to confirm that the Luddite fires were burning high, early in May Radcliffe intercepted a letter from "Peter Plush, Secretary to General Ludd" in Nottingham to "General Ludd Juner" in Huddersfield, expressing "extrem regret" at the loss of "the two *brave boys*" at Rawfolds, but adding:

> The Genral further auhtorises me to say that he trusts to the attachment of his subjects for the avenging of the death of the two brav youths who fell at the sege of Rawfolds. He also wishes me to state that though his troops heare are not at present making any ostensable movments that it is not for want of force—as the orgenisation is quite as strong as in Yorkshire—but that they are at present only devising the best means for a grand attack and that at present thay are dispatching a few indeviduals by pistol shot on of which fel last nite [a reference no doubt to the Trentham attempt].
>
> I am further otherised to say that it is the opinion of our general and men that as long as that blackgard drunken whoreing fellow, called Prince Regent and his servants have anything to do with government that nothing but distres will befale us there foot-stooles.

The "avenging" for Rawfolds had already taken place with Horsfall's murder. The question Radcliffe must have been pondering was whether the General's subjects around Huddersfield were now moving on to the "grand attack."

6

The Luddites

May 1812–January 1813

O<small>N</small> SATURDAY MORNING, May 9, 1812, this verse was posted in several places in the city of Nottingham:

> *Welcome Ned Ludd, your case is good,*
> *Make Perceval your aim;*
> *For by this Bill, 'tis understood*
> *Its death to break a Frame—*
>
> *With dexterous skill, the Hosier's kill*
> *For they are quite as bad;*
> *And die you must, by the late Bill,*
> *Go on my bonny lad!—*
>
> *You might as well be hung for death*
> *As breaking a machine—*
> *So now my lad, your sword unsheath*
> *And make it sharp and keen—*
>
> *We are ready now your cause to join*
> *Whenever you may call;*
> *So make foul blood, run clear and fine*
> *Of Tyrants great and small!—*

Two days later, in London, Prime Minister Spencer Perceval was shot.

On Monday afternoon the prime minister was scheduled to attend a Commons debate on the controversial Orders in Council, of which he was the major supporter, beginning at 4:30. A short, slight man, not quite 50, cleanshaven, mild, carrying a stick, he had left his home on Downing Street a few minutes before to walk to Westminster, but several people had stopped him on the way and so it was close to 4:45 when he stepped into the lobby of Parliament. Two dozen men or so were there standing around, talking, pressing their business on the MPs come for the debate (hence the term "lobbying"), one of whom was Samuel Crompton, inventor of the spinning mule, who was hoping to get Parliament to reward him with £20,000 for his genius (he was eventually granted £5,000). Off to the side sat a tall, well-dressed man, speaking to no one, who suddenly rushed to the front of the lobby as the prime minister appeared and, before anyone could stop him, pulled a long pistol from his coat and fired a shot point-blank into Perceval's chest. The prime minister staggered, strangled out something that sounded like "Murder!" and collapsed on his face onto the marble floor, dead.

The assassin made no effort to get away. He went to a bench against the wall while everyone crowded around the fallen leader, and sat there a few minutes until someone had the presence of mind to grab and search him, finding a second pistol in his pocket, unfired. He was entirely undemonstrative and without saying a word allowed himself to be taken away, with an escort party front and back, to the Parliamentary "prison-room" somewhere in the bowels of the building.

When reports of the assassination were first received in the land, it was generally assumed that Luddism had struck again, this time at the highest level. It took no more than two days, however, for the London authorities to determine that the assassin, John Bellingham, was a slightly deranged merchant who had lost £8,000 in some deal with the Russians and held the British authorities in Archangel, and by extension their superiors in London, to blame: no connections to Luddism, the authorities

said, to Paineites, to Jacobins, or revolutionaries of any kind, a
lone gunman operating out of private motives. In less than a
week he was tried and sentenced, and on May 18, just a week after
the murder, he was hanged. Among the witnesses to the execution, a vast crowd of several thousand typical of such events in
those days, was Lord Byron, who rented a small room on the second floor of a building on the square facing the gallows so that he
would have an unimpeded view.

The reaction of the British public to the death of their leader
had very little in it of sorrow, and even the professional Tories
responded with trepidation more than grief. The crowd that
gathered outside the House of Commons in the hours just after
the assassination had been quiet enough but by no means mournful, and when Bellingham was finally taken away in double chains,
there were "repeated shouts of applause from the ignorant or
depraved part of the crowd"; not far away, according to Robert
Southey, young Percy Shelley went into a "pothouse" in order to
relish how people were celebrating the event. And in the eyes of
much of the populace, especially in the industrial areas, Bellingham was seen as a savior—what matter his motives?—who, as
Cobbett later wrote, "had ridded them of one whom they looked
upon as the leader amongst those whom they thought totally
bent on the destruction of their liberties."

In Nottingham, a happy crowd "proceeded with a band of
music through all the principal streets," the *Nottingham Journal*
reported, "joined by a numerous rabble, who . . . testified their
joy at the horrid catastrophe, by repeated shouts, the firing of
guns, and every species of exultation" for several hours until the
Riot Act was finally read and the crowd forcibly dispersed. In
Newcastle, Staffordshire, according to a contemporary historian,
a man was seen "running down the street, leaping into the air,
waving his hat around his head, and shouting with frantic joy,
'Percival [sic] is shot, hurrah! ditto!'" And, as one manufacturer
reported to a colleague in London, "as the coaches [bearing news
of the assassination] arrived in various parts of the kingdom, the

intelligence of the murder of a fellow-creature had been received with more exultation than horror, and even in some places greeted with savage shouts of un-Christian joy."

Southey, dramatic as always, saw the killing as "but the opening of the floodgates." He wrote a friend: "This murder, though committed publicly by a madman, has been made the act and deed of the populace. Shocking as this appears, so it is and so it must be considered." And two days later he added: "I have often been grieved by public events, but never so depressed by any as this. . . . I can scarce refrain from tears as I write. It is my deep and ominous sense of danger to the country." Southey was no poet—but no fool, either.

Almost every historian of the period agrees that if there was ever going to be a revolution in Britain, it would have been at that moment. "Then, if ever, the seeds of a revolutionary situation existed," writes F. O. Darvall, not one to overstretch such a case: the prime minister slain, distress across the land, crop failures four years in a row, overseas trade and industrial production almost at a standstill, soldiers and resources siphoned off to a ceaseless war on the Continent, an obdurate government heedless of any means for redressing grievances, a lawless insurrection now into its seventh month destroying machines and their owners alike, and a military police force unable to restore order in the industrial heartland. "Then, if ever, a revolutionary attempt would have had a real chance of success," Darvall says. "Then, if ever in nineteenth-century England, there were grounds for revolution, hopes for improvement only in revolution, chances for the success of revolution."*

There were some, men like Southey and others professionally involved as well, who were alive to this threat. The vice lieutenant

---

* It is no doubt stretching, but it is not entirely errant to see in J. M. W. Turner's magnificent "Snowstorm: Hannibal Crossing the Alps," which went on exhibit for the first time this very month, some of the swirling turmoil and roiling rebellion that was affecting the country at that time.

of Yorkshire, Sir Francis Wood, declared in June that "except for the very spots which were occupied by Soldiers, the Country was virtually in the possession of the lawless . . . the disaffected out-numbering by many Degrees the peaceable Inhabitants"; the Luddites, he said, were leading the nation on "a direct Road to an open Insurrection." General Thomas Maitland, commander of the Nottingham and Lancashire troops, was quite convinced in May that there was "a combination to overcome all legal author-ity" at work, aiming at "nothing more or less than the subversion of the Government of the Country and the destruction of all Property," and he confessed his inability to uncover its plans or leaders. The commandant of the army militia at Sheffield the next month relayed to the Home Office a deposition from a source "intelligent and worthy of confidence" warning that the Luddites, with a series of committees "from Glasgow to Lon-don," were planning "to raise a few partial disturbances in this part of the country, to draw off as many troops as possible from the metropolis, and that then the great rising will take place there."

But the fact is that Luddism, and its attendant circumference of popular outrage, was not really revolutionary—or not revolu-tionary in a way that those whose thinking was confined to conventional notions of armies-in-the-street and governments-in-waiting could comprehend. Luddism's revolt at bottom was not against a government or a king, as previous revolts like those of Mary Stuart or Guy Fawkes had been, nor even against an antiquated aristocracy, as in France, but rather against the on-rush of the entire system of industrialism and the dislocations it entailed, the values it promoted—something more on the order of Joan of Arc's revolt, perhaps, inspired by restitution and resto-ration, legitimacy and tradition, justice and right. Yes, there were those who joined the Luddites or took their part because they sought to follow "the Noble Example of the brave Citizens of Paris," as the March 9 leaflet in Leeds had put it, or because they really thought now was the time to shake off "the Yoke of the

Rottenest, Wickedest and most Tyranious Government that ever existed," as the letter to Smith in Huddersfield had said; there was, as E. P. Thompson takes pains to point out, this kind of genuine revolutionary tradition in the area. And yes, there were surely those who had become persuaded in some way that Luddism was a prelude to a "general rising" that would end all their troubles, much as George Mellor undoubtedly had, conveyed in this speech of his as rendered in *Ben o' Bill's:*

> I'll call on every man that has a heart in his breast to join me in a march to London. We'll strike into the great North-road. We'll ransack every farm house by the way for arms and provisions. We'll take toll of every man in every town who has got rich by grinding down the poor. . . . We'll march with swelling ranks and a purpose firmer by every step we take, till we stand, an army, at the very gates of Westminster, and there we will thunder forth our claims and wring from an abject Parliament the rights, without which we are driven slaves.

But these kinds of revolutionary voices were in a decided minority, however much they may have been given a sympathetic ear just now in the pub or cropping shop, however much certain officials and their agitative agents may have wanted to dwell on them in their reports. The great majority of the workers, even in areas of the West Riding where "march with swelling ranks" talk seems to have been loudest at this time, had simply not developed a politics, a view of possibilities, that encompassed all that a revolutionary vision entails. Mellor's rhetoric may sound dangerous, but note that it still has to do with a reformative wringing of rights from Parliament, and there is no reason to suppose that most of those around him even articulated that much of a political dream. The fact that there was never any convincing evidence of a widespread revolutionary *organization* during these years— despite the House of Lords' imagining an overarching "Secret Committee" and all—and no signs of anything more than quite local groupings with an occasional delegate between them, suggests that there was probably no strong revolutionary intent at work either.

Indeed, if the disaffected workers thought in terms of rebellion at all, it would not have been one aimed against the Crown and Parliament in London, for those were more often regarded, on whatever slim grounds, as institutions that had been traditionally on the side of the plain English laborer and should be so again. That is why there is so much feeling about government *protection* for the trades injured by new machinery, lowered wages, "colting," and the like; so many appeals (even as the Luddite attacks were going on) to the House of Commons or the Prince Regent to enforce traditional rights; so much emphasis in the Luddite letters about "redressing their Wrongs" and restoring "ancient liberties." "Armies of Redressers" are concerned with "Machinery hurtful" and the "commonality," not Jacobinism and a free republic.

What was in the minds of the Luddites, insofar as their translucence yields, was probably fairly well indicated by three other snatches that the two Yorkshire historians of *Ben o' Bill's* offer:

We must arouse the conscience of our rulers [says John Booth, the young apprentice killed at Rawfolds]. They cannot, or will not, see how desperate is our plight. . . . Their sense of right will not move them: we must frighten them.

Th' poor ha' borne wi' slack work an' mullocked on as best they could [says a war veteran, Soldier Jack], as long as they thought th' wars and bad harvest were to blame. . . . But now th' mesters [manufacturers] are for makin' bad worse wi' this new machinery . . . and by gow, the lads about won't see their craft ruined, an' them and theirs pined to death, wi'out a blow struck.

For the great mass of the people [says Ben Bamforth], those who had to work for their living, they believed in General Ludd. In some way they could not fathom nor explain[,] the Luddites were

to bring back the good times, to mend trade, to stock the cup-
board, to brighten the grate, to put warm clothes on the poor shiv-
ering little children.

"In some way they could not fathom" catches a sense of it
well, I think, for this revolt, though it had clear and immediate
targets and purposes, was never formulated or designed, never
articulated in its underlying grievance or ultimate aim. But how
could it be, really, when the enemy was the impending end of the
settled and the known, the imposition of the new and ruinous,
the future that they could sense would deny their past? To articulate all that would have meant understanding, while it was happening, the whole epochal experience affecting them, this thing
only much later comprehended in its full transformative impact
as the Industrial Revolution—as if 16th-century American Indians could have articulated the consequences of European conquest when they saw the first few settlements arise.

If, then, Luddism did not represent a true revolution in conventional terms of overturning the institutions of society to some
clear-defined purpose, it was nonetheless a revolt, no matter how
ill expressed and ill directed, with real people acting out real dissent against forces they detested, some thousands of textile workers of middle England and their families clumsily resisting, for all
the kingdom to see, the future.

And somehow the kingdom knew. Somehow the sense of the
larger, latent meaning of Luddism, beyond its simple lawlessness
and apart from its possible insurrectionary threat, was understood, at least by the general range of those who made it their
business to learn what was doing in the industrial districts. That
is why there were so many who were quick to call it a rising or a
revolution, the literary types as well as the generals—because
they realized that a serious challenge had been declared but had
no other way to make sense of it. That is why these particular
machine breakers, of all the machine breakers that had operated
in Britain for a century, were fixed in the public mind and in sub-

sequent histories as the personifications of the opponents of technology, the antagonists of progress.

But it is just at this point—as the Luddites and their constituen-
cies try to come to terms with the escalation of violence symbol-
ized by the assassination of Horsfall and the destruction of the
Westhoughton mill—that Luddism takes a new turn that seems
on the surface to be genuinely revolutionary. No more the
machine breaking in cottages or the torching of factories, except
in rare and isolated instances: now it was nighttime raids for arms
and ammunition and money. No more the marching on the
moors and threatening letters: now it was burglaries of isolated
houses in the dead of night and blood oaths and secret plans.

This is not the contradiction it seems. What Luddism
becomes this summer—what it is forced to become by the frustration of its goals, the failure of its strategies, the implacability of
its enemies—is a kind of caricature, a grasping for those classical
fixtures of revolution on the part of a radical few when there was
in fact no revolutionary base to attach them to. For just as
Luddism could not come up with the words to articulate its
rebellion or define its goals, so it had no way to devise the kind of
strategies that would frame its insurrectionary purpose or the
kind of tactics, specific to the time and place and need, that
would carry it through. Failing that, it fell back on the tactics
borrowed from other times and places, suitable for strategies in
other rebellions with other aims, other targets, other populations.*

---

* This may be a predicament common to most incipient revolts. It has, at any rate, an
almost exact parallel with the American radical movement of the 1960s, when at the height
of its impact a great many within it wanted to move from resistance to revolution, beyond
opposition to war and racism to the overthrow of capitalism and its compliant institutions.
Unable successfully to articulate either means or ends that would be appropriate to the
populace within which it had to work or to the enormousness of the transformation it
wanted, this segment fragmented into competing factions, one of which then modeled
itself on old-fashioned industrial-shop organizing and another of which took to underground armed cells, both tactics borrowed from other times and places; predictably, both
failed.

One has to assume that fewer men were drawn into this new phase of Luddism. The failure of half a year's violent protests to arouse "the conscience of our rulers" must have discouraged some, and its success at arousing nothing but the vengeance of the rulers must have frightened or wearied others; some, too, will have become disenchanted by the level of violence and death on both sides, and not a few will have simply fled from the area to avoid arrest and imprisonment. And yet the pattern of arms raids indicates that in both Lancashire and Yorkshire enough men were moved to adopt this new tactic to be able to strike almost anywhere in the counties at will, from Bolton to Barnsley, for the greater part of the next six months, in the face of all that military presence, without a single arrest until September. In mid-June, that very active government agent in Stockport, John Lloyd, told the Home Office that "bodies of 100 and upwards of the Luddites have entered houses night after night and made seizures of arms"; in the West Riding Vice-Lieutenant Wood the same month reported that there had been "some hundreds of cases," mostly in the woolen towns between Huddersfield and Wakefield, leading him to fear it would all end "in open rebellion against the government of the country"; and a Parliamentary committee reported in July that Luddites were "exciting and keeping up perpetual terror in the country," with the "considerable" theft of guns and ammunition in most towns, and in Huddersfield of "all the arms."

The style of attack seems to have been fairly similar throughout the northern region. Bands of men, ranging from ten to fifty according to news reports, operated late at night, with no advance warning, against houses somewhat isolated from town, whose owners were thought to have arms (or cash or some kind of booty). Although occasionally shots would be fired into the house before the raid as a way of persuading locked doors to open and inhabitants to cooperate, and some homeowners were tied up with cloth or cords, there is no instance of anyone being injured in these attacks.

The skill and thoroughness with which these operations were carried out is suggested by the *Annual Register* account of West Riding raids in early June:

> At half past twelve a party of men, consisting of about twelve persons, surrounded the house of Mr. Butterfield, and demanded his fire-arms, threatening him with instant death if he hesitated; at two other houses they fired two musket-balls through the door. This lawless banditti then went down the common, where they entered every house likely to contain arms, and insisted upon their being delivered up, threatening to shoot the owners if the least delay was manifested. These depredators were armed with muskets and pistols. They obtained on this occasion about six stand of arms.

Lord Lieutenant Earl Fitzwilliam, the no-nonsense governor of Yorkshire, a little later expressed his dismay at their "sweeping off *every* gun at Clifton," saying it proves they had "a system of enquiry, and a means of information," and acknowledging that the "manner in which the business was done, proves also a great degree of tactic in execution." He was relieved only in that "there is no evidence whatever . . . of their having been assembled and drilling in a military way" with all the arms they collected.

The raid on the house of George Haigh in the village of Skircoats, near Leeds, is one about which we know some details because the raiders were later brought to trial. One of the raiders, Joseph Carter, testified (according to the judge's summary)

> that he and the three prisoners, and a number of other persons, in the whole nine or ten, assembled in a field, by appointment, on a Saturday at the end of August . . . and that the purpose of their so assembling was, to go about and take arms and guns from different people's houses; that they afterwards proceeded to different houses, and among others went to the house of Mr. George Haigh . . . somewhere near twelve . . . and some of them went to the front door, and some to the kitchen door, and knocked hard with guns and pistols, and demanded arms.

Haigh then testified (again in summary) that

> he was awakened by a loud rapping at both the front and back door
> of his house . . . and went down to the landing of his staircase. . . .
> He heard the voices of several people calling out . . . "Your arms"
> . . . and another voice said, "General Ludd, my master, has sent me
> for your arms." . . .
>
>   He then says that a man of his, of the name of Tillotson, came
> up to him and said, "Master you had better give them the gun, for
> they will shoot us." Upon that, Tillotson immediately went down
> stairs with the gun, and presently returned to him again; and when
> he returned again, he (Haigh) gave him a pistol, and then Tillotson
> went away.

Tillotson added that

> the people, to whom he gave [the guns] were armed, some with
> guns, and some with pistols in their hands; and that at the time he
> so gave the gun and pistol to them, some of them held the pistols
> and guns they had in their hands close to his person, and told him,
> if he would not deliver them the guns and the pistols, they would
> shoot him.

Then, taking a topcoat from the hall (which was returned the
next day!), the men strode off. If it hadn't been that Carter was
arrested on another charge that December, and for reasons of his
own saw fit to finger three of his comrades for this crime, this
would have been just one more of the hundreds of successful
Luddite raids that went unpunished.

It is impossible to figure how many guns were collected by the
Luddites in these summer months—the authorities spent a good
deal of time looking for caches rumored to be secreted away in
this woods or that moor without finding more than a few odd
pieces—but it must have been a sizable arsenal, considering that
"some hundreds" of raids must usually have yielded one or two
pieces per household. And to this was added stolen ammunition,
most of it apparently not in the form of actual bullets but of

everyday lead objects and artifacts that could be melted down for musket balls and bullets. "Every article of lead," wrote a correspondent from the West Riding, "such as pumps, water-spouts, &c. which can be readily conveyed away, is constantly disappearing"; another from Manchester said that "the churches are every where plundered for lead, to be converted into bullets."

At the same time, in actions separate from the nocturnal raids, armed attacks on individuals also continued throughout the north. No one was killed in any of them, but in the month of May alone three shots were fired at soldiers guarding the house of the army commander at Leeds, three men were shot at in separate incidents near Manchester and another injured with a rock, and the Huddersfield magistrate, Joseph Radcliffe, was fired upon in his home, the assailant fleeing safely. In addition, three people suspected of being informers were roughly handled: one man near Manchester, who was held upside down over a mine shaft until he proved his innocence; a woman near Leeds, who was set on by neighbors and had her skull fractured (not fatally); and a man near Huddersfield, who was shot in the eye by two men after he had implicated one of his neighbors, apparently incorrectly, in Luddism.

The new "revolutionary" turn of Luddism, though it had not yet produced the much-feared "rising," was extensive enough to cause serious worry in the populace: "The commotions . . . were never more alarming than at present," the *Annual Register*'s informant reported in June. One correspondent in Yorkshire put it rather eloquently that month, after noting that "the atrocious practice of stealing arms has been lately carried to an alarming extent": "The glaring violation of the laws of society and of private property, evinced in these nocturnal visits, though an evil of great magnitude, is, as it were, lost in the contemplation of the more atrocious purposes for which those instruments of death are collected." It did seem as if the bloodshed of true rebellion could really be in the offing.

*   *   *

It was just at this point that a threatened state showed what it was capable of, with its machinery of justice, in the cause of repression.

The annual spring assizes in Lancaster, which opened on May 23, were presided over by Justices Baron Alexander Thomson and Sir Simon LeBlanc, who had been selected with the help of the Home Office to ensure that there would be no repetition of the sort of "lenity" practiced by Justice Bayley at the Nottingham assizes in March (a lenity in which, be it remembered, seven out of ten defendants were shipped off to Australia in chains). The jurors, besides, were not to be any ordinary representatives of English citizenry but, by the designation of the trial as a "Special Commission," only the most well-heeled and aristocratic in the county, including some of the manufacturers against whom criminal acts had been committed.

Fifty-eight defendants were paraded before this tribunal. Six were brought up for the arson attacks on Daniel Burton's house at Middleton, but the evidence tying them to the fire, aside from their mere presence in the crowd, was so flimsy that they were all acquitted; undaunted, the prosecutor simply bound them over for a new trial on charges of rioting, and put them back in jail. Sixteen others were tried for having something to do with Luddite oaths, on the evidence of no fewer than nine spies, an army sergeant, and an informer, and despite the shakiness of the identifications and the certainty that the spies had been entrappers, all but one of them were sentenced to seven years' transportation to Australia. Two men were found guilty of breaking into a factory and stealing food—seven years' transportation—and seven women and a man were found guilty of rioting in various mill attacks—six months in jail.

The harshest penalties were for those involved in the Manchester food riots and the destruction of the Westhoughton factory. All four of the food rioters were found guilty of the terrible crime of taking property: three men who had been caught stealing bread, cheese, and potatoes from a house in Deansgate, and the woman who had led the crowd to grab potatoes for free and then buy butter at a shilling a pound. Of the thirteen West-houghton rioters who were captured and arraigned, only four could be identified by the supervisors and head workmen from the mill and they were found guilty of successful arson, though there was no evidence that any of them had done anything but be present in the crowd at the attack. All eight of these guilty parties were sentenced to death by hanging, including a 16-year-old boy, Abraham Charlson, who had played soldier by walking up and down in front of the Westhoughton plant as a sentinel; as a con-temporary account tells it, he "was a boy so young and childish" that when he was about to be hanged "he called out for his mother, thinking she had the power to save him."

Before it was all done, eight were hanged, seventeen trans-ported, thirteen imprisoned, and twenty—despite the state's obvious ability to use tainted evidence and uncertain identifi-cations—were acquitted. So successful were these outcomes in the eyes of the Home Office that the two judges here were selected to preside over the all-important assizes in York in mid-October, where, if the magistrates were able to come up with any legitimate suspects, the cases of the Rawfolds attack and the Horsfall assassination would be heard.

The Chester assizes, also a "Special Commission" held simul-taneously with Lancashire's and concerned with various crimes in the Stockport district, came to nearly as harsh a conclusion. Here the government was quite explicit about what it wanted, and it sent Henry Hobhouse, the Treasury Department solicitor, to Chester to get it: executions for those involved in extorting funds from people for Luddite causes, in food-riot robbery, and in machine breaking, with the understanding, it made clear, that "perhaps the guilt of the convicted was not of prime importance as long as the violated laws were upheld and sacrificial victims could be found as an example to the rest of society."

Little surprise, then, that of the twenty-eight people tried, five were imprisoned, eight transported for seven years, and as many as fifteen convicted of capital crimes whose penalty was hanging.

Of those fifteen, seven were guilty of "obtaining money contrary to the King's peace" (i.e., extortion by "Ludd's men" in April), six were guilty of stealing small amounts of food during the April food riots, and two were convicted of breaking machines, the first victims of the new law that Byron had protested. At the trial's end, only five of those convicted of capital offenses were in fact given the death sentence, and in the event only two men were hanged and the rest presumably were transported for fourteen years, that apparently being sufficient to communicate the state's warning to the public. The two unfortunates were Joseph Thompson, 34, a weaver who had been seen at the attack on John Goodair's house in April but was mostly guilty of stealing some silver articles from the house before it was torched (and he was the one who was found with them in his possession three days later), and John Temples, 27, also a weaver, who had broken into a house and stolen five silver teaspoons and some clothes, after a food riot in a Stockport suburb.

Some measure of the authorities' felt need to gain Luddite convictions at all costs is revealed in the case of one of the men sentenced to transportation, Thomas Whittaker, found guilty of administering an illegal oath. Whittaker, 44, a Stockport joiner, was regarded by the solicitor, Hobhouse, as a "man of superior ability and education" who should therefore be convicted as an example to others, but the only evidence against him was the testimony of one John Parnell, who had been picked up by the energetic John Lloyd during an extortion attempt on April 15 and was hoping to snitch his way to freedom. Not one of the other Luddites that Lloyd arrested would corroborate Parnell's story, despite all the pressure Lloyd could bring ("because it is evident," he complained, "they are so ignorant as to conceive themselves under the obligation imposed by the diabolical oath not to tell of one another"), but that didn't prevent the magistrates from bringing the case to trial, along with unspecified "various minute circumstances" for corroboration. Upon this shaky evidence, sufficient for the obviously compliant squires of the jury, Whittaker was sentenced to seven years in Australia.*

On Saturday, June 12, the eight people condemned at the Lancashire assizes were hanged in Manchester, not one of them repentant, until, a local paper reported, under the "pathetic exhortations" of the prison chaplain they "confessed their offenses" but implicated no others in the crimes. Three days later the two condemned at Chester were similarly dispatched, after a "solemn procession" through that city escorted by soldiers and "the proper officers" of the Crown, "followed by an immense crowd of people," and at one o'clock "they ascended the drop, and soon after were launched into eternity."

Within those three days the calculated judgment of the ruling powers of Britain was delivered unmistakably to the industrial heartland: Luddism and all attendant to it would be considered a capital offense, and judges would not shirk from exacting the maximum sentence for it.

The new government in London that took over in early June after Perceval's assassination was headed by Lord Liverpool, a political nullity christened by Benjamin Disraeli "the Arch Mediocrity," with the manipulative Viscount Castlereagh as foreign minister and one Henry Addington, the first Viscount Sidmouth, as home secretary. Sidmouth was of that stripe of men Cobbett called "the most cruel, the most unfeeling, the most brutally insolent," and it was etched in every line of his portrait: thin, pursed lips in a small, self-satisfied smile, cold, narrow eyes under

---

* Whittaker attempted to escape this fate by writing a long account to the warden of the Chester jail about how he had attended a secret Luddite meeting in Stockport and was "never more surprised in my life when I heard the Manchester Delegate lay down the plans and communications with other towns" by which "a fixed time would be appointed for a general rising of the people," including 500,000 in the North and Midlands. It was just the sort of information the authorities liked, for it fed their desire for increased powers of repression, but it did Whittaker no good. He was transported anyway and ended up teaching mathematics at a private academy in Sydney.

bushy eyebrows, a plain beardless face, head mostly bald but with close-cropped hair at the sides, and an air fitting the description of him in the *Dictionary of National Biography* as having a "pompous manner and sententious gravity." He turned out to be a man perfectly suited for the task of directing the Tory government against the Luddite revolt and indeed going on to conduct the business of political suppression with a firm and remorseless hand until he retired from office in 1824: "Under his vigilant superintendence," writes his official biographer and son-in-law, George Pellew, "every attempt to create disturbance, and to clog the wheels of government, was immediately repressed, and no sooner did sedition anywhere raise its head than it was crushed."

It was Sidmouth's opinion, as he expressed it in a speech to Parliament on June 29, that "although the conduct of the [Luddite] rioters might be, in some degree, traced to the high price of provisions and the reduction of work; still there was no doubt that these outrages were fomented by persons who had views and objects which it was the duty of government to counteract." Simple enough, made all the easier for one who was himself of the wealthy landed gentry and was often known to observe, with some smugness, "Man cannot create abundance where Providence has inflicted scarcity." (That this was not precisely true in his own case is shown by the fact that as a minister he managed to confer on his son, while still a schoolboy, a life-long government pension of £3,000 a year.) Hence it was that he immediately established committees in both houses of Parliament to come up with official reports denouncing Luddism in most fearful revolutionary terms so as to provide him cover for whatever measures he might unleash the magistrates or military to carry out. He then asked Parliament for laws giving magistrates increased powers to interrogate and confiscate in their districts and raising the crime of oath giving to a capital offense, both of which passed easily. What he did not ask Parliament about, but felt no constraint in authorizing, were policies giving increased license to the use of spies and informers to provide (or manufacture) evidence against the Luddites, encouraging troops in the industrial areas to be extra ruthless in coming up with Luddite suspects, and speeding up trials of those against whom any incriminating evidence could be produced.

No one embraced these policies more enthusiastically than General Thomas Maitland, now effectively in command of all the armies in the north (the less-belligerent General Grey in the West Riding having stepped aside and soon to be off on his honeymoon). Maitland devised a plan for a series of informers from other textile districts in England and Scotland to be sent to Lancashire and Yorkshire and to become "Active and Efficient Members" infiltrating the local Luddite committees, and he enrolled a large roster of spies (mostly supplied by the aggressive deputy constable of Manchester, Joseph Nadin) into his army and gave them freedom to act on their own in the search for evidence. On the military front he introduced the practice of having small squads of troops move around at night from village to village or neighborhood to neighborhood in an unannounced and haphazard fashion, in the hopes that they would come upon Luddite bands by surprise, and he established what he called his "Secret Service" of small units of soldiers on double pay operating under cover to infiltrate Luddite councils, identify oath givers and oath takers for local magistrates, and by any means see that enough men got arrested to instill fear in the rest.

One such secret unit was under the command of Captain Francis Raynes, who has left a considerable account of how he functioned—in fact he published a pamphlet on it in 1817, hoping to get the government to give him the reward for this service he felt he deserved—and it amounts to a virtual confession of legal terrorism. For example:

> In pursuance of my instructions, I continued marching and patroling every night. The system I adopted on the road, was to send two men in plain clothes, in advance; the first being desired, on meeting any person or persons, to let them pass, but give a signal to the

second, by whom it was conveyed to the soldiers in the rear, who
were marching in small bodies of six or eight; they, on receiving the
signal, immediately closed up, and the travellers, whoever they
were, found themselves in the midst of the soldiers, before they
suspected we were near. By this method, and observing the most
profound silence, we avoided the noise usually attending the march
of troops. We interrogated every one, and not unfrequently, on
these patroles, apprehended those of whom I had information.

And, he adds later, by arresting one person you can usually get
others to "tumble in" out of fear afterward.

Raynes also commanded a network of Maitland's special
agents, who were paid a rather handsome 21 shillings a week and
expenses and were empowered (with what legality is uncertain) to
gather intelligence for him, pay others for information ("I find
nothing will procure information but money"), and even make
arrests on their own. Two of those agents, posing as Luddites,
were actually successful in entrapping a Huddersfield weaver,
James Starkey, who was not a Luddite. Talking with him in a
pub, they had asked him what he thought was the best way to
destroy Cartwright's mill and he said he thought a barrel of gun-
powder would be best; a few hours later he was arrested at gun-
point and indicted for inciting His Majesty's soldiers to an act of
incendiary crime, punishable by death. (In the event, the whole
thing was eventually judged so absurd that it was never brought
to trial, but only after the poor man went through months of
agony.)

Home Secretary Sidmouth, at the apex of all this, was also
instrumental in two other important acts undertaken by the new
Liverpool government, both of which he saw as being useful to
establish order in the "disturbed areas." The first was the repeal
on June 23 of the Orders in Council that had effectively kept
Britain's ports closed to most foreign trade since 1809, a move
that was greeted with great joy by manufacturers and workers
alike—"churchbells all over the Riding rang out the glad news,"

Ben Bamforth noted—in the hope that trade, especially with America, would now be revived and put the disaffected populace back to work. Unfortunately, however, the United States had already declared war on Britain five days earlier in retaliation for its blockade, chose to ignore the repeal when news of it finally arrived there, and was to carry on fighting for another two and a half years before a peace treaty was signed and trading renewed. Some relief did come later that year in the wake of Napoleon's disastrous invasion of Russia and the virtual collapse of the Continental System that had officially closed European markets to Britain, but it was slow to have an effect and had no real impact on the textile trades for another year or more.

The second Sidmouth initiative was a Royal Proclamation added to the law making oathing a capital offense that offered clemency until October 9 to any wrongdoer who would step forward and name names, perhaps testify in court, so the authorities could get evidence against the ones administering oaths, presumably the Luddite ringleaders. This affidavit, before the Stockport magistrate Charles Prescott, in August, is representative of the kinds of results the clemency measure produced:

> The voluntary deposition of James Band, of Hollingworth . . .—
> Who saith, that on Sunday, in the month of March last, the day of
> the month he cannot recollect, he went to a place called Hobson-
> Moor, in Hollingworth, accompanied by Peter Ashton, of Hol-
> lingworth aforesaid, cotton-spinner, where they were met by two
> or three persons, whom examinant doth not know, who proposed
> to him and his companions to take a certain oath, which they said
> would do them no harm: but if they did not take it, they would be
> killed. That, thereupon, they consented, and one of the strangers
> produced a paper, and a book, which this examinant and Peter
> Ashton kissed, after repeating the words of the oath, read to them
> by the stranger. The precise words this examinant cannot recollect:
> but the purport of the oath was to bind the person taking the same
> to secrecy, and to put to death any traitors. At the same time, the

174 REBELS AGAINST THE FUTURE

stranger delivered to the examinant, a paper, containing the words
of the oath which he had taken, and told him to *twist-in* as many as
he could.

There was not much for Prescott to go by with testimony of that
sort, but that was about all that the new strategy produced: by
October something like a thousand men availed themselves of
the clemency—without, it seems, a single criminal oath giver
being turned in or tried. At least some of the men, including the
fifty-eight from Manchester who testified in September and the
twenty from Bolton who testified in October, had apparently
been twisted in by spies or agents of Constable Nadin of Manchester or Colonel Fletcher of Bolton, so their identifications
didn't do much to advance the government's cause; and most of
the other men, like James Band, became completely blank when
asked to remember who it was who had twisted them in ("It
appears that the men who administered the oath to these people,"
a Lancashire magistrate reported, "were either Strangers or Men
who have left this part of the Country"), so their testimony got
the authorities no further. Captain Raynes complained bitterly
that in his district the clemency seekers simply used the opportunity as a way of getting off the hook after they realized their meetings had been infiltrated by his spies, and they "then went home
and boasted how nicely" they had cheated the magistrates.

Ultimately, three trials against oath givers were held after June,
but in none of them was any testimony used that had been produced by the clemency. In Chester in August a man was found
guilty of having administered an oath to one of Captain Raynes's
spies; in York in January 1813 one man was condemned by the testimony of an informant who had been paid £10 for his trouble;
and six others at the York assizes were convicted for giving or wit-
nessing an oath to two of Joseph Nadin's spies. And in every case the
men could be sentenced only to transportation for seven years, since
the crimes were committed before oathing was a capital offense.

*   *   *

Sidmouth's anti-Luddite plan, then, for all the wiliness of its deceit, turned out to be essentially useless. Indeed, what is so striking about the various forms of repression devised by the British government in these months, even under the energetic Sidmouth, is that they produced so little in the way of prosecutions or convictions. As of September, though there had been any number of detentions and arrests, only a dozen or so had produced evidence sufficient to take to court, the murderers of Horsfall were still loose, and no one had been caught for the Rawfolds attack. London even decided not to go ahead with the assizes scheduled for October 19 in York because there were too few cases to bring and the grounds in those were so flimsy that it was felt better to postpone the trials than risk a series of acquittals.

Which is not to say that the heavy hand of the government at all levels did not have an effect on the Luddite triangle. From May on, there were no more attacks on factory buildings for the rest of the year (a calico plant in Stockport burned in September, but the fire was eventually thought not to be arson), only seven incidents of machine breaking were reported (five in Nottinghamshire in November and December, two in the West Riding in September), and even the nighttime arms raids tailed off in late summer. There were food riots in several cities—Barnsley, Leeds, Rotherham, Sheffield, and Nottingham—but only the ones in Leeds and Nottingham, both led by women who called themselves "Lady Ludd," had any Luddite overtones, and none led on to marches or attacks on factories as had happened in April. It would be too soon to say that Luddism was over, but the authorities could feel by the fall that it had at least been fractured and contained with some success. Early in November General Maitland could even report that he thought there was "no real bottom in all this Luddite system."

During these same months much of the effort of the textile workers throughout the area was once again being diverted into the familiar, often frustrated, patterns of reform. "We petition no more that won't do fighting must" was surely the credo of many

Luddites in March, and there were many out raiding through the summer who obviously still believed it. But for thousands of others, those who had been in Luddite gangs as well as those who had never taken part, the hope of relief from Parliament or Regent, even of Parliamentary reform, was revived once again. It was almost as if, when one part of Luddism went underground into nighttime arms raiding, another part went overground into Parliamentary petitioning, and the whole strategy of machine breaking in between, after half a year of intensive and escalating attacks, no longer seemed to find support.

Reformism was always an open option, even at the height of Luddism, and many never deviated from it. One of its most ardent and well-known advocates was Major John Cartwright (brother of the man who perfected the power loom but no relation to the master of Rawfolds), then a man of 72, gray and imperturbable, committed to a diet of raisins and weak gin-and-water and to a platform of direct manhood suffrage. Cartwright had begun a group called Friends of Parliamentary Reform in late 1811, which developed into the Union for Parliamentary Reform this next year, and he was indefatigable in promoting its cause, particularly in the industrial districts where he sensed he could get support among the disaffected workers. He traveled to Derby and Leicestershire in January (and would have spoken in Nottingham if he had been allowed to by the city council), then to Manchester, Halifax, Sheffield, and Liverpool, asserting his opposition to machine breaking and working "for turning the discontents into a legal channel favourable to Parliamentary reform."

He certainly had some effect. In March several thousand workers in Bolton sent a petition for peace and Parliamentary reform to London: "It is the humble opinion of the petitioners, that if the House consisted of representatives of the people only, it would not . . . consent to expose the people of this country to the certain misery, ruin, and starvation, which the continuance of the war must bring upon them." In Manchester a succession of committees, some infiltrated by spies, were meeting from January on to figure out ways to win broad support for reform. One such meeting, on June 11, was invaded by Manchester's constable, Nadin, who arrested thirty-eight men on trumped-up charges of administering oaths, for which, as General Maitland later said ruefully, "we might not be able to get legal proof"—nor did they, since all Nadin found at the scene was an address to the Prince Regent and a petition to the House of Commons. All thirty-eight were subsequently acquitted at a trial in August in which the government was held up to ridicule for its ineptitude and to contempt for its use of spies, but the experience of arbitrary state power soured the reform movement in Manchester for quite some time.

Meanwhile, in Nottinghamshire, the tireless Gravener Henson was continuing with his campaign to have parliament pass a bill that would end the major abuses in the stocking and lace trades—and would prove, incidentally, that quasi-unionism, even at a time when formal union combinations were forbidden, worked better than Luddism. After months of traveling and drumming up support, and the expenditure of several thousand pounds on legal and administrative costs, Henson finally got a draft of the bill before the House of Commons in late June, where it was summarily stripped of all references to hosiery and all but the flimsiest relating to lace (allowing manufacturers, Henson said bitterly, to "Cheat, Rob, Pilfer and Oppress now to their hearts content") and was finally passed in late July. Even that thin gruel was too strong for the Lords, however, and on July 24 the bill was thrown out without a single word in its favor (Byron at this point was off basking in fame and the illicit love of Caroline Lamb), Sidmouth adding that he "trusted in God" that no such bill interfering with the perfect freedom of manufacturers to do as they pleased "would be again attempted to be introduced" to that chamber.

Henson, to the credit at least of his tenacity, did not fold up. As early as January of the next year he was back with a new

Society for Obtaining Parliamentary Relief, and he continued to counsel the discontented stockingers, as he later said, to give up "the breaking machinery, which generally ended in some other cause of vengeance," and instead to go on with forming "clubs and combinations." But many of his followers were understandably disillusioned with Henson by then and the new organization had rocky going. Reformism was by no means destroyed—it would resurface in various forms, industrial, political, and social, in the years to come—but for the moment at least it seemed as dead an end as machine breaking.

In mid-October Joseph Radcliffe brought in George Mellor and Benjamin Walker, the croppers, to be questioned at Milnsbridge House about the assassination of William Horsfall, and told them he had two other men under arrest for the crime as well. Since William Thorpe and Thomas Smith, the two other actual accomplices, were still at large, the bluff did not serve to break either Mellor or Walker, but something of the incident got back to Walker's mother. Fearing for her son, who would be condemned if one of the other assassins was the first to buy immunity by turning his comrades in—fearing also, it must be presumed, that someone else would then get the £2,000 reward—she confided her dilemma to a friend, who told someone else, and the story got back through one or another agent to the ears of John Lloyd, who had left Stockport just then to work for Sidmouth throughout the north. Lloyd having no scruples whatsoever, he simply decided to kidnap Mrs. Walker ("a particular mode of examination which I made use of in this neighborhood," he boasts) and very shortly forced her to give evidence against her son. With this information he then went to the cropping shop of John Wood, where Walker and Mellor worked and where they had plotted the assassination, and after extensive questioning broke one of their fellow workers, William Hall, who not only confessed to supplying one of the assassination weapons but would go on to name sixteen men who had been in on the Raw-

folds raid and nine others who had been with him on a raid near
Huddersfield on March 15. At long last, a breakthrough for the
constabulary.

Around October 21, Radcliffe arrested Walker, who quickly
confessed, apparently with some relief as well as pecuniary hope,
and eventually fingered the others. The next day Mellor, Thorpe,
and Smith were arrested (Mellor, it is said, raised his hands in
shackles, shouting "Three cheers for General Ludd") and,
brought before Radcliffe, were charged with murder. The *Leeds
Mercury* for October 24 reported:

> A man [Walker] has been taken up and examined by that indefati-
> gable magistrate, Joseph Radcliffe, Esq., and has given the most
> complete and satisfactory evidence of the murder of Mr. Horsfall.
> The villains accused have been frequently examined before but
> have always been discharged for want of sufficient evidence. The
> man charged [Mellor] behaved with the greatest effrontery till he
> saw the informer, when he changed colour and grasped for breath.
> When he came out of the room after hearing the informer's evi-
> dence, he exclaimed, "Damn that fellow, he has done me."

Indeed he had. And with him, in a sense, Luddism.

In December more arrests were made, with little regard for
legal niceties, in the effort to get the intimidated to talk and the
implicated to impeach, and at the end of the month sixty-four
men were being held in the castle jail at York, awaiting trial at the
January assizes. Even so, except for the assassination charge, the
cases were weak, resting as they did on the word of one or two
accomplices and several spies and informers, with virtually nothing in the way of corroborative evidence. Only eight men could
be indicted for the Rawfolds raid, out of the more than sixscore
who had taken part, and their identifications hinged on the word
of Walker and Hall and a few circumstantial witnesses with none-
too-certain memories: thin stuff to go to trial on, as even the law
officers in charge admitted. The government, prodded by Sidmouth, nonetheless decided there would be no advantage in

waiting and, by turning the assizes in York into another Special
Commission, by installing a nervous squirearchy in the jury box,
and by assuring the presence of inflexible judges (Thomson and
LeBlanc again) on the bench, determined that this session would
be an unmistakable example of British justice on the line.

York Castle, where the trials were held, was ringed with soldiers,
mounted and afoot, on the drear and snowy January 6, 1813,
when the Special Commission of Oyer and Terminer opened for
the Luddite trials. But the crowds that came to the courtyard in
front and jammed the ornate courtroom inside were more sullen
than threatening, "of a very ill Complexion," Henry Hobhouse
wrote, but generally receiving the daily parade of cases "with perfect Silence." Hobhouse was there once again to manage the
prosecutions on behalf of the government, following a cynical
but rather clever strategy Sidmouth had devised of taking on the
Horsfall murderers first and getting them executed, too, even
before the other trials were over so that the awful punishment for
the awful deed would hang over the entire proceeding and lend
the weight of somber rectitude to the government's cases. Then,
when a sufficient number of the major Luddites had been disposed of and made an example of to the country—and it was "of
infinite importance to society," Sidmouth believed, that it be
done without mercy—the prosecutors should simply dismiss or
hold over most of the rest of the cases, so as not to create any further "social antagonism" or a pro-Luddite backlash by pursuing
verdicts where "the Evidence was next to nothing" in any case.
Above all, the prosecution at all times should avoid raising, or
having the witnesses inadvertently raise, any question of *motive,*
any hint of political or social purpose to these deeds, so that the
Luddite cause would seem to be empty and groundless, something akin to simple hooliganism. This is why the Home Office,
though it well knew that the attitudes of a number of the
Luddites it had on hand might make such charges stick, did not
bring a single charge of treason, preferring to limit the charges to

disembodied acts like oathing and burglary without raising messy and potentially volatile questions of intent. Hobhouse, it must be said, handled all this masterfully.

The trial against Mellor, Thorpe, and Smith, buttressed by testimony from Walker, William Hall, Joseph Sowden (another fellow worker), and several witnesses who saw the three men just after their crime, was over in a day. The three were found guilty after twenty-five minutes of deliberation and were immediately sentenced by Justice LeBlanc—"This may be pronounced a crime of the blackest dye"—to be hanged on Friday, January 9, at nine in the morning. "During the whole of the trial," wrote the correspondent of the *Annual Register*, "and even while the solemn sentence of the law was passing, not one of the prisoners shed a tear; but their behaviour was perfectly free from any indecent boldness or unbecoming levity." Mellor in particular seemed stolid, "as tho' he did not hear what passed around him," according to his cousin Ben Bamforth, "his eyes being fixed, not upon the judge but beyond him, with a far away gaze as tho' scenes were acting in a theatre none but he could see, and which concerned him more than what passed around."

Awaiting death, none of the three condemned men recanted or provided information for the authorities.* According to the Huddersfield minister who attended him the night before he was to go to the gallows, Mellor said "that he would rather be in the situation he was then placed in, dreadful as it was, than have to answer for the crime of his accuser; and that he would not change places with him, even for his liberty and two thousand pounds." On the Friday morning, reported the *Annual Register*, "two troops of cavalry were drawn up in front of the drop, and the avenues to the castle were guarded by infantry," but although

---

* Mellor did write a letter that was smuggled out of prison and later fell into the hands of Radcliffe. It urged the people who had given him alibis to stick to their evidence, and to it was appended the signatures of thirty-nine fellow prisoners who wished their names added to "a Pettitioning for a Parliamentary Reform" that the recipient was circulating. It was not apostasy, exactly, but it was an extraordinary gesture for one recently talking about marching "to the very gates of Westminster" to "thunder forth our claims."

the crowd was far larger than normal, in the end "not the slight-est indication of tumult prevailed, and the greatest silence reigned." The three men, "on whose countenances nature had not imprinted the features of assassins," each gave a short speech, or prayer, that part of the crowd nearest the gallows sang a hymn, and "they were executed in their irons."

In the week after the Horsfall case, seven others were brought to trial: two oathings, three burglaries, an assault, and the Rawfolds affair. (One case was tried before the Horsfall trial, in which four colliers were found guilty of "plundering," but this was not a Luddite suit.) It would be wrong to say that the gov-ernment prosecutors railroaded the convictions through without evidence, but it is safe to say that without the two judges bending over backward to burnish the testimony of extremely dubious witnesses and without an extremely compliant set of jurors (including six peers of the realm) who looked very kindly on the state's entrapment and very skeptically on the defendants' alibis, the state would not have won the day. As it was, eight of the twenty-five men in the dock were acquitted, four other cases involving thirty-five prisoners were not even put to the court (although they had spent months in jail), and one trial (of the unfortunate Joseph Starkey who had been entrapped by Raynes's soldiers) was put over to the next assizes. Still, for the seventeen men who remained, the verdicts were as harsh as the law allowed: six men were found guilty of late-summer arms raids (total take: two guns, a pound note, and some silver) and were sentenced to death; six men from Halifax found guilty of administering or wit-nessing an illegal oath were given seven years' transportation (including old John Baines of the St. Crispin Inn "thirty years" speech); and five men found guilty of the Rawfolds attack, which Judge Thomson called "one of the greatest atrocities that was ever committed in a civilized country," were sentenced to death. (The Rawfolds victims were Thomas Brook, the one who had lost his hat, Jonathan Dean and James Haigh, who had come under sus-picion when wounded, and John Ogden and John Walker, who were seen with pistols in Mellor's company after the attack.) Together with three of the colliers tried earlier, fourteen men in all were scheduled to be executed. The prosecutor asked Judge Thomson if he thought all the men should be hanged on a single beam; "No, sir," he replied, "I consider they would hang more comfortably on two."

On Saturday, January 16, the fourteen victims were executed, seven by seven as the good justice suggested, in York Castle courtyard. Frank Peel wrote:

> The criminal records of Yorkshire do not, perhaps, afford an instance of so many victims having been offered, in one day, to the injured laws of the country. The scene was inexpressibly awful, and the large body of soldiers, both horse and foot, who guarded the approach to the castle, and were planted in front of the fatal tree, gave the scene a peculiar degree of terror.

Four of the men were croppers, three colliers, two woolen spinners, two cotton spinners, and one each a tailor, a woolen weaver, and a canal worker. Their average age, as near as we can tell, was 25.*

Two days after the poison of execution, the milk of amnesty. On January 18, the Prince Regent, acting on Sidmouth's advice, offered a pardon to anyone who would confess to taking an illegal oath or stealing firearms, "hoping that the example of the just and necessary punishments which have been inflicted in the counties of Lancaster, Chester, and York, upon certain offenders lately tried and convicted in those counties, may have the salutary effect of deterring all persons from following the example of their crimes by a renewal of the like atrocities." It is not known that there were any takers.

The fate of the turncoats upon whom the government depended for its convictions was predictably unhappy— "All things betray

---

* Percy Shelley, then living in Wales, was so upset over the fate of these men that he immediately began a fund for their children, to which he forced all his friends to contribute.

thee, who betrayest Me" was quoted in more than a few pubs—
and the government itself was predictably parsimonious. The spy
who turned in the six Halifax oathers was paid £50, somewhat
less than he expected, and released from a prison sentence; two
more informers were paid £10 each and expenses for setting up
the Barnsley oathing, though one later complained loudly that he
never got any money; and Benjamin Walker, the vital Judas for
the vital Gethsemane, apparently was given nothing more than a
few pounds by John Lloyd to settle him far away from his wrath-
ful community—the £2,000 promised by the manufacturers'
committee was somehow never forthcoming—and years later he
was said to be a beggar in London.

The fate of the various government officers was slightly rosier.
Constable Nadin, though he complained often that London was
not paying him his due, continued to serve as a very well-
connected official in Manchester until 1821, when he retired to a
vast estate. John Lloyd, immediately taken off his rounds at the
end of the York trials lest he fire up the very resentment that Sidmouth now sought to dampen, was rewarded with what was said
to be "a handsome purse" by some of the grateful Stockport mill
owners. And Joseph Radcliffe, thanks to the unrelenting efforts of
Lord-Lieutenant Fitzwilliam (and over the opposition of General
Maitland), was honored with nothing less than a baronetcy as a
reward for "that loyal, zealous, and intrepid conduct which you
have invariably displayed at a period when the West Riding of the
county of York presented a disgraceful scene of outrage and plun-
der," as Sidmouth put it in September 1813 in forwarding the news.

The fate of William Cartwright was, in the nature of things,
appropriately mixed. The manufacturer had attended the York
trials, where he gave evidence of the attack without being able to
identify any of the prisoners in the dock, but in his typical
fashion he refused to intercede for clemency for any of the condemned men unless they were prepared to confess and disclose
the names of others: "A sense of Duty only having guided me
up to the present moment I cannot step out of that Line by

interfering with the course of justice until after the most satisfactory disclosure." None was forthcoming: "If any of these unfortunate men possessed any secret," the *Leeds Mercury* reported, "they suffered it to die with them."

Cartwright himself was afflicted little. Although he complained in early December 1812 of "the miserable prospect of Ruin," he was awarded several hundred pounds by the government that month, a donation engineered by Lord-Lieutenant Fitzwilliam ("It would be a very acceptable thing in this country, if this man was noticed by Government"), and not long after was given an additional £3,000 put together by the local manufacturers—who now, after the trials, were even more inclined to regard him as a champion—probably at the instigation of Joseph Radcliffe. His mill continued to use the shearing machines quite successfully—Horsfall's father, by contrast, never went back to using the machines that had caused his son's death—and in time, with the return of trade, Cartwright became a prosperous man. It was said, however, that he never would talk about the attack on his mill, now become legendary throughout the kingdom, and that he gradually grew resentful of the general ostracism he received from the Huddersfield community, where many refused to speak to him, eventually even declining to go to church.

7

The Luddites

1813– . . .

IT IS NEARLY as difficult to say when Luddism ended as when
it began: movements—processes—are not like Beethoven's Fifth,
with crashing final chords, but more like Haydn's *Abschiedssym-*
phonie, with musicians gradually leaving the stage one by one
until the last instrument is silent and the music over.

It could be said that Luddism's last gasp was the string of
frame breakings in Nottinghamshire between April and October
of 1814, after more than a year in which nothing was heard from
Luddites anywhere in the country. In that series more than a hundred frames were destroyed, mostly in Nottingham and mostly
belonging to manufacturers who were paying less than what the
stockingers, and their proto-union organization led by Gravener
Henson, determined were the going rates. Under the pretext of
tracking down Luddites, the city authorities in July captured two
members of that organization (and all its books and papers), and
their prosecution and imprisonment for violating the Combination Acts effectively ended attempts at trade unionism there for
another several years. In retaliation, another two dozen frames
were broken, and then in October, in another attack on a shop
where the local constables were lying in wait, two men were
killed, one of the Luddite attackers, Samuel Bamford (not the Lancashire weaver), by the officers, and a next-door neighbor who
came to see what the shooting was about, by the Luddites; a royal

proclamation offering a £220 reward was issued, but no one came forward, and no one was ever caught. After that, all was quiet.

Or it might be argued that it was not until the spectacular attack on John Heathcoat's lace factory in Loughborough in June 1816 that Luddism came to an end. That had elements of classic Luddism about it. At midnight on June 28, seventeen men with their faces covered with kerchiefs and their coats turned inside out pushed their way into the factory, shot at and wounded an armed guard inside, and proceeded to go through the three floors of the building tying up millhands still at work, burning cloth in the machines, and smashing frames with hammers and axes: "Ludds, have you done your work well?" shouted one man at the end. "Yes," came the reply, "and it was a Waterloo job, by God!" They disappeared into the night within half an hour leaving behind fifty-five destroyed machines and a considerable amount of worthless lace—one source said £7,500 worth of damage in all, the clothier-historian William Felkin thought between £8,000 and £10,000, and the government subsequently awarded Heathcoat £10,000 in recompense. The attack effectively put the factory out of business, Heathcoat thereafter preferring to set up shop in Devonshire rather than deal with the Luddites.

A certain arrogant carelessness marked this job, a number of the men having frequented the area beforehand and been remarked upon in the local pubs, and the leader, James Towle, 36, a well-known "old Ludd" in the area, having not even bothered to replace his kerchief when it slipped. Not much surprise that Towle was arrested not long after, somewhat more so that he seems to have named a number of confederates ("among those whom they know to be well inclined to Ludding") before he was executed in November at the Leicester courthouse, singing hymns at top voice even as the platform was dropped beneath him. Five months later another eight men were tried for the same attack, turned in by two accomplices, one of whom had actually done the shooting that night; the following April six men were executed (average age, 32) and two transported. As classic a

Luddite affair as Loughborough may have been, it is tarnished
not only by this snitching but by the story later told by some
defendants that they had been paid more than a hundred pounds
for their work that night, said to come from other manufacturers
in the district who resented the fact that Heathcoat was paying a
third less to his men than they were.*

Or the demise of Luddism might more truly said to have coin-
cided with the pathetic failure of the "Pentrich rebellion" in June
1817. Certainly that was presumed to be a true part of a "general
rising" at last, and some of its leaders—including the charismatic
Jeremiah Brandreth, a weaver done out of work by a change in
London fashions—were veteran Luddites. But the whole enterprise seems to have been largely controlled, if not entirely instigated, by a government spy working for Sidmouth, "Oliver"
(W. O. Jones), who duped a great many men into marching out
from Pentrich, Derbyshire, on the road to Nottingham on the
night of June 9, supposedly to meet "a cloud of men" sweeping
down from Scotland and Yorkshire on their way to London. A
mile and a half from the White Horse Inn in Pentrich, where the
brave army of some two hundred men began their march, what
they met instead were two mounted magistrates and a company
of Dragoons; forty-six of the marchers were arrested and ultimately brought to trial, and three of them (including Brandreth)

---

* The Loughborough raid inspired some tossed-off verse from Byron, to his friend
Thomas Moore, just before Christmas 1816:

> As the Liberty lads o'er the sea
> Bought their freedom, and cheaply, with blood,
>   So we, boys, we
> Will die fighting, or live free,
> And down with all kings but King Ludd!
>
> When the web that we weave is complete,
> And the shuttle exchanged for the sword,
> We will fling the winding-sheet
> O'er the despot at our feet,
> And dye it deep in the gore he has pour'd.

It is an imaginative, and rare, attempt to get into the minds of the Luddites, but it fails as
much as projection as poetry; still, as Byron said to Moore, he wrote it "principally to
shock your neighbour," a Tory parson.

were executed, fourteen transported, and nine imprisoned. Oliver's name was never mentioned at the trial, and he escaped punishment from the Luddites, but the *Leeds Mercury* eventually revealed his odious story and he soon became infamous throughout Britain as an example of the worst of governmental transgressions against ancient rights and freedoms.

But in truth, since these last twitches of Luddism seem so fitful and sparse, it does seem as if it could really be said that the neck of Luddism was broken as those fourteen men were dropped below the gallows platform at York Castle on the dark January Saturday in 1813. One might wish to make more of Luddism, if one were to see their agony and understand their purpose, but cold analysis gives little reason for extending the dates of the movement beyond those wild, unprecedented fifteen months between November 1811 and January 1813: virtually all the Luddite letters, most of the clearly concerted and clearly political actions, the characteristically Luddite trappings of oaths and marches and disciplined raids, and all but one of the violent, angry factory sieges, occurred between those dates.

It is no doubt futile—but inevitable—to wonder why Luddism effectively ended after little more than a year, a year in which it successfully embedded its name in the hearts of the entire industrial population, whether alongside fear or pride or some combination of the two. Surely the massive power of the British government unleashed upon it, with at least fifteen (and more probably three dozen) souls killed in action, twenty-four strung on the gallows, fifty-one sentenced (and at least thirty-seven actually shipped) to Australia, and two dozen clapped in prison, plus the daily presence of an occupation army, had its intended deterrent effect. Surely, too, both the successes and the failures of the movement took their toll: the successes that deflected men of limited aims or interests after those were taken care of, the defeats that frightened or disheartened others after they were lost. And the turn to revolutionary tactics, too, with the hardening of purpose and heightening of violence—espe-cially, no doubt, the assassination and attempted assassinations—surely discouraged many without the inclination or the ideology to lead them down that perilous route.

Luddism at its core was a heterogeneous howl of protest and defiance, but once that cry was heard in the land and the only response of officialdom and merchantry was indifference, indig-nation, or inhibition, it hardly knew what to do, how to con-tinue, where to move, and at that juncture only a few in its ranks were persuaded of the need to arm and murder and march in a "general rising." In a sense Luddism ended because in fifteen months it had made its point, and indelibly so: the progress of industrial capitalism, and the misery and pain and humiliation and displacement that came with it, was hurtful and odious to the English working family and demanded resistance and rebel-lion, at least by those thousands courageous enough to act out the resentment of the millions. If that point was then to be sub-merged beneath the tide of ebullient Progress, if their howl was to be drowned out by the deafening noise of the factory engines (and the marching boots), who would have had an analysis that told them how else to act, who could have come up with any other way to protect the past and forestall the future?

Perhaps it is surprising that a movement lasting so short a time should gain such a place in history. But an assessment of just what Luddism achieved, and what it represented even when it failed to achieve, suggests why it struck a historic chord, and why that chord resonated through the social edifice of Britain, then and afterward, as few others before or since.

The first and most immediate effect of Luddism was the toll of its violence. It is impossible to be very precise about it, but we can estimate that in terms of property alone, Luddites destroyed something over £100,000 worth between 1811 and 1813: perhaps £50,000 of machinery in Nottinghamshire, probably £30,000 of

machine and factory damage in the West Riding, and £25,000 of
machines, houses, and factories in Lancashire.* That does not
include the cost to the government of maintaining the vast numbers of soldiers in the affected areas for the better part of two
years, which could not have cost much less than £500,000 a year
in salaries alone, to say nothing of food, lodging, and equipment;† or the cost of prosecuting the Luddite cases at nine different assize sessions; or the expenditure on special constables, spies,
and informers (which in the case of Colonel Fletcher came to
£122 for three months' payments for spies alone). Nor does that
include, on the private side, the costs borne by individual manufacturers or home owners in defense of their property or losses
sustained in production when mills and machines were inopera-
ble. All that totaled together might come to losses of around £1.5
million that could be laid directly to Luddite activity.

A second and equally obvious effect of the movement was the
gain of some practical victories of a unionistic kind, if sometimes

---

* I estimate that 1,200 stocking frames were broken in the Nottingham area between
November 1811 and January 1813, with an average value of £33 (since town records say the
prices varied from £16 to £50 in 1812), which equals £39,600, plus an uncertain number of
lace machines, perhaps 50 simple machines valued at £30 each and 50 bobbin-net machines
valued at £120, for something around £7,500. In Yorkshire's West Riding, one factory was
destroyed (£8,500 estimated value at the time), one was damaged to the amount of £700,
and £500 worth of cloth was destroyed in one shop, which comes to £9,700; in addition a
very uncertain number of shearing frames and gig mills were destroyed, but certainly not
less than 200, and since these were new and costly machines an average value of £100 is
conservative, totaling £20,000, and thus £29,700 for the West Riding. In Lancashire and
Cheshire, two factories were totally destroyed, one of which was said to be valued at
£6,000 independent of machinery and cloth, and a number of others were damaged representing perhaps half that value, for a minimum of £18,000; two large houses were burned
down (maybe worth £3,000 each, including possessions), the Manchester Exchange was
badly damaged (£500 minimum), and shops and stalls were damaged and food stolen in
fifteen different food riots (£100 each would be an underestimation), making £26,000 for
the counties together at the very least. The total for the Luddite triangle would then be
£108,300. This tallies well with the estimate of F. O. Darvall, a pioneer Luddite scholar,
who, without providing much in the way of detail, has suggested "upwards of one hundred
thousand pounds' worth of machinery and other property."
† The average soldier's pay was said to be £29 a year around this time, an officer's £139; if
we estimate that 13,000 of the troops were regular soldiers and 400 were officers, the total
would be £432,600.

only temporarily. For a time wages were increased for outworkers in those areas, especially around Nottingham and Manchester, where manufacturers thought it a prudent investment against further destruction. A hosier with a dozen frames rented out, for example, and no control over their safety, could easily reckon the value of raising wages a couple of shillings per dozen pairs, at least as long as the Sherwood lads were making good on their threats, and according to William Felkin this is exactly what happened in most of the stocking-frame areas. Many manufacturers, too, who had been using machinery drawing Luddite wrath—particularly the cut-up machines in Nottinghamshire and the shearing frames in Yorkshire—agreed to stop working them, sometimes until all danger was past, in some cases permanently. In the West Riding there were many like the Wakefield factory owner who, after a few threatening letters and a rock through his window, "thinking discretion to be the better part of valour, quietly took down his machinery after these unmistakable warnings, and laid it on one side, till the disturbances were over, when it was again set in motion"; there were also some, like William Horsfall's father, who after his son's death immediately discontinued the use of finishing machines at Ottiwells and invited the croppers back. In Lancashire, though most of the cotton factories did not shut down (unless because of a lack of orders)—the Burton family closed their plant at Middleton rather than risk working power looms again, but this was an exception—wages for handloom weavers did increase a bit for a time and some of the worst abuses against factory hands were checked. In addition, the attention drawn to the plight of workers in the Luddite triangle led to an increase in Poor Law rates and food allowances in almost all the affected parishes—it was charity, and it was meager, but it was something—and a national Association for Relief of the Manufacturing and Labouring Poor was established at the end of May 1812 to send aid from private sources to the distressed areas of the heartland.

Luddism may also have had some residual effect in slowing down the adoption of new machinery by the manufacturers, at least in some regions and some trades. Several contemporary historians suggested that in fact it was the fear of a revival of machine breaking that worked to retard the adoption of new equipment in the textile trades, outside of cotton at any rate, for several decades after the spasms of 1812. An 1819 account of the woolen industry says that "machinery of the most perfect kind" existed but was not introduced because it was "so directly opposite to the inclination and interest of the able workmen"; and as late as 1842 one traveler reported that almost no cotton was worked in Westhoughton, where the vast factory had been destroyed in April 1812, because of "the fear of Luddism." And it may have been the sense of the latent power of Nottingham stockingers that kept the hosiery industry from experiencing the wholesale change from cottage to factory that took place in the cotton and woolen trades from 1810 on, making this industry, in technological terms, among the most backward in the country.

Another residual effect, this one political rather than industrial, may be seen in the gradual revival of reformism among the textile workers after the Luddite repression: if violence doesn't work, and violence had always been the last resort of misused workers, then all that's left are the old ameliorative recourses of paternal law and fraternal association. Luddism represents almost the last time that concerted violence is attempted in England—there was machine breaking in industrial disputes in 1826 and in the "Captain Swing" protests of 1830, but they were short outbursts rapidly contained—and therefore its demise marks the effective starting point for the twin movements of reformism: legislative reform through broadened Parliamentary representation and electoral modifications on the one hand (as with the Reform Bill of 1832 and the Chartist movement in the 1840s), and economic reform through unionism and workplace improvement on the other (as with the Trade Union Acts of the 1820s and the

Ten-Hours Movement into midcentury). From this time on the workforce is largely resigned to an industrial future, many workers going with Major Cartwright and William Cobbett for increased suffrage and legal redress, many with Francis Place and Robert Owen for repeal of the Combination Acts and the dream of a Grand National Consolidated Trades Union. It also must be said, however, that many, perhaps most, were simply resigned, submitting to the inevitable squalor and privation of their lives and the destiny of trades no longer wanted, talents no longer marketable, whole villages no longer needed. *Their* history, ignored by Whigs and Marxists alike in their enthusiasm for reform, is probably the basic one of the next fifty years.

The corollary of this renewed reformism was in effect the death of radicalism, the end in England of anything that might seriously challenge or overturn the accepted order of things. Political sensibilities that turn toward unionism and reform may be oppositional and even angry, but by definition they are not radical insofar as they accede to the given system of power and seek a larger place within it, insofar as they are not rebels against the future but participants in it. Whether or not the Luddites could ever have been seriously revolutionary, could ever have hoped to replace the institutions that imposed industrialism, they were nevertheless expressing something of fundamental dissent from all that those institutions were doing to their lives, and with their passing there were none left to dare that dissent again.

But among the important effects of Luddism the most lasting may perhaps have been the lessons that were absorbed and the strategies that were learned by the sectors of British society that may be said to have been the victors in this war.

Chief among these, though hardly noticed at the time, was the alliance forged between the British government and British industrial enterprise. Not that the British establishment, even the Tory squirearchy, had ever been exactly hostile to the rise of the new industrialists, but now that it had proved willing to support their cause with all its powers of force and repression in the name not merely of order but of laissez-faire order, it was acknowledging for the first time an identity of interests that was to become the dominant theme of the nation's 19th-century experience. On the one hand, the Whiggish mill owner who despised the Orders in Council and the prolonged war and the pompous Prince Regent understood very quickly, as wool merchant William Dawson wrote in May 1812, that "gentlemen of respectability" had now to present "a united front" against that Luddite "threat to society." On the other hand, the Tory ministers who looked condescendingly on the "liberality" of the merchantry discovered how vital such mill owners as William Cartwright were at the local level for establishing control over the numerous laborers and welcomed their expressions of loyalty and gratitude to the Crown. In general, the phenomenon of Luddism, perhaps because it indicated a dangerous potential for solidarity on the part of the workers, served to create a bond between aristocrat and plutocrat that was never really to be sundered. The repeal of the Orders in Council in June 1812, coming as it does in the middle of the Luddite period, may stand as the clear symbolic orb of this new alliance, and the repeal of the Elizabethan laws against apprenticeship in 1814 as the subsequent cross upon it.

Not coincidentally, a crucial instrument that this alliance would wield with devastating effect was also being forged around this time: the creation of the idea of "class," as in ruling/upper class and working/lower class. I do not mean that this is the "making" of the working class, as E. P. Thompson tries so hard to prove, but rather the making of the *idea* of it, not any true "class consciousness," which is really nowhere to be seen during this period, but rather a *class concept*, which as it turns out is a very useful construct for social manipulation and stratification. Once an idea like "class" can be established to explain how society operates, it becomes a way of seeing the proper, or at least ordained, segmentation of the populace, the division between rich and poor, as an eternal and acceptable given of Britain, like

bad weather and abundant coal. As such, then, it is a useful tool
for those in power, relegating some populations to labor and poverty as if it were God's will ("good servants in agriculture and
other laborious employments to which their rank in society had
destined them," as the House of Commons was told in 1807),
and then serving to create or strengthen those institutions—
unions, schools, "friendly societies," churches—that would keep
them there, adjusted to the industrial system around them and its
fundamental values. This was, to be sure, a lengthy process, but
we can see in the alignment of manufacturing and governing
interests during the Luddite crisis one of the crucial early steps
along this path.

For the industrialists, Luddism's other main effect, after order
was established, was to have opened a permanent breach between
worker and master, who traditionally had had certain bonds
and obligations that drew them together despite their different
standings. The obduracy of the mill owners and the resistance
of the workers, escalating to include murder on both sides—of
men whose only crime was hunger and fear, or running new
machines—represented not only a transgression of all previous
understandings but an indelible statement that things could
never be the same again. The events of the Luddite years were
like acids that ate into and deteriorated the fabric of mutuality
that had existed, in however imperfect a form, between men and
manufacturers in the past; once destroyed, very few paternalistic
obligations were any longer felt in the countinghouse, where
from now on the only relationship was one of wages.

For its part, the government learned from Luddism the techniques of quelling rebellion and establishing civil order, which
would prove very useful at home over the next two decades
(though such measures were never again as necessary as in this era)
and in the colonies for another century. Working without precedent or policy other than that might makes right, it proved that
the use of overwhelming army manpower, and attendant spies
and bribes and arrests and hangings, was effective in breaking

worker resistance; and that, at least in the ranks of those who mattered, this did not call forth the kind of outrage and denunciation that a nation supposedly devoted to individual rights and legal niceties might expect. Yes, a Cobbett here and a Carlyle there, some complainers like Byron and Shelley on the fringes, but by and large the opinion-making elements of the kingdom did not mind the demonstration that the principal art of government is the maintenance of order at all costs: Jane Austen, busily transcribing the dreams of the delicate gentry, and Walter Scott, busily creating the dreams of a mythical past, had nothing to say on the matter, and some historians have surmised that the whole Luddite furor went on without their even knowing of it.

The one last great consequence of Luddism, and the one that traditional historians have tried all along to ignore, was that it raised what was called in the 19th century "the machinery question" in stark and unavoidable terms that had to be acknowledged right there at the start of the Industrial Revolution but would continue to persist and vexate forever afterward. The burden of it was quite simple: who would determine what would be the technology of production for Britain? by what criteria would they decide? how would the consequences of this be judged?

The answer of the innovators, the owners of capital and production, was that, in the words of an anonymous commentator on the Luddite trials, "the improvement of machinery is beneficial, instead of being detrimental, to the interest of the labouring manufacturer, as well as to the community at large." The question, put in entirely material not to mention selfish terms, was answered by an equation in which improved machinery meant decreased costs, which meant increased production and profit, which meant continuing employment for those not done out of work, result happiness. It did not matter, though it was inevitable, that there were fewer jobs, for, as the prime apologist Andrew Ure put it, "It is in fact the constant aim and tendency of every improvement in machinery to supersede human labour altogether, or to diminish its cost, by substituting the industry of women and children for that of men"; or, as the prime theorist David Ricardo put it, "The opinion entertained by the labouring class, that the employment of machinery is frequently detrimental to their interests, is not founded on prejudice and error, but is conformable to the correct principles of political economy." The battle lines couldn't be drawn more clearly.

The innovators and their theorists were also putting it about at this point that what was of benefit to the manufacturers was also to the good of the country. For if industrialists grew richer with their new machines they would find new markets and produce more and expand their plants and therefore add on more jobs than before, so even the "superseded" humans would be able to work and to buy, and in a ceaseless round of production-consumption everyone would prosper. As a *process,* something like this did eventually happen in Britain—but only after several generations of the superseded lived in the most destitute poverty, only because the little kingdom established an empire and control over world shipping that enabled its markets to expand and workers to work while others overseas suffered, only at a cost to the environment of Britain and its colonies from which they have not yet recovered today. But as a *theory,* applicable anywhere, the notion that new technology somehow creates new jobs and increased wealth is hogwash (as E. P. Thompson among others has infuriated orthodox economists by pointing out), never close to being proven, and the experience of most of the rest of the world in the past two centuries, particularly those countries without empires, belies it utterly.

The answer to the machinery question that the workers of the early 19th century, by contrast, might have given—the answer that seems to have inspired Luddism—was of course quite different. "Improvement of machinery," as workers had seen it in the first quarter century of the Industrial Revolution, had had two effects, neither one much to their benefit. First, it threw people out of work—the spinning machines, the scrubbing engines, the

gig mills, the power looms, the lot of them—an invariable
tragedy not only for the individual families thus cast adrift but
also for the nation as a whole, since (as a wool workers' spokesman put it to Parliament in 1806) "a trade or manufacture is valuable to a country in proportion to the number of hands it
employs." And second, it made people who wanted jobs succumb
to a factory system that turned them into little more than atten-
dants on Stygian forges, a grueling process of deskilling, deper-
sonalizing, demoralizing, and degrading even under the best of
its conditions, whose primary economic achievement was not
even productivity but labor discipline. And if in the long run
those two effects were supposed to redound to the workers' benefit, however unlikely that might seem, they would do so only in
the crude material terms the Feelosophers liked to set, leaving organic and communal ones, those that had been the underpinning
of society for some centuries, in tatters. "Unrestrained machinery
demoralises society" is the way one pamphleteer of the post-
Luddite era said it, and "substitutes idleness for industry—want
for competence—immorality for virtue . . . *and unless restrained,
will, ere long, involve this country in every horror and calamity
attending the bursting of all the bonds that hold society together.*"

But whichever way the machinery question might be
answered, it was a question that could no longer be ignored,
raised as the Luddites had raised it, nor could its problematic
moral implications be dismissed, however much the gloss of
Regency rakery might try to conceal them. The simple, overarching fact is that technology always has consequences, far-reaching
consequences, usually more so than anyone can predict at the
beginning, and this truth is exactly what lies at the heart of Luddism—and is the reason why in fact the name and idea lasted
beyond its brief fifteen-month course. For most of its lexiconic
life it has been used in the pejorative sense, of course, with a great
deal of condescension toward those who might try to hold back
progress, because it was the prophets of progress who won the day
and have continued to set the terms of the discourse ever since.

But there have been throughout these last two centuries, and there are today as perhaps never before, any number of serious minds that have come to see the point of the Luddite challenge, to ask questions about progress and its values, to wonder where the victory of unimpeded technology-for-profit has gotten us. Luddism, then, did not die on the scaffold with the Luddites: it has lived an inextinguishable existence with "the machinery question" at its heart.

Luddism did, however, lose.

Insofar as it is possible to determine its varying aims, from an increase in wages to the abandonment of a machine to the restoration of rights to the "just republic" that understood machinery, it never realized any of them in the long run. Hated machines continued to be used, oiled and squared after the Luddite furor passed, and new ones were introduced wherever the climate permitted, and their application depended rather more on whether they were economical or efficient than on whether they would put people out of work. Owners combined successfully to keep wages down in all but a few trades and positions, and in most of the handworked trades, again when the Luddite threat was over, to reduce wages steadily until they no longer needed such cottage labor anymore. Factories continued to be built and to adopt the steam engine, in all of the lines of the textile industries whose economics justified it, as if Luddism had never existed; as Edward Baines was proud to point out in 1835, "It is by iron fingers, teeth, and wheels, moving with exhaustless energy and devouring speed, that cotton is opened, cleaned, spread, carded, drawn, roved, spun, wound, warped, dressed and woven"—as well as bleached and printed.

Economic conditions for labor in the Luddite areas did not improve after 1813, nor would they, except in short fits and starts, until well past the middle of the century. Juggle the standard-of-living figures any way you like—which is in fact the enterprise of a considerable academic coterie these days—and there is still no

way to come up with anything but sequential misery: workers in
the Luddite triangle were just as badly off in 1816–17 as they had
been in 1811–12, and in 1819–20, 1829–30, 1836–37, 1841–42,
and 1849–50, save only that some of them did better in the peri-
ods in between and some were absorbed into the factory system
to stay alive by its harsh and pinching terms. E. P. Thompson's
judgment here still stands, and no one who reads the evidence
of the parliamentary inquiries in this period, imperfect as they
are, can doubt it: "During the years between 1780 and 1840 the
people of Britain suffered an experience of immiseration, even if
it is possible to show a small statistical improvement in material
conditions." Moreover,

> any evaluation of the quality of life must entail an assessment of the
> total life-experience, the manifold satisfactions or deprivations, cul-
> tural as well as material, of the people concerned. From such a stand-
> point, the older "cataclysmic" view of the Industrial Revolution
> must still be accepted.

Inhuman as its conditions were, the factory system triumphed.
By 1820 there were as many as 126,000 workers in the cotton
factories, by 1835 there were 219,000, and by 1844 there were
340,000, the great majority of them being women and children
paid negligible wages, on average no more than a fifth being adult
men. The woolen trade took somewhat longer to industrialize,
but the number of factories grew from 258 in 1811 to around 600
in 1835 and 1,298 in 1850 (with only a quarter of those employed
being men), and the number of power looms from 2,778 in the
West Riding in 1835 to 11,458 in 1841 and 23,800 in 1850. The
stocking trade took to the factory system unevenly, and not in a
wholesale way until the 1840s, but the lace industry moved
quickly (970 net machines in 1817, 2,469 in 1826, 3,842 in 1829)
and in 1835 there were as many as 31,000 people in the lace
mills, only about a tenth of them men. The conditions within
these "many-windowed fabrics" were every bit as bad as the
Dickensian images and Factory Act statistics would suggest—no

need to rehearse them here—and every bit as horrible as the Luddite fears had depicted, but nothing stopped their march across the land.

Handcrafters clung to their perilous existence for a surprisingly long time—men for the most part, keeping to their old tools in squalid and crumbling cottages, working for so little money that they would sometimes be cheaper for the manufacturers to use than machines—but slowly and inevitably they faded away. Workers in any number of lines followed this sorry fate in the first half of the century—nail making, boot making, tailoring, farm labor—but the great majority were in the textile trades that had populated Luddism. In 1849 the London *Morning Chronicle* sent a reporter out to portray the conditions of these families in the textile regions. In the cotton towns, he found, where "the streets were filthy and mean, the houses crumbling, crazy and dirty," lived the last of the handloom weavers, "taken altogether . . . a wretched and hopeless set," living on potatoes and bread and weak tea, on whose faces were stamped "the most unequivocal marks of stolid, hopeless, apathetic despair." The woolen towns were if anything worse, and the croppers and wool combers and handloom weavers so "very ill-off" that one woman said flatly, "I don't call it living. We kept ourselves alive but that was all." And yet it was the stockingers, the poor souls whose desperateness had sparked Luddism in the beginning, whom the reporter found most pitiable:

> There can be no doubt of the miserably depressed state of the framework knitters. They appear to labour without either energy, or hope, or heartiness. In point of personal appearance and decent comfort of attire, the framework knitters must take the very lowest rank in the social scale connected with the textile industry.

It is, all in all, a pathetic and deplorable chapter in Britain's history, a future that the Luddites were justified in resisting. It passes, yes, and gradually men find other work to do, or die, families move, factories enlarge, Poor Rates increase, the worst conditions improve, and by the last quarter of the century the cottage outworkers are no longer there in sufficient numbers to be reminders of the ravages of the industrial system. But the worst part of it is that this tragedy was not an anomaly, a peculiarity of this first experience of industrialism, a stage that, once anticipated, could be eliminated. In one way or another, displacement, dislocation, impoverishment, and misery have attended this process, in every country that has given itself over to the factory, no matter what its political system or previous history, across the globe. There are many who have suffered, who are suffering, the fate of the handcrafter and the cottager, in rich countries as well as poor, in metropoles as well as colonies, all of whom might say, with the wool comber in 1840: "Our homes, which were not many years ago the abodes of comfort and domestic enjoyment, have now . . . become dwelling places of misery and receptacles of wretchedness."

And so Luddism lost, and all that it foretold, or at least apprehended, came to pass. The industrial future was not abated, the dawn of modernism was not held back. Eventually, after the last Luddite lad had grown old and died, and the secrets had been kept forever, the laissez-faire abutments of it all crumbled, one by one, in Europe and then elsewhere, and various forms of open governmental protection and assistance took their place, from state socialism to state capitalism in all sorts of guises and variations—but industrialism triumphed everywhere. Indeed, it could be said to have conquered the world, only a few small regions excepted, as has no other system of human organization and production save hunting-gathering.

Of course, it has had only two hundred years of triumph. The Luddite tradition, of custom and community, of resistance to "machinery hurtful," lasted far longer than that.

8

The Second Industrial Revolution

IT IS NOT CLEAR when "Luddite" begins to take on a secondary meaning and comes to be applied not only to the machine breakers of 1811–12 but generally to anyone who is opposed to new technology, not necessarily with violence and sabotage. The earliest use I can find is a report of a British Parliamentary debate about the new phenomenon of automation in the 1956 *Annual Register*, in which "a Labour spokesman . . . assured the Minister that organised workers were by no means wedded to a 'Luddite' philosophy,"—suggesting that by then the word had already acquired a modern connotation, though still new enough that the *Register* reporter felt quotation marks were necessary. Three years later, C. P. Snow in his famous lecture on "The Two Cultures and the Scientific Revolution" accused most people in the literary culture of being "natural Luddites," by which he meant nothing having to do with machine breaking at all but an opposition to science in general and industrial technology in particular, which these intellectuals have never "tried, wanted, or been able to understand." Dictionaries do not begin to record this secondary meaning until as late as 1988, when the *Chambers English Dictionary*, published in Britain, is apparently the first, followed by the 1989 *Oxford English Dictionary*, which gives "Luddite" as "one who opposes the introduction of new technology," citing first a 1967 reference in the *Sunday Times* ("Systems men . . . susceptible to Luddism") and then a 1970 reference in the *New*

Scientist on the need "to overcome the professional and official luddites."

All this indicates that the extended use of the word is quite surprisingly recent, having begun sometime in the years after World War II when an onrush of new technologies began a transformation of the 20th century similar to that which had taken place in the 19th, and to forestall criticisms its champions needed to call forth a symbolic opponent, one who could be dismissed as both unsuccessful and somehow irrational, a role the Luddites were very neatly pressed into serving.

Just when that second Industrial Revolution begins is difficult to say. Some might want to choose 1945, the date of the first explosion of a weapon made possible by the alteration of the very atoms of existence by a man-made energy source, a towering feat of technological mastery; or 1949, when the United States invented a new imperial concept for the word "underdeveloped" and set off on a crusade to make "the benefits of our scientific advances and industrial progress available for the improvement and growth of underdeveloped areas"; or 1951, the date of the first transcontinental television broadcast, followed by the invention of fiber optics in 1955, and the first communications satellite in 1976; or 1970, with the first gene synthesis, leading to the first genetically engineered bacteria in 1971 and recombinant DNA in 1973. A case for any one of these could be made, since they all mark important points in different phases of technological domination. But I think it can be truly said that nothing has had as reticulate and reverberating an effect on industrial society as the electronic digital computer, the "master technology" that stands behind so many other inventions and processes of our lives, which has many antecedents but is appropriately dated from the perfection of the microchip and microprocessor in 1971.

Obviously to isolate the precise date or even the particular technology is not so important. What is important is to realize that since about midcentury, and especially in the last two decades, a powerful and sweeping alteration of the industrial world has taken place as a result of technological changes that go to the very core of our lives, creating a revolution in work and thought, politics and markets, culture and leisure, at least as profound as that of the first Industrial Revolution. That storm swirls around the world—most particularly the industrial nations of Europe, North America, and East Asia, and nowhere more completely than in the United States—with effects that many have seen as sweeping: computers and electronics have wrought a "Digital Revolution" is the way a magazine called *Wired* put it in 1993, with "social changes so profound their only parallel is probably the discovery of fire"; computer-aided design and manufacturing has created "a new industrial revolution," said a *Fortune* cover story in October 1981; molecular science and biotechnology have created what the American Medical Association alerted its members to in 1993 as "a genetics revolution" from which "there is no turning back"; electronic information technology, according to the National Science Foundation, will have altered every institution of American life with "transformative effects" by 1998. It is unquestionably, as the historian David Noble has put it, a "second Industrial Revolution" in which "capital is moving decisively now to enlarge and to consolidate the social dominance it secured in the first," only now on a global scale and with "the new technology as a weapon . . . in the quest for more potent vehicles of investment and exploitation. . . . Once again the machines of industry have taken center stage in the historical drama, as the drive for ever more automatic processes becomes a historical stampede."

Some, incidentally, would like to call this revolution "post-industrial," presumably meaning that it depends less on smoke-belching factories and more on computer-using offices, in which "information" rather than textiles or steel is the prime commodity and the old manufacturing jobs give way to new "service" jobs. But though the nature of many trades and businesses has certainly changed, the economy is still *industrial* in all meaningful ways, and the processes and policies that shaped the industrial system at the start—including specialization, mechanization, commodification, mass production, expanding markets, large and impersonal units, intensive capital investment, and monetarization of worth—are still at work, even if the technologies have changed and the air is cleaner. Tourism, though mainly based on service employment and only secondarily dependent on factory products, is every bit an industry, indeed the world's largest, as are filmmaking, gambling, investment banking, advertising, and selling real estate, though none is much involved with assembly lines or smokestacks. "Postindustrial," in fact, is an intentional misnomer, a sociologist's sleight of hand intended to direct attention away from the often unpleasant truths of the ongoing economy, which is, now in its second revolution as in its first, thoroughly industrial.

It is remarkable how the new period resembles the old in many little ways: the early 19th century was a period of vulgar theater, elephantine buildings, public obsession with murders and executions, increasing fear of street crime, great enthusiasm for boxing and other violent spectator sports, and passions for running, ballooning, and gambling of all kinds, including lotteries. But it is remarkable also that the large characteristics that served earlier to define the first Industrial Revolution can be applied, though with the same caution of erring toward the schematic and reductive, to the second as well.

THE IMPOSITION OF TECHNOLOGY

This time around the technology is even more complex and extensive, and its impact even more pervasive and dislocating, touching greater populations with greater speed and at greater scales. No one voted for this technology or any of the various machines and processes that make it up; no one explained or even thought much about what the consequences of any of them would be, singly or synergistically, on individual, society, or environment;

and no one took responsibility for the transformations they have wrought, except insofar as governments were ultimately asked to care for the most ruinous results (poverty, pollution, unemployment). It "just happened," in an onrush of industrial creation, swiftly and powerfully and inescapably. But the effects are profound, maybe more profound than we know.

About fifteen years ago the executives of IBM got together the biggest academic and intellectual mandarins they could find, best hotels, all expenses paid, to discuss the question of the long-term implications of the computer for American society. After a week of discussions the experts threw up their hands and said they couldn't possibly foretell the range of impacts the computer would have in even the short run, much less the long. As one of the historians there pointed out, if Henry Ford in 1910 had assembled the best minds of his age to ponder the implications of the automobile in America, they could not possibly have predicted even one of the personal, familial, social, architectural, cultural, industrial, economic, or environmental effects that it actually has had—and, he said, the computer is far more versatile and intrusive than the car. Indeed, since then, the computer has allowed a profusion of so many other technologies and functions—think only of faxes, robots, microwaves, photocomposition, credit cards, airline reservations, word processors, supermarket scanners, compact disks, lasers, supertankers, spacecraft, CAT scanners, and satellites—that it is no wonder there is a widespread sense that, in fact, technology is in the saddle and rides humankind; as the sign above the portals of the 1933 World's Fair in Chicago put it presciently, "Science explores: Technology executes: Man conforms." But that, as it turns out, is highly appropriate, for cybernetics, the science of computers, comes from the Greek *kubernetes,* "helmsman" or "governor," meaning simply that the machine is in charge.

More and more, it seems, human decisions get made because of technology rather than the other way around. As, for example, when Chrysler engineers invent power steering because they have stuffed so many new gadgets and parts into their car that it is too heavy to turn; as when microcomputer "notebooks" are created not to meet any known or expressed need but because miniaturization at some point has made it possible to put immense amounts of information on a very tiny silicon chip; as when space shuttle missions are repeatedly launched, at a cost of $6 billion a year, not for any remotely scientific purpose (missions have been devoted to the study of jellyfish, slime mold, and frog eggs in zero gravity for want of anything else to do) but because NASA has the capability of doing so. Once again, it is the technological imperative, expressed by Robert Oppenheimer as "When you see something that is technically sweet you go ahead and do it."

But the kind of technology shaping the second Industrial Revolution has its own special and inescapable logic, just as the one wrought by the steam engine had its, that goes beyond the proliferation of its machines and methods. Automation, for example, is an inevitable consequence of computerization and robotics, and serves to replace human endeavor in more and more ways in more and more settings. Simplification and routinization are similar consequences in tasks where humans are still involved, deskilling and often dehumanizing the operatives and making them subject to minute monitoring and discipline. Massification and quantification are also built-in biases of the computer, indeed were probably the reason computers became so important in the first place, as necessary adjuncts to a mass society and its mass production, mass marketing, mass consumption, mass communications, mass education, and mass culture. Add to these such other attributes of high technology as centralization, order, speed, uniformity, regularity, linearity, and passivity, and it becomes clear that when a civilization buys into the computer's logic it buys much else besides. In the words of the Canadian philosopher George Grant, "Computers do not present us with neutral means for building *any* kind of society. All their alternative ways lead us towards the universal and homogenous state."

Indeed, it is the imperative to *control,* whether by the state or other institutions, that may be the most decisive characteristic of computerization, since the possibilities of amassing information on such a large scale over such a wide population, and using that information then to identify, follow, manipulate, and regulate, are so clear. Information (or at least data-supply—whether it "informs" anything is another matter) is the fodder of the computer maw, and as more bits are fed into the machine the more it can know and use and administer. If what is in store for us, as many say, is an "information age" with "information highways" and "information supermarkets" then it is the computer and those who feed and handle it who reign supreme: in the country of the sighted, the all-seeing one is king. Control of information is control of power.

That is disturbing enough, and unprecedented, but what seems to generate even more anxiety is, paradoxically enough, the *lack* of control throughout our technological society, the fragility of the systems, the constant uncertainty and instability. Computers are always "down" when you need them, automatic teller machines go blank, savings-and-loan banks are suddenly bankrupt, long-standing corporations no longer exist, no one around knows how to program the VCR, nuclear missiles are almost triggered by a full moon, the stock market collapses because of computerized institutional trading, men who spent their boyhood under the hood of a car are baffled by new computer-diagnosed automobiles. It is not just that the machines seem to be beyond our individual control, though that is demeaning enough— nothing is fixable, everything says "No serviceable parts"—but that, separately and collectively, they seem to be beyond anyone's control, operating at such speed and complexity that it defies human competence to manage them regularly and infallibly. As we are repeatedly reminded, not only by the many technological disasters of our age (Chernobyl, Bhopal, DDT, Times Beach, the Challenger, Three Mile Island, chlordane, *Exxon Valdez,* Love Canal, Mars Observer, PCBs, and on and on) but by the less dramatic technological malfunctions that recur (acid rain, radiation leaks, ozone depletion, environmental cancers, airplane crashes, electricity blackouts, oil spills, and the like).

But ultimately it is not even a question of whether late-industrial technology is stable or fragile: the point is that it dominates and pervades, it is imposed throughout our lives in such a way that it mediates experience to a degree no society before has ever undergone. Less and less is human life connected to other species, to natural systems, to seasonal and regional patterns; more and more to the *technosphere*, to artificial and engineered constructs, to industrial patterns and procedures, even to man-made hormones, genes, cells, and life-forms. In one of the profound insights of one of the profound minds of the 20th century, Herbert Read paused at the end of *The Grass Roots of Art* to say:

> Only a people serving an apprenticeship to nature can be trusted with machines. Only such people will so contrive and control those machines that their products are an enhancement of biological needs, and not a denial of them.

This society serves no such apprenticeship, alas, nor does there seem much hope that it would ever know how to do so, so immersed is it in industrial culture that it has difficulty understanding experience in any other form than the technological.

Let us take, for example, the industrial view of nature to which technology inclines us and by which many of us understand the nonhuman environment. It argues, with the full power of industrial science, that most of nature is inert and lifeless—rocks and mountains, winds and rivers—and that other species, without our form of consciousness, are innately inferior. All of those may therefore be considered "resources," for the human species to exploit in such ways as improve its condition, or at least its material amassment, and technologies should be designed to make the maximum use of such resources as completely as possible by as many people as possible. In the technological worldview it would be meaningless to talk of rocks as being alive, mountains as having souls, winds as gods; it would be absurd to consider a river system holy or an insect species sacred, or either one as having inherent rights; it would be mistaken to adopt as an ethical philosophy the position that "a thing is right when it tends to preserve the integrity, stability, and beauty of the biotic community, wrong when it tends otherwise"; it would be insane to assign greater priority to old trees than new logs, to leave wetlands undeveloped while people need space to build on, to consign someone to death if a machine would provide life, to allow food to spoil if chemicals would preserve it.

An industrial society, it becomes obvious, has its own inevitable logic, simply because its needs and values are determined by its technology. In such a society the artifacts are not something added on, like a coat of paint or a caboose; they are basic, central, the revelation of its mind and heart.

THE DESTRUCTION OF THE PAST

A high-tech society is by and large present-minded, just as its machines are—a computer's "memory," after all, is only regurgitation, not the recreation of experience, and it exists only in the present, when it is being transmitted. A high-tech society is ever-changing and unsettled, always caught in that rush of improvement and innovation that generally goes by the name of "progress," regardless of which direction it is hurtling in. And a high-tech society values solitary life and experience over communal, the mediated experience over the direct, and the mechanical expressions of a shared culture (networks, programs, electronic games) over the personal (taverns, schools, parks).

Put those together and it is obvious that such a society will find the idea of the past—the institutions of its history and the values that adhere to them—either irrelevant or, worse, impedimental. In particular the historic elements that tend toward social cohesion and stability—the small community, the small town, the stable neighborhood—will be seen generally as incompatible with those that encourage individuality, mobility, consumption, growth, and change; hence the corner grocery gives way to the supermarket, Main Street to the mall, the cul-de-sac to the arterial road, the meadow to the development. The past is by definition imperfect, inadequate, impoverished.

The extraordinary suburbanization of America in the last half century has been one principal way by which the places and values of the past have been destroyed or enfeebled. People have been sucked from neighborhoods and villages by government building and road policies, tax incentives, bank practices, consumer propaganda, and other devices of a modernizing society, and relocated in sterile enclaves where the cohesive arrangements of the past, much less the ancient connections to the natural world, are not only missing but impossible to create. Such places are not accidental, inevitable phenomena, mind: they are the quite explicit expression of a mass-production, consumer-directed, relentlessly mobile technological society, producing the anomie and atomization that make good workers and citizens, the dependence and emptiness that make good consumers. But so little do they provide the fertile soil for roots and stability of family or community that, statistically speaking, fully a fifth of the population over the last twenty years has changed homes every single year.

One other crucial demographic means of undermining the past, and this one with striking parallels to the enclosure movement in industrializing England, has been the destruction of the family farm. This, too, was not happenstance, "just one of those things": it was a deliberate undertaking of state and federal governments with conscious policies and laws, abetted by commercial and savings banks and other real estate institutions, designed to create an agriculture dependent on high-tech fertilizers, seeds, pesticides, equipment, and marketing, regardless of the depopulation that would accompany it. It began as early as the New Deal, but it was really after 1960, when mechanization began to change agriculture into agribusiness and large (especially corporate) farmers were enabled to drive out tenants, sharecroppers, and small family units, that the full effects were felt. The Department of Agriculture adopted a specific policy of "get big or get out," enforced through the Farm Bureau Federation and its compliant banks and propagandized by the land-grant agricultural colleges, and massive subsidies (tax breaks, cash outlays, price supports, etc., making up at least a third of all farm income since 1960, $13 billion in 1992) ensured that the policy would be followed. From 1950 to 1990 the American farm population declined from 23 million to less than 5 million, the number of one-family farms from 3 million to 1.4 million, the number of farm laborers from 7.2 million to 3.2 million.

The driving force by which this was accomplished was largely technological, a mechanization of the farm on a scale so vast, if invisible to the urban dweller, that by the 1980s American agriculture was actually much more mechanized than the manufacturing sector.* Factory husbandry (particularly of chickens), center-pivot irrigation, mechanical tomato pickers (three workers do the work of sixty), cotton strippers (one worker does the work of fifty-six), grain and beet combines (one worker does the work of eighty), automated milking machines, cattle feedlots, computer bookkeeping, helicopter spraying—American farms have become almost entirely industrialized, corporations of great size and complexity (and therefore debt: about $80 *billion* a year in recent times). But, as always, mechanization serves the interests primarily of the largest firms, and those who cannot afford the latest expensive technology (or cannot repay the loans for it)

---

* Not long after John and Mack Rust in Texas patented the spindle-picker machine for cotton harvesting in 1928, they realized that it could put at least "75 per cent of the labor population out of employment." To avert that tragedy they proposed to adapt their machine to small farms, sell it only to community cooperative farms, restrict its use on larger farms, and set aside some of their profits to assist unemployed cotton workers. "None of the schemes proved practical, however," according to the dry account of *Scientific American* in September 1982, "and all of them were swept aside when the effects of World War II [high demand and high prices] brought several more companies into the business of manufacturing cotton harvesters." Of course: the spindle-picker was in the saddle, riding even its inventors.

inevitably fall behind, and the number of farms inexorably dwindles. The human tragedies caused by that process were material for nightly news stories in the 1980s when farm debt reached beyond $100 billion a year and foreclosures were as common as harvests—40 percent of the farms in Kansas, for example, went under in the 1980s—but in fact the wrenching depopulation of the American countryside has been going on steadily for four decades, and is continuing.

The calamity is double. Rural communities decay; half the young families who inherit farms cannot afford to keep them because the inheritance taxes or accumulated debts are so large; the investment required to start up a new farm is beyond the reach of all but a handful of families, and there are always absentee corporations in the wings. Displaced populations leave the land and make their way, uselessly, to the cities; urban ghettos swell and fester; families without skills recognizable in the cities compete for the few available jobs or go on the public dole, using food stamps to buy what they once knew how to grow.

How such a double calamity became a social policy of the United States—and many other nations that have gone for technological agriculture—is a mystery only to those who do not realize that technologies have logics of their own.

THE MANUFACTURE OF NEEDS

Obviously the destruction of past settlements and past values is as advantageous for the second Industrial Revolution as it was for the first, and if it leads a society into an emphasis on the material over the intangible this can only be a boon to the progenitors of technology. But this time around the array of incentives available for the creation of needs, within the industrial world and without, is staggeringly varied and effective—in fact, taken as a whole, it may be the most powerful element of the computer age, rivaling the computer itself.

Advertising, of course, is primary; in the United States it has been for some time an enormous industry of more than $100 billion a year ($150 billion in 1994), more than is spent on all public higher education, whose impact is made inescapable by an annual barrage of 21,000 TV commercials, 1 million magazine ad pages, 14 billion mail-order catalogues, 38 billion junk-mail ads, and a billion signs, posters, and billboards. To it must be added a number of ancillary industries affecting popular taste and spending, including promotion, public relations, marketing, design, and above all fashion, not merely of clothes but many other consumer products—another $100-billion-a-year enterprise. The total is an exercise in mental manipulation of a most extravagant kind, in service to the definition and fulfillment of consumerist needs.

Television, the most important medium of this manipulation, is also very seductively selling a way of life that declares from a whisper to a shout that consumption is *good,* fulfilling, fun, moral, empowering, all the certainties that are so elusive in the rest of life. It is the medium that almost perfectly expresses the high-tech society: simplistic and forceful, capable of no complexity of thought whatever, designed for limited and graphic impacts (best if short and violent, like football and commercials), and sending pulses continually at that psychological nexus that Freud, doctor for the consumer society, called the "pleasure principle," where desires, always created, are always insatiable.

The global effect of television, a blue genie now shining out of more than 850 million sets worldwide, is to implant the vision of the commodified life in every corner of the world; TV shows are the number-one American export by dollar volume. This is enhanced of course by global advertising (a $250 billion industry in 1990, surpassing the GNP of India), franchising, jet travel, "free" trade, and runaway factories and offices, but above all by tourism, which spreads everywhere the artificial image of the industrial citizen as a carefree, well-heeled sybarite. Within less than a generation vast populations across the globe have thus been brought into the range of the industrial monoculture, including such formerly resistant empires as those of Russia and China, and anthropologists believe that by the 21st century there will not be a single culture anywhere that will have escaped its impact.

It is to assure the continued expansion of this transnational commissary that the industrial corporations in recent years have pushed through global free-trade agreements and World Bank "development" loans that have drawn virtually every nation of the world into the industrial net; right behind them are the compliant industrial governments, primarily that of the United States, which has deliberately devoted itself in its myriad ways, as the Clinton administration has put it, to "the enlargement of the world's free-market democracies."

One essential part of this global rialto is the immense growth in recent years of its cities, urban conglomerations of unprecedented size—and dependency. By the year 2000, for the first time in human history, more people will be living in cities than in rural areas, and at least twenty-one of those cities will have populations of more than 10 million; in the United States by then 80 percent of the population will be living in metropolitan areas, up from only 30 percent in 1950. Just as in the first Industrial Revolution, these populations are ready-made markets for all kind of industrial detritus, including the food they eat, and it should not be overlooked that even the worst by-products of these places— crime, civil unrest, alcoholism, drug addiction, disease, disintegration—are each themselves growth industries.

And as in the first revolution, war and military spending have proved to be additional marvelous engines of need. No reliable dollar figure can be put upon the amount laid out in the years since, say, the end of the Vietnam War, but from a global perspective it can be said that no year has gone by without at least fifty full-scale military conflicts, many very extensive, and that arms exports in those years have averaged $30 billion a year, rising to a high of $45 billion in 1989 before the Soviet Union splintered. In the United States, Pentagon expenditures have averaged $250 billion a year, at least half of which goes to lines on the budget marked "Construction," "Procurement," "R & D," and

"Operations," creating and maintaining enormous quantities of equipment, much of it (thankfully) unused and eventually junked.

It is impossible to detail the rest of the miraculous manufactory of needs of the high-tech society, so vast and complex has it become. Suffice it to note that among its essentials are waste and throw-away consumerism (fifty-two tons of garbage per person in an average American lifetime); planned and built-in obsolescence and shoddy production; unnecessary packaging and product differentiation; consumer credit (and debt), discount rates, and tax incentives; malls and shopping centers (33,000 in the United States by 1994, more than the number of high schools), development of new products (at the rate of $80 billion a year in the United States) and then the production of them (at the rate of 17,571 new entries in 1993, going up around 10 percent a year). Put them all together they spell "consumer," as in "consumer society," which is what the West is acknowledged to be.

Only one measure need be applied to ratify that title: according to the Worldwatch Institute, more goods and services have been consumed by the generation alive between 1950 and 1990, measured in constant dollars and on a global scale, than by all the generations in all of human history before.

THE SERVICE OF THE STATE

The doctrines of laissez-faire have long ago been discarded by governments of all the industrial nations, even in the United States, where the rhetoric of getting Big Government "off the backs" of private enterprise has continued to be a popular campaign idea despite the fact that it is entirely devoid of meaning. But the extent to which the nation-state not merely builds the muscles of the successful modern corporation but has been responsible for its high-tech brains and nerve system is seldom appreciated.

In addition to overseeing all the basic functions that states have all along performed in the interest of commerce and trade,

modern governments have been largely responsible for supporting higher education, fostering basic scientific research, assigning
specific subsidies to electronic, aerospace, and defense industries,
and guaranteeing patents and "intellectual property rights"—all
of which has been essential to the development of the high-tech
revolution. After all, most of the ideas and hardware that shaped
it originated in government-sponsored military projects in the
years during and immediately after World War II—control systems for automatic guns, microelectronics for radar and missile
systems, computers for targeting bombs and ballistics, and countless devices to perfect the business of destroying people and places
and keeping track of who was doing what to whom. In order to
adapt these techniques to civilian uses—especially where large
numbers of people had to be accounted for, mass-scale calcula-
tions had to be made, and large and complex projects had to
be undertaken—state subsidies (cost-plus contracts, tax breaks,
tariffs, R & D money, etc.) were given to corporations in fields
ranging from petroleum to electronics, chemicals to aircraft,
communications to cookery.*

   The United States was not the most aggressive nation in
building up government-corporate partnerships—Germany and
France were early leaders and Japan (with its famous MITI)
became the most successful—but since the U.S. was the first and
had by far the largest military and aerospace budgets (the largest
single source of R & D in the world) it has played a decisive role.
This is why the initial development of the matrix of the computer
revolution happened first in the U.S., why so many of the pioneer
firms were American, and why so many of the components of

---

* For example, taking 1984 alone the National Science Foundation received between $6
million and $9 million for automation; NASA, $6 million for robotics; the Army, $56 mil-
lion for computer-aided manufacturing (CAM); the National Bureau of Standards, $4 mil-
lion for computer-aided design and manufacturing (CADCAM); and the Department of
Defense, $283 million for a Manufacturing Technology Program, around $100 million for
integrated circuits, about the same for a "next-generation" computer, and $90 million for
microchips. In all, twenty-seven government bodies were directly supporting high-tech
development that year.

computer technology are to be found in the U.S. business and consumer culture—even if so many of them are in fact made elsewhere.

It should not be assumed that government, particularly military, influence is somehow benign, or neutral, or blandly Medician. Research is generally restricted to areas that are expected to provide improvements in the movement of missiles rather than, say, the movement of foot soldiers, or, unlikelier still, the movement of sidewalk pedestrians. Performance is more important than cost, thrust and mass and power more important than efficiency, and waste, pollution, depletion, and degradation are simply not factored in at all. Speed of information is, strangely enough, a far more important factor than usefulness or even accuracy, since the basic principle of cybernetics is the feedback mechanism (developed originally for anti-aircraft guns) by which improvements and corrections can always in theory be made, provided only that enough information is available quickly enough. Other biases of military research are, not surprisingly, toward centralization, command hierarchy, routinization, and the replacement of (fallible) humans by (infallible?) machines.

With the end of the Cold War the influence of the military on technology is certain to wane somewhat, but there is no sign that overall government sponsorship of technology will slacken. The U.S. has committed itself to funding something called the Human Genome Project, for example, designed to reveal, and make profits from, all the information in human cells, ultimately thought to be a trillion-dollar investment; and under the Clinton administration the government has begun to switch R & D money from the military directly to corporate computer technology: $7 billion has been transferred in the first term, with more promised. The government has also already embarked on paving the "electronic superhighway" that is supposed to allow corporations to computerize and connect almost every aspect of daily American life, from movie watching to scientific research, schoolroom teaching to medical diagnosis, grocery shopping to banking.

If the superhighway is in fact developed, a considerable part of it will have to be funded by the federal government in what is thought will become the largest public works project ever undertaken.

Interestingly, however, though the servile state remains important, perhaps crucial, as the funder of high technology, it has less and less influence on the actual behavior of the corporations benefiting from it. Partly this is because the principal corporations of the industrial world have become so rich and powerful that they cannot be effectively monitored or directed by any state agency, however large or motivated. After all, the annual sales figure of a company like General Motors ($123 billion in 1991), is larger than the Gross Domestic Product of all but fifteen countries in the world and that of Royal Dutch Shell is as great as South Africa's. Partly it is because these multinational giants have operations all over the world and therefore are accountable to and have loyalties to no particular nation, no particular location, and can elude controls and restraints by moving (or merely threatening to move) a plant overseas or transferring a couple more million dollars offshore. And partly it is because the very technology itself opens directions and creates opportunities that have never existed before, allowing high-tech global markets trading $1.5 trillion a day to determine the fate of national economies and currencies far beyond the reach of any single government, its regulators or legislators, far beyond any existing supranational system of control.

At the same time, real policy-setting power seems to have largely been consolidated upward, beyond the reach of any individual state, in the instruments of global industrial development, chiefly the World Bank, the International Monetary Fund, the General Agreement on Tariffs and Trade (and its smaller continental counterparts), the World Trade Organization, and the "G-7" summits of Northern industrial countries that advise them. A particularly glaring demonstration of this fact was the much-heralded "Earth Summit" in Rio de Janeiro in 1992, where some

143 nations sent officials (two thirds of them heads of government), much grandiose rhetoric was offered, and several modest agreements were signed, but long-term influence over the world's environment was put in the hands of a new Global Environmental Facility, effectively controlled by the G-7 nations and administered by the World Bank, whose primary mission is to be continued industrial development within cursory ecological constraints. But such an outcome would not have come as a surprise to anyone who had followed the increasing supremacy of the World Bank in the global economy since the early 1980s, particularly its influence over the nations of the South, where (to take but one example) it had by 1990 forced more than seventy governments to sell off state-owned enterprises worth more than $185 billion to private, very often Western, corporations.

In short, what the major multinationals of the modern world have apparently achieved is not merely the nation-state grown servile, in its old 19th-century ways as well as new high-tech 20th-century ways, but nearly, except in the continued provision of money, impotent.

THE ORDEAL OF LABOR

The impact of technology on employment in all industrial nations has been dramatic and severe for the last two decades, but by the mid-1990s it was clear that what had been happening was evidence not of "a transitional or temporary or cyclical problem," as Stephen Roach, the chief economist of Morgan Stanley, has put it, but of "a lasting and structural problem." The problem is technology.

It is an axiom of capitalism that employers will try to lessen the expense of production in order to increase profits, and historically the easiest way has been to reduce labor costs, either by cutting the workforce or paying it less. With the advent of industrial technology in the 19th century it became possible to do both, and with the development of computer technology it became possible to do so across a wide range of employment and on a global scale.

The story of the last quarter century in the West is this "lasting and structural" displacement of labor by ever more sophisticated forms of automation, an acute reduction in farm and manufacturing jobs (U.S. manufacturing employment shrank from 29 percent of the workforce to less than 16 percent), and an increase in largely nonproductive "service" employment (16 percent to 27 percent), much of it low-paying, temporary, and insecure.

For most of the time the effect of this displacement has been disguised by government funding and government employment—the public trough, as it might be called—fueled by increasingly onerous debts. In the United States, for example, there was a steady expansion of jobs in all levels of government, in government services like schools, hospitals, prisons, and welfare, and in public boondoggles like the defense, aerospace, and computer industries. Those who were not absorbed by those means were kept by greatly expanded welfare, training, and entitlements programs. This took an immense amount of money, naturally, and it quickly drove the United States into becoming the world's largest debtor nation by 1985, as it ran up debts in quite mind-boggling trillion-dollar figures to try to keep it all together.

But the Ponzi scheme obviously couldn't last, and sometime in the mid-1980s it began to unravel, here and throughout the industrial world, effectively collapsing entirely with the end of the Cold War in 1989. Governments could no longer sustain their bloated budgets and mounting deficits, corporations under pressure from environmental and social obligations reduced payrolls further and sent jobs overseas, unemployment payouts and welfare costs grew steadily, and worldwide recession rolled across the industrial landscape. Beginning in about 1986, unemployment rates soared to 10 and 15 and in some cases 20 percent of the workforce, discouraged and no-longer-looking percentages were thought to be at least two or three times those figures, and underemployment and involuntary part-time work was pushing toward 50 percent. Technology and its relentless drive toward automation, coupled with its ability to move and control employment anywhere in the world, could finally be seen as the culprit, eliminating, as it was always intended to do, the annoying cost of production known as labor.

Now in theory—the theory first propounded during the British Industrial Revolution—technology, however many jobs it may eliminate in the short run, is supposed to increase them in the long. Factories and offices are supposed to be more productive, turning out more for less and less, stimulating a demand that should eventually require new jobs, either in the shops that expand to meet the new demand or in those that arise to produce and improve the new technologies themselves. (Or as Bill Clinton has put it, "We cannot turn away from the idea that modernization is the key to employment.") As we have seen, the cruel fact is that this theory does not work and never has—jobs have always been lost to technology, and war, colonialism, and government spending have been what created new ones—but in the crisis of the last decade it is clearer than ever that the technological trade-off is quite mythical.

To begin with, it is indisputable that automation has eliminated vast numbers of jobs across all sectors of the economy in all industrial nations, maybe 35 million of them in the last decade. The example of the United States, still the leading economic power in the world, is revealing. From 1988 to 1994 the number of jobs lost was estimated to be 6.5 million, far higher than in any other postwar period, and fully 85 percent of them are thought to be permanently lost to machines and overseas transfers. Automation is held to be responsible for the loss of half a million manufacturing jobs *every year* in this period and close to 3 million in the decade before—the completely automated factory is only a few quarters away—but it has also begun to make deep cuts into service jobs and seems likely to make its biggest future impact there. Most routinized service jobs have already been mechanized—bank tellers, data clerks, back-office filers, messengers, receptionists, elevator operators, gas pumpers, dishwashers—and new technologies will shortly displace at least 100,000 telephone operators and maybe as many as 3 million data typists, post-office sorters, and other human impedimenta. In fact, a 1992 Carnegie Institute study concluded that 6 million more manufacturing and no fewer than 38 million office jobs were at risk to automation, with no sign that anyone has any idea where to fit the displaced workers. As Wassily Leontief, the Nobel economist, has put it trenchantly, "The role of humans as the most important factor of production is bound to diminish"—and, he adds, "in the same way that the role of the horse in agriculture production was first diminished then eliminated by the introduction of tractors."

Bad enough, but the effects of technology go beyond automation. It is technology, and the fierce global competition it engenders, that forces the abandonment of product lines made unprofitable and the closing of plants made obsolete and indeed the elimination of entire industries made unprofitable—all with immense effects on employment, as American steelworkers and coal miners, among others, can attest. It is also this sort of competition that has caused the flight of so many factories and businesses from the industrial metropoles to outposts in East Asia and Latin America in particular, not merely for cheaper and more docile workforces but for newer and more efficient plant and machinery; new technology now enables home offices to establish direct and immediate communications with these distant workers, both white- and blue-collar, in any part of the world, effectively doing away with the need for any but a few executive jobs at home. As Western corporate investment overseas has increased dramatically in recent years—up by nearly 100 percent from 1987 to 1993—employment has automatically followed, and seems likely to reach a near stampede in the future if the purposes of the global free-trade agreements are fulfilled.

And all the new jobs that technology is supposed to create at home? They have simply not appeared, except in those few industries still sustained by government boondoggles. "Automation roars ahead, letting industries grow and prosper," as *The*

New York Times said on Labor Day 1993, "but no one sees the emerging industries that can take on the workers they are letting go." In the United States, large firms, even high-tech giants like IBM and Xerox, are getting rid of people at unprecedented rates—getting higher every year since 1986 and reaching an all-time high of 700,000 in 1994—and making it known that they have no intention of filling those slots again.

Moreover, most of the new jobs that have been created in the last decade are part-time and temporary jobs, with lower wages, reduced benefits, fewer hours, and no security—"disposable" jobs they are called because they exist at the whim of management, there when employers need them and gone as soon as computerization or a sales downturn makes them unnecessary. (Thus a neat parallel with the 19th-century handloom weavers, hired on for a pittance when factory capacity reached its limit, abandoned as soon as orders slackened.) According to the U.S. Labor Department some 46 million workers were stuck in these disposable jobs as of 1993—that's *40 percent* of the total workforce— and at least half of them were in the lowest-paying, least-protected slots, typically retail stores, restaurants, sweatshops, warehouses, supermarkets, and nonunion assembly lines. A 1993 *New York Times* front-page analysis called "Jobs Without Hope" said that what "makes this recovery different from any other" was that the "regular jobs that people would lose in past recessions and reclaim when business picked up" have simply disappeared.

Not quite disappeared: machines have them.

Only one last point need be added about the economic effect of what *Time* magazine (which a decade earlier had nominated the computer to be its "Machine of the Year") in 1993 called "the relentless and accelerating pace at which technology is changing work as well as every other aspect of life," and that is the below-the-line finality of income. Everywhere in the industrial world the split between rich and poor, professional and clerical, skilled and unskilled, is wide and widening. Computer technology enables a small number of highly educated and inventive and enterprising people to operate old businesses in new ways and new businesses in exponential ways, and many of these companies have generated fortunes in the past decade and will continue to do so; it also requires, for a time at least, a sizable workforce at the bottom of the heap in routinized and low-paying jobs in the electronic offices and factories. This produces two clear results. First, as the U.S. Census Bureau keeps reporting, the rich get richer and the poor get poorer: the most affluent 20 percent of the population took in 48 percent of the total income of the nation in 1993, while the bottom 20 percent got less than 4 percent, and this disparity has *increased,* by as much as 70 percent, every year in the last twenty years. Second, the middle stagnates and declines: median family income adjusted for inflation has not changed at all since 1973 (except for those under the age of 45, who earn about half of what their parents did) and 44 percent of the population had a decline in real income in the 1980–90 decade.

In 1992—as typical a year as any other—37 million Americans were below the official poverty line, 19 million more were below the line adjusted for real costs, 8 million were officially unemployed, 36 million were said to be discouraged from looking, and 46 million were in disposable jobs: it seems a slim triumph indeed if the nation has bought its microwaves and laptops and ATMs with this.

THE DESTRUCTION OF NATURE

It is characteristic of industrialism, of course, to make swift and thorough use of nature's stored-up treasures and its living organisms, called "resources," without regard to the stability or sustainability of the world that provides them—a process ratified by such industrial ideologies as humanism, which gives us the right, materialism, which gives us the reason, and rationalism, which gives us the method. But it was not until industrialism grew into its high-tech phase, with the immense power-multiplier of the computer, that this exploitation of resources escalated onto a new plane different not only in *degree,* with exhaustion, extermination, despoliation, and pollution at unprecedented and accelerating rates, but in *kind,* creating that technosphere so immanent in our lives, artificial, powerful, and global, and fundamentally at odds with the biosphere. What Carlyle saw as the economy's "war with Nature" in the 19th century has, like all warfare, become a vastly more thorough force in the 20th. That this has happened so quickly, effectively within a few decades, has prevented a true understanding of the fact and its magnitude, but it is undeniable, and undeniably tragic.

Voices of doom can be foolish and self-serving at times, and often misguided. But the array of such voices in recent years is so broad and deep that it is no longer possible for the sentient mind to disregard the doom inherent in the war between technosphere and biosphere, a contest in which the bad news is, in short, that we are winning. Out of that array I offer but two. In 1991 a worldwide gathering of environmentalists—scholars, scientists, activists, writers, tribal representatives—met in Morelia, Mexico, and at the end of a week of reports on the myriad threats to the earth issued a declaration warning bluntly of continuing "environmental destruction" and stating, "Independently, but without exception, each participant expressed concern that life on our planet is in grave danger." And in 1992, the U.S. Union of Concerned Scientists, in a statement endorsed by more than a hundred Nobel laureates and 1,600 members of national academies of science around the globe, proclaimed a "World Scientists' Warning to Humanity" stating that the present rates of environmental assault and population increase cannot continue without "vast human misery" and a planet so "irretrievably mutilated" that "it will be unable to sustain life in the manner that we know." These are sober voices, not alarmist, not self-interested, and if their somber words have not received the attention they deserve and the actions they demand, have in fact been overwhelmed in the

cacophony of a computerized culture, that affects their validity
not a whit.

The technosphere produces environmental costs in every
phase of its daily operation—extraction, cultivation, transportation, manufacture, production, storage, marketing, use, and dis-
posal—that are paid only by the biosphere. Some of them have
become glaring, the stuff of headlines: *resource depletion,* typified
by the loss of 26 billion tons of topsoil a year around the world,
and dwindling supplies of copper, lead, nickel, iron, bauxite,
mercury, zinc, phosphate, manganese, uranium, tin and tung-
sten, all of which, it is thought, will be exhausted within another
generation or so, even at present rates of use; *deforestation,* which
has so far laid bare two thirds of the earth's surface that was covered by trees when the first Industrial Revolution began, and is
proceeding now at the rate of 56 million acres a year and will
effectively deplete the world's old-growth forests in the next
decade; *pollution,* of air, water, groundcover, and soils, which has
already (among much else) wrought havoc with the ozone layer
and may change climate irretrievably, has damaged significant
sections of the oceans and the vital reefs within them, has made
half of the world's drinking water unhealthy or downright poison-
ous, and has destroyed whole species at an estimated rate of 5,000
a day in the last twenty years; *desertification,* which has already
made three quarters of the once-arable land of the earth into bar-
ren and dehydrated waste, and now threatens an additional 8 billion acres around the world. Some of the costs are less obvious:
overpopulation, which has nearly doubled the world's human
stock since the computer revolution began in 1971 and will, growing now at a rate three times as fast as ever before, expand it to 7
billion as early as 2010; *organochlorine poisoning,* from a wide variety of industrial chemicals, which has clearly affected both male
and female reproductive systems worldwide and is thought to be
the cause of a 300 percent increase in testicular cancer in men in
the United States since 1983 and a drop in the sperm count of 42
percent in men throughout the industrial world; *depletion of*

fishing stocks in every part of the world's oceans, despite increasing bans and regulations, to the point that in 1994 thirteen of
the seventeen major fisheries were regarded as being in serious
decline and not more than a decade away from exhaustion; and
consumption of photosynthetic energy, the basis of all life on the
planet, by a single species—the human—at a rate that now
assigns nearly 40 percent of the basic global food supply to ourselves, leaving all other plants and animals to use the rest, a per-
centage that is increasing every year.

Now these and similar calamities have been well established
over the last thirty years, surveyed and verified, and presented to
the world by various media, and some have even been made the
subject of laws and regulations worldwide. But not one of them
has been halted, not even significantly slowed: as the Worldwatch
Institute put it in 1993, there is not one life-support system upon
which the biosphere depends for its existence that is not severely
threatened and getting worse. The pace and range of the technosphere, it seems, is unstoppable, as if it had a will of its own that
no form of public protest or restrictive rule or moral caveat could
appreciably affect, as if it were literally unable to understand that
the planet cannot perpetually absorb its wastes like some infinite
sink, that the destruction of nature's species and systems cannot
proceed forever without bitter consequences. Before this altar of
the god of Progress, attended by its dutiful acolytes of science
and technology, our modern society has presented an increasing
abundance of sacrifices from the natural world, and now we seem
prepared even to offer up the very biosphere itself.

This is not accidental. It is inherent in the machines themselves that this high-tech civilization has chosen to express itself
with—above all the computer. Computers are designed to work
by a kind of linear, fact-based logic that is the language of science,
to fulfill the scientific desire for understanding and ordering
nature, ultimately reducing all its "secrets" to reductive analysis
and manipulation; but more than that, they are designed to give
humans not merely analytical but physical control over nature,

putting all its elements to human use wherever possible, altering its systems and even its species for human enhancement, ultimately changing its atoms to create new compounds and life forms for human aggrandizement. The fact that they can go such a long way to achieving what they are designed to do is stark evidence of the technological imperative at work: if we *can* destroy this only living planet, as von Neumann might have put it, we will.

One last characteristic of the second Industrial Revolution, which has no exact parallel with the first, is *the instability of global society.* Not that early industrialism was without global effects, or impoverishment and warfare in far-flung lands, but because both population and development were on such a smaller scale it did not create as great inequalities and disparities, or the resulting social dislocations and bloody conflicts, as the current industrialism has.

In the two centuries between industrial revolutions the population of the world has grown from about 950 million (1800) to around 6.2 billion (2000), a species bloom of 650 percent totally unprecedented in the earth's history, and due almost exclusively to the products and priorities of industrialism. But even though the earth has been plundered repeatedly and increasingly to sustain this immense throng, there has never been enough to go around—or, put another way, there has never been the will to divide it equally. As of 1990 it was estimated that at least a billion of these people live in abject poverty and another 2 billion eke out life on a bare subsistence level. Another billion and a half, it is thought, live modest lives on incomes under $5000 a year, part of the commodity economy but without being able to accumulate enough land or wealth to leave anything to their children. And a billion people enjoy a dissipative life at various levels of prosperity, having what is called a higher standard of living, measured by material accumulation and the prolongation of life, including two hundred (U.S. dollar) billionaires and more than 3 million millionaires.

This inequality, an inherent consequence of industrialism, and to a degree unknown before, has been greatly increased rather than lessened since the advent of the second Industrial Revolution. Not only, as we have seen, have disparities grown within every nation, as some enjoy the fruits of modernism and many receive only the pit of a life beyond childhood, but in a most pronounced way they have grown between nations, as the industrialized states of West Europe, North America, and East Asia, containing a quarter of the world's population, command 85 percent of the world's personal income, and the other 4.5 billion divide the remaining 15 percent. The gap between rich nation and poor, already alarming at the end of World War II, has more than doubled since then; in 1960 countries of the North were twenty times richer than those of the South; in 1990 they were fifty times richer. And no amount of aid, trade, lending, or catch-up industrialization seems able to change or even slow down that differentiation.

For forty years it has been the professed policy of the industrial West to try to close the gap by what it calls the "development" of the rest of the world's nations, by which is meant their adoption of industrialism and the thoughts, philosophies, practices, and products of the Western monoculture, with the express purpose of assisting them to the "take-off" stage where they might develop thriving industrial economies of their own. This attempt has been a dismal failure. Westernization has indeed penetrated everywhere, with a resulting loss of cultural, linguistic, and social diversity and the destruction of age-old tribal and communitarian societies, but with minor exceptions the poor nations have not become rich—and in fact, though it is kept quiet by the benefactors, there has been a continuing net flow of money from the poorest nations to the richest, amounting to $19 billion by 1993. The actual products of "development" have been greater disparities of income within the less-developed lands, increased emigration, a sharp rise in illicit trade (particularly drugs), a catastrophic growth of urban excrescences, repeated internal clashes and coups usually ending with military control, and everywhere an immense assault on natural species and systems that is destroying forests, farmlands, and fisheries, all in the name of progress, at an alarming and unsustainable rate. "Development," far from increasing wealth and happiness, has turned out to be a modern plague.

There is no chance that the rich-poor gap can be reduced by Western aid, global trade, or any other form of industrial expansion. This is because the industrial nations already consume almost all of the earth's available treasures—more than 75 percent of its chemicals, paper, iron, aluminum, timber and energy every year—and there is no way that the rest of the world, with its huge populations, will be able to live at that level because the resources simply do not exist. Nor could the earth's environment, already so threatened, possibly survive an attempt to do so: if the billion-plus people of China, for example, were to achieve living standards at American technological levels they would be adding 20 billion tons of carbon pollution to the atmosphere each year, more than three times the amount now so polluting the globe and threatening severe climatic change. Thus the conclusion, the awful truth that must lie at the heart of industrialism, is that inequalities, within nations and between, must exist and persist, in fact must grow.

There is another, attendant truth: societies, singly and together, cannot survive such inequalities long without severe disruption. This is why so many countries in the last two decades have fallen into civil war, tribal and ethnic conflict, rebellion and revolt, civil unrest and sheer disintegration, at such alarming and unprecedented rates; this is why the number of wars and skirmishes being fought in 1990–94 was greater than at any other period since the end of World War II; this is why the number of refugees around the world has mounted steadily during this same period and stood at an all-time high of at least 50 million people in the mid-1990s. Just how long it will be until those disruptions begin to spill across the borders into the major industrial countries, how long poor people will endure the death from hunger of 40,000 of their children every year without blaming those nations where obesity is a serious health problem, is an open question, but pending. Just how long it will be before the have-not castes of the developed nations, tired of the thin pap from the hindmost teat and no longer pacified by alcohol, drugs, sports, TV, police, and religion, will direct their anger, and weapons, at the have-much castes, is also open, also pending. But they are questions that the increasing disparities of the world make no longer unaskable.

Suppose the second Industrial Revolution were to be judged by the standards historians tend to use for any revolution in human affairs, like the French, or the Agricultural. Has it brought more happiness than there was before? More social justice? Democracy? Equality? Efficiency? Were its means benign, or legitimate? Its ends valuable, or consistent? At what price have its benefits been won, and are they sustainable?

The record, so far, is not very positive. The best that could be said for it is that it has increased material prosperity among that favored fifth, increased the flow of capital and information around the world, and enabled perhaps a third to be born and survive to somewhat greater ages. Three fifths of the remainder are forced into an existence marked primarily by deprivation, often by wretched misery, probably at levels never known to them, however inequitable their past, before the 20th century. Those who live at the top, with material power unparalleled in history, might be assumed to be happier than they were a generation ago, except that no social indices validate that assumption in any advanced society, and some evidence exists—increased rates of stress, depression, mental illness, alcoholism, drug dependency, crime, divorce, occupational disease, political anomie— that seems to contradict it.

Neither the means nor ends of this revolution make any pretense to nobility, nor does it claim to have a vision much grander than that of prosperity, perhaps longevity, both of which have seriously damaging environmental consequences. By and large its adherents would disclaim grand-sounding motives or methods, arguing them irrelevant: enough that progress may be presumed meritorious and material affluence desirable and longer life posi- tive. If industrialism is the working out in economic terms of certain immutable laws of science and technology, of human evo- lution, the questions of benign-malignant hardly apply. Those who want to wring hands at this inequity or that injustice are essentially irrelevant, whether or not they are correct: the terms of the game are material betterment for as many as possible, as much as possible as fast as possible, and matters of morality or appropriateness are really considerations of a different game.

Viewing the issue on its own terms, the question would then seem to come down to the practical one of the price by which the second Industrial Revolution has been won and whether it is too high, or soon will prove to be. The burden of this chapter is that there are no two ways of answering that question: the price, par- ticularly in social decay and environmental destruction, has been unbearably high, and neither the societies nor ecosystems of the world will be able to bear it for more than a few decades longer, if they have not already been overstressed and impoverished beyond redemption.

9

The Neo-Luddites

IN MARCH 1990, a New Mexico psychologist named Chellis Glendinning published "Notes toward a Neo-Luddite manifesto," an attempt to give legitimacy to those who in one way or another are troubled by, and resistant to, the technology of the second Industrial Revolution, and to prepare the ground for a statement that would articulate their critique and goals.

"Neo-Luddites have the courage to gaze at the full catastrophe of our century," she began, which is that "the technologies created and disseminated by modern Western societies are out of control and desecrating the fragile fabric of life on Earth." And to underscore the link of present with past, she added, "Like the early Luddites, we too are a desperate people seeking to protect the livelihoods, communities, and families we love, which lie on the verge of destruction."

Arguing that effective resistance to this destruction "requires not just regulating or eliminating individual items like pesticides or nuclear weapons" but "new ways of thinking" and "the creation of a new worldview," she set out three basic principles of neo-Luddism:

    1. Opposition to technologies "that emanate from a worldview that sees rationality as the key to human potential, material acquisition as the key to human fulfillment, and technological development as the key to social progress."

2. Recognition that, since "all technologies are political, the technologies created by mass technological society, far from being
   "neutral tools that can be used for good or evil," inevitably are
   "those that serve the perpetuation" of that society and its goals
   of efficiency, production, marketing, and profits.

3. Establishment of a critique of technology by "fully examining
   its sociological context, economic ramifications, and political
   meanings . . . from the perspective not only of human use" but
   of its impact "on other living beings, natural systems, and the
   environment."

She ended with a "program for the future" that envisioned "the
dismantling" of nuclear, chemical, biogenetic, electromagnetic,
television, and computer technologies; the creation of new technologies, by those who "use them and are affected by them," that
promote "political freedom, economic justice, and ecological balance," community-based, decentralized, organic, and cooperative; and the achievement of a "life-enhancing worldview" that
would let "Western technological societies restructure their mechanistic projections and foster the creation of machines, techniques, and social organizations that respect both human dignity
and nature's wholeness."

"We have nothing to lose except a way of living that leads to
the destruction of all life," she concluded. "We have a world to gain."

Glendinning's remarkable document was inspired by her
experiences in writing a book she had finished only a few months
before called *When Technology Wounds,* the result of an in-depth
study of what she called "technology survivors," people who had
suffered injury or illness in recent years after being exposed to
various toxic technologies in their homes and workplaces. All had
succumbed to technological assault inflicted under the guise of
some advance of progress or other—nuclear radiation, pesticides,
asbestos, birth-control devices, drugs—and they had all begun to
question not only the processes that maimed them but the world
that forced those processes on them with such unfounded prom-

ise and such blithe indifference. These people know, "in the most intimate and compelling way," Glendinning found,

> what dangerous technologies can do to life. They know the disrup-
> tion, loss, and uncertainty. They feel the breach of trust, and these
> experiences can catalyze them to question accepted beliefs about
> technological progress. . . . They see them as symptoms of a whole
> system gone awry.

This is what made Glendinning think of the original Luddites, people who similarly suffered from technology, saw themselves as the victims in a "system gone awry," and were engaged in "an ideological struggle" against an onrush of progress that was a threat to "longlived social relations." These modern-day survivors were, as she saw it, legitimately in the Luddite line, part of a new Luddistic movement.

The idea that there might be such a movement right here in the Land of Technophilia is not as far-fetched as it might seem at first, for the second Industrial Revolution has always had its critics and skeptics, always had an underside of anxiety and distrust. Even in the societies that have succumbed to the new technologies most fervently—or perhaps especially there—a persistent feeling of disquiet, edging toward fear, has always existed about their immense power and sweep, their capacity for accident and misuse.

In part this anxiety goes back to the 1950s and the reaction, at the fringes of the culture at least, to science's awesome and awful achievements at Hiroshima and in the German death camps. Postwar science fiction was dominated by notions of technology gone awry, either out of control or in the hands of evil forces, and postwar films, particularly of the horror genre, by stories of irradiated monsters or invasions by outer-space species even more technologically developed than earthlings. The apprehension was fed by revelations of environmental dangers in the 1960s and '70s—DDT and other everyday chemicals, oil spills, cigarettes, PCBs, toxic wastes, radiation leaks, and so on—which called the

wisdom and the truth of scientists, experts, and official government sources into question, producing a partial dissociation from
the ruling technocracy for many. At the same time a considerable
coterie of disenchanted intellectuals on both sides of the Atlantic
produced the analyses that served to challenge the technocratic
mainstream: Lewis Mumford beyond all others, particularly with
his masterful *Myth of the Machine (Technics and Human Development,* 1967, and *The Pentagon of Power,* 1970), Paul Goodman,
Jacques Ellul, E. F. Schumacher, W. H. Ferry, George Parkin
Grant, Rachel Carson, Ivan Illich, Herbert Marcuse, Doris
Lessing, Robert Jungk, Henry Geiger, and some few others.

When the 1980s brought the two most disastrous failures of
modern technology to date, the 1984 Bhopal plant explosion in
India and the 1986 Chernobyl nuclear plant disaster in Ukraine,
followed by revelations of global warming and destruction of the
ozone layer, both by technological by-products that had once
been touted as harmless, the sphere of disquiet and apprehension
certainly enlarged, global now in scope and touching all levels of
society. Again this was reflected in several elements of popular
culture, in the novels of Kurt Vonnegut, Thomas Pynchon,
Farley Mowat, and Edward Abbey, and particularly in movies like
ET, War Games, Gremlins, and above all *Return of the Jedi,* the cli-
max of the *Star Wars* series. (In which, be it remembered, the triumph of the natural, not to say the primitive, over the machine is
manifest in the Ewoks' use of sticks and stones to defeat the
supertechnocratic forces of the Evil Empire.) And again there was
the learned support of a new wave of technology critics, now
from an even wider range of disciplines and with even greater
impact, academics like Langdon Winner, Stanley Diamond, and
David Noble, ecologists like Edward Goldsmith, David Ehrenfeld, and Arne Naess, activists like Dave Foreman and Jeremy
Rifkin, and Wendell Berry, Jerry Mander, Carolyn Merchant,
John Zerzan, Theodore Roszak, Susan Griffin, Gary Snyder, Paul
Brodeur, Stephanie Mills, Thomas Berry, Bill McKibben, Paul

Shepard, and a surprising number of others, trenchant and occasionally widely received commentators.

Within this context, then, it is not surprising that we should be able to identify something that, if perhaps not always so purposeful as a movement, gives expression in many ways and with growing force to a range of ideas and sentiments that are unquestionably Luddistic. If this neo-Luddism is apt to demonstrate its resistance to technology and the forces of modernism behind it less by actual machine breaking than by opposing the corporation making the machines, nevertheless it is directly linked to the spirit of King Ludd and to the underlying motives and causes of his original followers.

This contemporary neo-Luddism, strongest and most self-conscious in the United States but indeed global in scope, can be seen to span a considerable spectrum—ranging from narrow single-issue concerns to broad philosophical analyses, from aversion to resistance to sabotage, with much diversity in between—that is pertinent to examine at some length.

It can start with those of Glendinning's "survivors" who have organized to send out warnings about technological assaults (almost always denied by the assaulters, usually for decades) and have successfully formed a variety of networks to trade information, plan strategies, raise funds, hire experts, and fight legal battles. There are probably three dozen such groups on a national scale in the United States alone, among them the Asbestos Victims of America, Aspartame Victims and Their Friends, Citizens Against Pesticide Misuse, Dalkon Shield Information Network, DES Action National, National Association of Atomic Veterans, National Committee for Victims of Human Research, National Toxics Campaign, and the VDT Coalition. Their members are people who in the course of healing their own wounds have come to a Luddistic sensibility that the problem lies not only with the particular industrial "advance" inflicted on them but with the

wider addiction of society to what one DES mother calls "technological hubris." Or, as one man who got lung cancer after
exposure to asbestos on the job put it to Glendinning, "What I
learned is that our technology is killing us."

Next along the spectrum are members of those groups that
have grown up to resist one computer age technology or other
not as victims but as concerned and fearful citizens—as for
example the campaigns against toxic wastes, biotechnology, incin-
eration, pesticides, clear-cut logging, automobiles, animal testing,
and industrial chemicals. The most successful here have been the
antinuclear activists who have been opposing nuclear weapons
and nuclear power for decades, and more recently nuclear wastes.
Their tactics have included everything from mass marches and
demonstrations to scientific papers and legal suits, and some have
had a distinctly Luddite air: the attack by a woman in 1987
against a missile-system computer at the Vandenberg Air Force
Base in California with a crowbar, bolt cutters, and a hammer,
for example, and the fifty "Plowshare" actions since 1980 in
which pacifists have used hammers and paint to attack planes,
missiles, submarines, and weapons at various military bases. The
reasons for the comparative success of the nuclear-power part of
this movement, particularly in the United States, where no new
nuclear plants have even been commissioned since 1978, are especially instructive: for one thing, it managed always to show the
connections between nuclear reactors and the larger industrial
culture, its militarism (nuclear weapons), its pollution (nuclear
wastes), and its authoritarianism (planning power stations without public participation); for another, it could always point to the
"worst-case scenario" of the obliteration of two Japaneses cities by
nuclear explosions, whereas most other technologies are introduced in clouds of unequivocal acclaim without their dangers or
difficulties ever being so fully exposed. Thus it has been one of
the few movements that can actually claim to have retarded, if
not altogether halted, a major technology favored by the powers
that be.

Another kind of opposition has been directed not against whole technologies as such but against specific projects on the general high-tech menu. In the United States, for example, active resistance, in some cases with explicit Luddistic overtones, has been directed against the supersonic transport plane, synthetic fuels, the antiballistic missile system, the supercollider, the Strategic Defense Initiative, food irradiation, bovine growth hormone, and any number of high-tech dam projects. Even with a Congress willing to buy into almost any technological boondoggle, and corporate and big-science establishments promising moons, victories have been won in a remarkable number of instances, most notably against the SST and supercollider projects and dams in Grand Canyon and James Bay. The surprisingly vigorous opposition to the North American Free Trade Agreement as it was being extended to Mexico in 1993—shown in some polls to be joined by two thirds of the public—was another project-specific fight, and specifically Luddistic in that so much of it was instigated by a fear over a loss of jobs to a Mexico where not only are wages lower but resistance to new labor-displacing technologies is negligible. In that opposition, accounting for an unusual alliance between Ross Perot conservatives and liberal populists, was also a strong sense that only powerful multinational corporations stood to benefit, a tacit comprehension that in the industrial culture it is the corporation, the technological form created by 19th-century industry, that reaps the rewards.

Something of that same sense animated similar protests in Europe against two specific agreements that were seen as promoting large-scale technocratic, particularly antitraditional and anti-local, interests, destroying regional and communal associations and doing away with jobs and pastimes that have endured for centuries. The first, resistance to the European Union formed in 1992, was expressed in many countries throughout the subcontinent—most vociferously in Scandinavia, Ireland, and Britain—and the Maastricht Treaty certifying that union was passed by very narrow majorities and only after dubious high-pressure

campaigns by corporate and government forces. This was followed by even greater opposition to the General Agreement on
Tariffs and Trade, widely viewed as a boon to corporations that
could cross borders in a nanosecond and move jobs and products
and profits around the world at their whim, leaving workers and
communities at their mercy. Here protests broke out into active
demonstrations against the Uruguay-round provisions, most viv-
idly in France in 1992 and 1993. French farmers, their existence
threatened by agribusiness provisions in GATT that would do away
with the subsidies that have kept them small and independent,
set up barricades of burning tires and hay bales, or ran their
trucks across the road to disrupt traffic, sometimes clashing with
police; and they were at the core of the 40,000 farmers from all
over Europe and parts of Asia that massed before the European
Parliament in Strasbourg in December 1992 to burn an effigy of
the U.S. GATT negotiator for agriculture policy. They were naturally derided in press and parliament for being Luddites, anti-
modern and antiprogress—and in some real sense they are,
arguing for other values than those of capitalist enterprise, including rural communities and rural lifeways, just as their English
predecessors had—but, confoundingly, this stance met with
enough sympathy to win them wide popular support and help
them gain some concessions on subsidies in the final agreement.

It is in the non-Western countries, however, where GATT's effects
are likely to be most strongly felt—free trade, we must remember, is free only for those who run the trade—and where the
greatest protests have been waged in recent years, and it is here
that today we most often see a clash of industrial modernity and
organic tradition that bears many resemblances to the experience
of the original Luddites. Farmers in Korea, India, Ceylon, and
Malaysia have marched, demonstrated, and petitioned against
GATT provisions that they see as allowing a "genetic invasion"
from the West, enabling such American grain-marketing giants as
Cargill and W. R. Grace to appropriate indigenous seeds and

species, alter them in some minor way, and then patent and sell the resulting variety back to the farmers, even forcing them to pay royalties. In India the Cargill offices in Bangalore were raided in 1992 and its files set on fire, a Cargill seed factory under construction was burned down in June 1993, and in October 1993 half a million people demonstrated in the state of Karnataka against the GATT provisions, the largest outcry against the effects of free trade—and specifically against the incursion of multinational technologies—anywhere in the world.

Indeed, it has been in the non-Western world that the Luddite spirit has been particularly vigorous in recent years against the industrial world's invasions, very often led by indigenous peoples who are trying to resist not only the machines and projects of industrialism but its culture as well. Peasants have refused to take part in various "development" schemes foisted on them by pliant governments usually at the behest of the World Bank or U.S. State Department, as for example the farmers in Mali in the early 1980s who destroyed dams and dikes being built for a rice-growing program they wanted no part of. Communities have mobilized to stop dam projects that threatened to drown their age-old settlements, sometimes successfully, as in the case of the villagers who protested the Narmada Dam in India in the early 1990s, sometimes less so in many other cases, as with the people of eastern Java who marched against the Nipah irrigation dam that was to flood their homeland, four of whom were killed by Indonesian security forces in 1993. Tribes have organized to fight tree-cutting and road-building schemes that invaded their territories, most famously with the Chipko "tree-hugging" movement in India in the 1970s and '80s, which eventually halted government clear-cutting efforts there; similar protests have also taken place in Malaysia, Australia, Brazil, Costa Rica, Solomon Islands, and Indonesia, among others. And at places all around the Indian subcontinent, in Malaysia and Indonesia, and several ports along the Pacific shore of South America, including Ecuador and Colombia, traditional fishermen have taken actions against industrial fishing fleets invading their waters and threatening their catch, even ambushing and setting fire to the mechanized trawlers in several instances.

These kinds of protest actions do not necessarily involve the destruction of machinery, though sabotage is not unknown (as in the destruction of a high-tech chemical plant in Thailand in 1986), but the motivating sentiment behind them is exactly Luddistic in its desire to maintain a traditional way of life and livelihood, in the face of an industrial capitalism that intends to draw them into a wage-and-market system. A more exact parallel is found in a story from eastern India (there are probably many such, but few become international news) of a joint Indian-Australian mining project at Piparwar, on the Damodar River. People there have been resisting outside destruction of their cultures for two centuries—what used to be done to them in the name of "civilization" is now done in the name of "development"—but in the late 1980s the Indian government forced many of them off the common lands from which they had wrested a self-sufficient living for generations and began opening up the hillsides for highly mechanized—and highly polluting—coal extraction. The project naturally promised jobs to the locals, an available workforce now that their lands had been confiscated, but in the event only a few of the positions were for unskilled workers and most of the men had to be assigned to other government projects outside the region, forced to leave their families behind. One of the few nonmechanized jobs available was loading coal onto railway cars at a siding, which men would do with large baskets on their heads, but late in 1990 this task too was mechanized. The affected workers and some fifteen thousand local supporters immediately began a ten-day sit-in, stopping all work at the siding, and did not resume work again until January. On January 22, when some of the workers started loading coal with baskets, ignoring the detested machinery, company officials called in the police, who opened fire on the crowd, killing one man and wounding six. Sometime in the next two days the mechanical loaders were disabled (one would like to think by the great Enoch hammers, though the means are not specified), but they were eventually repaired or replaced and, despite protests at the site for the next two years, the coal loaders, like the croppers, were out of work forever.

This kind of resistance in the non-Western countries has led one writer, Claude Alvares, a Goa-born journalist and farmer, to argue recently that "it is the luddite response of the third world that is the most instructive and indicative of future directions." He believes that it is against "the dual oppression of science and development" that this Luddite opposition will be mounted and that the power behind such a movement comes on the one hand from traditional religious beliefs that reject the "scientific ratio-nality" of the West and on the other from a general antagonism to "further colonization of popular consciousness" at levels both popular and intellectual in all these countries. Indeed, he is impressed enough by such resistance to predict that these forces are powerful enough to succeed in defeating some projects of the Western nations in the short run and that "eventually all may suc-ceed, aided by modern science's own crumbling foundations."

There is no question that an anti-Western sentiment and dis-enchantment with Western industrial culture has informed many of the rebellious movements in parts of that "third world" in recent decades. In all the Moslem fundamentalist movements, from Morocco to Pakistan, a pronounced anti-Western strain operates as well as a thoroughgoing critique of Western rational-ism and science, even if it seldom extends to a rejection of Israeli machine guns or American oil rigs or Japanese transistor radios. And some of the armed uprisings in such places as Somalia, Algeria, Egypt, Nepal, Indonesia, Central America, and the Phil-ippines have stated their opposition to Western industrialism, its specific corporate agents, and the regimes forcing it upon them. A leader of the Zapatista rebellion in Mexico, for example—which began, not coincidentally, on the day that NAFTA became official, January 1, 1994—was explicit in announcing its effort as "against the whole neo-liberal project in Latin America," by which he meant foreign trade, privatization of state enterprises, agriculture for export rather than local consumption, and free-market capitalism. It may be that such sentiments are only contributary as motive forces in these rebellions, but there seems no doubt that antipathy to the industrial nations' "neo-liberal project" plays a role seldom acknowledged.

But it is not only in the non-Western world that examples from this part of the neo-Luddite spectrum are to be found. In the West, and even in the North American core, protest against industrialism in general and environmental onslaughts in particular has spawned an active resistance that goes by the name of "ecotage."

Starting in the 1970s, environmentalists of several stripes began to sabotage the machinery and products connected with industrial projects that threatened to invade wilderness areas, clear-cut old-growth forests, block free-running rivers, or interfere with settled lives and homes. In the mid-1970s farm families in northern Minnesota, in protest against power lines that represented both health and environmental risks, used bolt cutters to try to topple the electric towers being forced through their area and were defeated only by arrests, beatings, and a daily police presence. A few years later a man in Chicago known only as "the Fox" drew some attention with his environmental sabotage, plugging polluting factory smokestacks and shutting off industrial waste-drain systems without ever being caught.

It was in the 1980s, though, that ecotage was raised to an art, largely through the efforts of Earth First!, a radical environmental organization whose slogan was "No compromise in defense of Mother Earth." Its strategy was to stop environmental intrusions by any means available, legal and otherwise, including slashing tires and disabling engines of earth-moving machines used to cut timber roads, blocking roads to prevent logging trucks from entering wilderness areas, and, most famously, drilling spikes into trees in wilderness forests to prevent them being logged by chain-saws. The specific purpose of these actions, as outlined in the group's freely available publications (their works were printed, not coincidentally, by Ned Ludd Books and their bookshop carried T-shirts saying "Ned Ludd Lives!"), was "the dismantling of the present industrial system," as one Earth Firster said (shortly before being arrested for trying to topple an electric-power tower), not just to protect nature but to "throw a monkey wrench" into the industrial machine. They have not quite achieved that, although one estimate in 1990 was that they were doing the industrial system between $20 million and $30 million worth of damage a year.

Other environmental groups have also employed forms of eco-tage in these years. Some animal-rights groups invaded laboratories where animal experiments were being performed, destroying cages and other equipment and in most cases freeing the animals when they could. Activists protesting the hunting of seals and seal cubs in the Arctic disabled hunters' vehicles and in one instance attacked and disarmed a group of men employed to club seals to death. Perhaps the most outstanding work of this kind has been done by Paul Watson and his Sea Shepherd Conservation Society, which has taken responsibility for incapacitating at least seven vessels engaged in illegally hunting whales, including sinking two of Iceland's four whaling ships in Reykjavik harbor in 1986 and inflicting $2 million worth of damage on the country's whale-processing plant; Sea Shepherd has also used ecotage against ships hunting for dolphins in Japanese waters and loggers attempting to clear-cut Canadian forests.

Ecotage has also surfaced elsewhere in the industrial world, sometimes spontaneously, sometimes in direct imitation of American Earth First! tactics. In Australia protesters challenging the cutting of the Big Scrub forest in New South Wales in the 1980s tied cables between trees in the hopes of disabling earth-moving equipment and camped out in trees to prevent their being cut, actions that eventually forced the government to make the forest a national park; elsewhere, damage to heavy equipment said to amount to more than $1 million forced some timber contractors to close down. In Europe protests against nuclear power plants have involved ecotage against power lines and transmitters at sites in France, Germany, Portugal, and Scandinavia, and a Basque attack on a nuclear station in Bilbao in the late 1970s was said to have done more than $70 million worth of damage and caused the death of two plant workers. Spontaneous actions by villagers in both Spain and France have led to the sabotage of heavy equipment at several places where locals objected to high-tech plants being built in their areas.

About here on the spectrum one might expect to find those who, directly affected by automation and technical displacement, have turned to forms of sabotage at least as inventive as the environmentalists' in trying to secure their jobs and livelihoods. In fact, though, the economic dislocations of the second Industrial Revolution are taking place with—so far—very little of the indignant fire and fierceness that marked the first.

It is true that in the earliest days of automation in the United States in the late 1950s, some union protests were effective in slowing down the pace of worker displacement or, more often, in providing compensation for those laid off as a result—the 1959 steel union strike of 116 days was largely over this issue, and was largely successful—but there was never any serious attempt to attack the machines themselves. And in the second wave of automation in the early 1970s there were isolated incidents of resistance that occasionally included sabotage, the most famous being at the General Motors assembly plant in Lordstown, Ohio, in 1970, where workers used "creative sabotage" to disrupt parts of the new automated production system for nearly a year, and at *The Washington Post* in October 1975, when pressmen threatened with the loss of their jobs to computer-run "cold type" technology broke into the pressroom and damaged most of the old hot-type presses. But these incidents, though having clear overtones of Luddism (*Time* called the *Post* pressmen "Washington Lud-dites"), were not made part of any larger union campaign and were isolated because they failed to build this instance of techno-logical displacement into a larger political issue about the general impact of technology in the workplace.

There was enough workplace resistance to automation by this time, however, to prompt the federal government to devise a national policy. "The impact of technology has been acutely felt by the blue-collar workers," reported a special Health, Education, and Welfare task force in 1973, resulting in markedly low pro-ductivity, "as measured by absenteeism, turnover rates, wildcat strikes, sabotage, poor quality products, and a reluctance of work-ers to commit themselves to their work tasks." The corporate response, HEW advised, should be to give workers thus threat-ened more "participation" in decision-making and to reassure them about the positive gains in productivity that "will come about mainly through the introduction of new technology."

Remarkably, American workers and their unions bought in to this strategy almost without a peep. One after another, unions threatened with sharp job losses from automation sought merely to ensure that the bulk of the workers who would be fired would have financial cushions and the rest of them "participation." The longshoremen's union, for example, once one of the most power-ful, rolled over in the face of automation, negotiated handsome deals by which their workers would get guaranteed annual wages for life whether they were on the job or not, and allowed ship-ping companies (strongly backed by the Pentagon) to use con-tainerization on the docks and cut the workforce by 90 percent. There was no protest from the ranks, no sabotage by loading hook, and the union proceeded complacently, as one rank-and-filer later observed, to "run interference for the new technology." As it happened, the union very quickly became powerless as the shipping companies expanded their profits and operations, the few remaining men on the job (mostly crane operators) were given less and less responsibility, eventually succumbing to computerization

themselves, and the lively shoreside communities that once surrounded the work sites and hiring halls (cf. *On the Waterfront*)
atrophied and died. (A decade later, longshore union leaders
eventually acknowledged that the whole thing had been a mistake.) Whether by agreement or coercion, the American workforce quite quickly succumbed to mechanization, with only a
brief flurry of strikes in the early 1970s to show its resistance.
In 1974, the number of strikes reached its highest level since
the 1930s—with automation at the core of many of them—but
the number of walkouts and of workers involved plummeted
sharply after that, down to less than half the 1974 figure by 1980,
and a tenth by 1990. Unions, diminished, were increasingly
impotent—in 1994 they represented just 13 percent of the workforce—and the second Industrial Revolution swept on as powerfully as the first.

Of course isolated examples of machine breaking in the workplace can be found, corks bobbing in the ocean. Many plant and
office managers will tell, off the record, stories of petty sabotage
of new machines that either deskill tasks or permit speedups, but
they try to keep news of such actions from spreading around to
other workers and only rarely is it publicized. Occasionally a few
stories surface, like the one about a computer in the Department
of Justice in Washington that was disabled by being saturated
with urine, or the farmworkers in California who put sand in the
gas tank and incapacitated one of the first automatic tomato-
pickers. But nowhere on the record is there any serious concerted
machine breaking challenge to the new technologies of the computer revolution, not even from the 6 million people terminated
in the doldrum years of 1988–93, most of whom did not find
other comparable work.

Somewhat more opposition surfaced in Europe and Australia
as computerization took hold there in the 1970s and early 1980s,
largely because the union movements were traditionally stronger,
but even there the usual weapon was only the strike and the usual
outcome defeat. In Australia telecommunications workers went

on strike in 1977 against a new computer system that threatened a number of jobs—"Our members will not move over for a computer," the union boasted—and an officer of one of the unions even summoned up "that spectre, that special understanding of the Luddite Martyrs" now "coming back to haunt the heirs of those who transported them in irons to the shores of Botany Bay." That dispute ended in a brief moratorium on new machines; but the computers were eventually installed with a few job-termination trade-offs. In England, workers at the Lucas Aerospace plant, famous for their attempts in 1980–81 to convert their work from military to civilian products, were also involved in efforts to influence the pace and design of new computerized machines in their shops, but the best they too could get was a moratorium that lasted less than a year. In Denmark, when in 1982 municipal workers in the town of Farum struck to demand veto power over new technology, they gave expression to an idea that was quite widespread then in Scandinavia, although their central union and the government refused to support their action and it eventually collapsed. In the end, the failure of central unions to align themselves against new technologies turned out to be as common, and as devastating, in Europe as it was in the United States.

A study carried out in the 1950s by Clark Kerr and a team of scholars and published in 1960 as *Industrialism and Industrial Man* found that "protest was not such a dominant aspect of industrialization, and it did not have such an effect on the course of society, as we once thought." Everywhere around the world, they found, resistance to industrialism, whether the machine or the factory or the culture, is likely only at the start and only where traditional values are strong and communities intact. But in light of the sophisticated ways that corporations have to control or suppress protest, workers tend to concentrate more on how to accommodate to the industrial order and get a share of its pie. "Experience has tempered visionary aspirations and sobered expectations" among all types of workers, they concluded, "thereby constraining worker protest." In the succeeding thirty-five years their analysis has held largely true, and there's no reason to think it won't hold for the near future as well.

Last along the spectrum comes a diverse set of social critics, activists and intellectuals for the most part, who accept the neo-Luddite label without demur and are consciously working to adapt certain of the Luddite fundamentals to contemporary politics. A good many of them have been drawn into a loose "neo-Luddite" group first put together in 1993 by the Foundation for Deep Ecology in San Francisco, coordinated by two antitechnology veterans, Jerry Mander, the author of *Four Arguments for the Elimination of Television* and *In the Absence of the Sacred,* a scathing attack on "megatechnology," and Helena Norberg-Hodge, whose work to preserve the Ladakhi culture of the Himalayas has led her to a broad-ranging campaign against the invading Western monoculture there and its technological and economic penetration everywhere.

A roster of some of those in this rough circle suggests the range of contemporary neo-Luddism. John Mohawk is a Seneca activist and lecturer in American Studies at the State University of Buffalo, New York, who was the principal author of the Irokwa Confederacy's recent statement setting out Indian culture's defiance of industrial society and its assertion of a biocentric, animistic, organic worldview. Jeremy Rifkin is the president of the Foundation on Economic Trends, a Washington citizens' lobby fighting the spread of biotechnologies and the threat of global warming, and the author of a number of books attacking the foundations of industrial society. Vandana Shiva, who has a doctorate in quantum mechanics, has been an activist in southern Asia for more than twenty years, where she has worked to resist the penetration of Western culture, particularly its science, and its destruction of local agriculture, genetic diversity, and traditional communities. Sigmund Kvaloy, a farmer and writer in Norway, is a critic of industrial society who has been instrumental in developing the Green movement in Scandinavia and in leading resistance to Norway's participation in the European Community. Charlene Spretnak, an early leader of the U.S. Green movement (and co-author with another neo-Luddite, Fritjof Capra, of an early analysis of Green politics), has been an ecofeminist critic of modernism through teaching and writing. George Sessions, a professor of philosophy at Sierra College, California, is the leading American spokesman for the ideas of deep ecology, which teaches the equality of all species and the need for the human to live in greater harmony, and in far fewer numbers, with the rest of nature. A disparate but distinguished lot indeed, and there may be another several dozen of similar stature and mind.

Now it must be said that what links these diverse people is essentially a philosophical kind of Luddism. Although many have been involved in direct-action protests of one kind or another, they are not known as people who have gone out and broken offending machines, or burned down noisome factories, nor for the most part are their livelihoods immediately threatened by the onrush of high-tech industrialism, however much they realize their societies and environments are. Indeed, that may be what makes them fittingly *neo*-Luddites, as Chellis Glendinning's definition suggests, rather than true replicas of the originals. Charles Cobb, an economist with the Society for a Human Economy ("Economics as if people mattered"), has drawn the distinction this way:

> Neo-Luddites do not propose to overcome subtle forms of enslavement to technology by physically smashing machinery. . . . In contrast to the original Luddites, who focused on the particular effects of particular machines, the Neo-Luddites are concerned about the way in which dependence upon technology changes the character of an entire society. . . . They are asking us to reflect on the entire configuration of modern technology instead of isolated pieces of it.

Of course the original Luddites were feeling the changes in the character of their society as well, and more keenly perhaps because they knew the old ways so intimately, but they were able to see only two decades of the industrial onslaught rather than two centuries of it and probably had greater faith, at least at the start, in the ability of frame breaking to stop it. The neo-Luddites understand the protean and far-flung nature of the technosphere, its pervasive power shot horizontally and vertically through modern society, in ways that the originals could not have begun to, and that is why their work takes them in so many different directions: Green politics, ecological restoration, anti-GATT organizing, wilderness preservation, alternative technology, cultural survival, food safety, historical research, and much else besides.

That is also why so many of them are willing to use, at least in the near future, the technologies at the heart of the system they oppose, including telephones, faxes, jet planes, and photocopiers; as John Davis says, though he is one of the neo-Luddites and editor of *Wild Earth* quarterly, he "inclines toward the view that technology is inherently evil" but "disseminates this view via E-mail, computer, and laser printer." It is a contradiction and a compromise, however, that sits easily with no one and is justified only in the name of the urgency of the cause and the need to spread its message as wide as possible. For there is another understanding that neo-Luddites generally share: that there is, in Jerry Mander's words, "an *intrinsic* aspect of technologies" that affects what happens regardless of who uses them or with what benign purposes; any technology, any artifact, has certain inherent attributes, its givens, impossible to change or correct, and these, the product of the political context that gives them birth, inevitably determine the ways it is used and the consequences it has. As Mander says, you can't have a "good" nuclear power plant, even if saints are in charge of it, because it will be fragile, dangerous, expensive, large, centralizing, and environmentally noxious by its essential nature—any more than you could have a "good" bomb or a "good" pesticide or a "good" automobile. This also means that in a real sense every use of a technology, particularly such a piece of quintessentially high technology as the computer, no matter how supposedly benevolent the ends, embeds its "intrinsic aspect" deeper and deeper into the soul of the user however wary or self-conscious, in fact embeds the values and thought processes of the society that makes that technology, even as it makes the user insidiously more and more a part of those values and processes. The neo-Luddite dilemma, then, is that though it may not be possible to avoid all aspects of the industrial world and still function effectively, there is a real question as to how effectively one can ever fight fire with fire.*

Indeed, among the neo-Luddites are some who, in reaction to this dilemma, take a stronger, more purist position. Wendell Berry, the essayist and poet who also runs a small farm in Kentucky, says, "As a farmer, I do almost all of my work with horses. As a writer, I work with a pencil or a pen and a piece of paper—in the daytime, without electric light." Of course the fact that his manuscript is then typed by his wife on an old Royal typewriter—she criticizes as she goes along, and they work together in what he calls "a literary cottage industry"—somewhat diminishes this technological purity, and the typescript is subsequently put through any number of computers in setting, printing, and marketing it. Nonetheless there is a certain logic to Berry's method: he won't use a computer because it represents the system

---

* About computers, over which much dispute rages, it suffices to say that they have two fundamental, fatal flaws—quite apart from the fact that a great deal of pollution and sweatshop labor is involved in their manufacture, some real risks to health and bodily functions are connected to their operation, considerable deskilling and job displacement result from their corporate use, and increasing surveillance and invasion of privacy attend their proliferation. First, in the hands of the large centralizing corporations and bureaucracies that devised and perfected them in the first place, and in service to the goals of production, profitability, and power, computers are steering the world toward social inequity and disintegration and toward environmental instability and collapse, and doing so with more speed and efficiency with every passing year—regardless of how many people on the Internet believe they are saving the planet. Second, computers interpose and mediate between the human and the natural world more completely than any other technology—they are uniquely capable of reproducing *another* nature through biotechnology and many "virtual" ones—and are the instruments that primarily energize the technosphere that not merely distances this civilization from nature but sets it at war with nature for its daily sustenance. Next to that it is quite insignificant whether some individuals find that the values of a technological society—speed, ease, mass information, mass access, and the like—are served and enhanced by such machines.

he opposes in his writing. "I do not see," he says, "that computers are bringing us one step nearer to anything that does matter to me: peace, economic justice, ecological health, political honesty, family and community stability, good work." It hardly comes as a surprise to hear Berry say, in his soft mountain drawl, "I am a Luddite."

Actually that kind of claim is not as rare in the last years of the century as one might think. Fritjof Capra, who is a physicist by training, has said it. Katharine Temple of the Catholic Worker movement has said it, calling on her comrades to "find even more ways to be latter-day Luddites." Thomas Pynchon, the novelist whose pervading paranoia applies also to the technological realm, has said it, adding that he takes comfort "however minimal and cold" from Byron's lines after the Loughborough raid, "Down with all kings but King Ludd!" And even Joseph Weisenbaum, a professor at the Massachusetts Institute of Technology, has said it, thus:

> I think we need a period of detoxification with respect to our science and technology. They have become toxic to our spirit. We need a moratorium on progress. If such thoughts are Luddite, then I am a Luddite too.

And who knows how many there may be, troubled by the onrush of arcane technologies and esoteric systems, bewildered by procedures unknown but a decade before, threatened by machines that make them exposed or servile or useless, or worried by a world growing every day more anxious, unstable, and befouled, who have said, perhaps only to themselves, "I am a Luddite."

The neo-Luddite spectrum, then, is surprisingly broad and far more multifarious and interesting than one might have been led to think. Not yet an ordered movement, perhaps, but it contains multitudes of those who have in common an awakening from the technophilic dream and resistance to one aspect or other of the industrial monoculture, and that is a sociological fact of considerable importance. It also seems capable of developing along more self-conscious lines in the years ahead, particularly as the kinds of tenuous links now being made among previously separate groups grow stronger and as the sorts of issues once regarded as distinct—biotechnology and free trade, clear-cutting and tribal extinction—are increasingly seen as parts of the same rough beast.

It is impossible to put a figure on the number of people who could potentially be drawn into such a movement. The only attempt I know of was made in 1992 by a Russian scholar, Dr. Felix Rizvanov of the Russian Academy of Sciences, who estimated that there were as many as "approximately 50 to 100 million people in the USA, Russia, Europe and worldwide, who have rejected the scientific, technocratic Cartesian approach with its 'laissez-faire' economy." Whether that figure has any validity, and how many of those who have made that rejection would see themselves as purposeful neo-Luddites, it is not possible to say. But even from a survey as limited as the one I have attempted here, it is not unreasonable to think that the audience for a neo-Luddite message is wide and must be growing daily—or even that a resuscitation and new appreciation of the original Luddites might provide exactly the kind of instructive parallel from which such an audience might learn how to become rebels against the future they face, and find a world to gain.

10

Lessons from the Luddites

IT MAY BE that even those who do remember the past are condemned to repeat it, such is the regularity of the human condition, but at least those who learn from it may fashion the weapons with which to triumph the second time around. Armed with an understanding of the past, perhaps that can allow them to be rebels against the future.

Much there is to be learned from the experience of the Luddites, as distant and as different as their times are from ours. Just as the second Industrial Revolution itself has its roots quite specifically in the first—the machines change, but the machine*ness* does not—so those today who are inspired in some measure to resist or even reverse the tide of industrialism might best find their analogs, if not their models, in those original Luddites.

As I see it, these are the sorts of lessons one might, with the focused lenses of history, take from the Luddite past.

1. Technologies are never neutral, and some are hurtful.

It was not all machinery that the Luddites opposed, but "all Machinery hurtful to Commonality," as that March 1812 letter stated it, machinery to which their commonality did not give approval, over which it had no control, and the use of which was detrimental to its interests, considered either as a body of workers or a body of families and neighbors and citizens. It was machinery, in other words, that was produced with only economic consequences in mind, and those of benefit to only a few, while the myriad social and environmental and cultural ones were deemed irrelevant.

For the fact of the matter is that, contrary to the technophilic propaganda, technology is not neutral, composed of tools that can be used for good or evil depending on the user. As we have seen, it comes with an inevitable logic, bearing the purposes and the values of the economic system that spawns it, and obeying an imperative that works that logic to its end, quite heedlessly. What was true of the technology of industrialism at the beginning, when the apologist Andrew Ure praised a new machine that replaced high-paid workmen—"This invention confirms the great doctrine already propounded, that when capital enlists science in her service, the refractory hand of labour will always be taught docility"—is as true today, when a reporter for *Automation* could praise a computer system as "significant" because it assures that "decision-making" is "removed from the operator [and] gives maximum control of the machine to management." These are not accidental, ancillary attributes of the machines that are chosen; they are intrinsic and ineluctable.

Tools come with a prior history built in, expressing the values of a particular culture. A conquering, violent culture—of which Western civilization is a prime example, with the United States at its extreme—is bound to produce conquering, violent tools. When U.S. industrialism turned to agriculture after World War II, for example, it went at it with all that it had just learned on the battlefield, using tractors modeled on wartime tanks to cut up vast fields, crop dusters modeled on wartime planes to spray poisons, and pesticides and herbicides developed from wartime chemical weapons and defoliants to destroy unwanted species. It was a

war on the land, sweeping and sophisticated as modern mechanization can be, capable of depleting topsoil at the rate of 3 billion tons a year and water at the rate of 10 billion gallons a year,
as we have seen demonstrated ever since. It could be no other
way: if a nation like this beats its swords into plowshares they will
still be violent and deadly tools.

The business of cropping wool cloth with huge hand-held
scissors was an arduous and tiring one, which the shearing frame
could have done almost as well with much less effort and time,
and the croppers might have welcomed such a disburdening tool
if it had had no history built in. But they knew, and became
Luddites because they knew, what they would have to give up if
they were to accept such a technology: the camaraderie of the
cropping shop, with its loose hours and ale breaks and regular
conversation and pride of workmanship, traded for the servility
of the factory, with its discipline and hierarchy and control and
skillessness, and beyond that the rule of laissez-faire, dog-eat-dog,
buyer-beware, cash-on-the-line. The shearing frame was so obviously not neutral—it was machinery hurtful.

It does not seem hard in a modern context similarly to determine when machinery is hurtful or to define a commonality
whose members might have something to say about a technology's introduction or use. Wendell Berry, the Kentucky essayist,
has produced a list of criteria that would serve well as a guide: a
new tool, he says, should be cheaper, smaller, and better than the
one it replaces, use less energy (and that energy renewable), be
repairable, come from a small, local shop, and "should not replace
or disrupt anything good that already exists, and this includes
family and community relationships." To which need be added
only two other crucial standards: that those "family and community relationships" embrace all the other species, plants and animals alike, and the living ecosystems on which they depend, and
that they be considered, as the Irokwa have expressed it, with the
interests of the next seven generations in mind.

2. Industrialism is always a cataclysmic process, destroying the past,
roiling the present, making the future uncertain.

It is in the nature of the industrial ethos to value growth and production, speed and novelty, power and manipulation, all of which
are bound to cause continuing, rapid, and disruptive changes at
all levels of society, and with some regularity, whatever benefits
they may bring to a few. And because its criteria are essentially
economic rather than, say, social or civic, those changes come
about without much regard for any but purely materialist consequences and primarily for the aggrandizement of those few.

Only three decades into the Industrial Revolution the Luddites already had a good sense of the magnitude and severity of
the changes it was bringing, though they could not have imagined where it was ultimately heading. The British scholar Adrian
Randall has said:

> Directly and indirectly the process of change affected and
> impinged upon whole communities. . . . Family economies were
> disrupted. And over all hung the threat of wholesale restructur-
> ing. . . . [The] opponents of change might not have realised that it
> was an "Industrial Revolution" they were experiencing but they
> recognised that the ways and the values of the past were about to be
> overturned [with] deep and profound consequences.

We can see something of the same process at work today in
those societies where industrialism has more recently been introduced, particularly in its Western-capitalist form, from Eastern
Europe to southern Africa, from Mexico to China. The shock
waves of change shoot through stable communities and settled
regions, disrupting families, clans, tribes, traditional relationships
and behaviors, often setting tribe against tribe, religion against
religion, race against race, in ways and with intensities never
known before, often dragging societies into successive dictator-
ships if not perpetual civil war.

Whatever material benefits industrialism may introduce, the familiar evils—incoherent metropolises, spreading slums, crime and prostitution, inflation, corruption, pollution, cancer and heart disease, stress, anomie, alcoholism—almost always follow. And the consequences may be quite profound indeed as the industrial ethos supplants the customs and habits of the past. Helena Norberg-Hodge tells a story of the effect of the transistor radio—the apparently innocent little transistor radio—on the traditional Ladakhi society of northwestern India, where only a short time after its introduction people no longer sat around the fields or fires singing communal songs because they could get the canned stuff from professionals in the capital.

Nor is it only in newly industrialized societies that the tumultuous effects of an ethos of greed and growth are felt. What economists call "structural change" occurs regularly in developed nations as well, often creating more social disruption than individuals can absorb or families and neighborhoods and towns and whole industries can defend against, and during times of rapid technological growth the result is almost certain to be disastrous for large sections of the population, no matter what public protections may exist. And when those protections are meager or ineffective—as with health insurance in the United States, say—structural change will have widespread and onerous costs.

3. "Only a people serving an apprenticeship to nature can be trusted with machines."

This wise maxim of Herbert Read's is what Wordsworth and the other Romantic poets of the Luddite era expressed in their own way as they saw the Satanic mills and Stygian forges both imprisoning and impoverishing textile families and usurping and befouling natural landscapes—"such outrage done to nature as compels the indignant power . . . to avenge her violated rights." Mercantile capitalism showed scant regard for nature and

perceived the earth's treasures as resource and bounty, but until the
19th century it had not developed many technologies capable of
wholesale destruction or an unreflective ethic committed to development and progress at all costs. With the Industrial Revolution
there was not even a pretense that British society was paying attention, much less serving an apprenticeship, to nature, nor was there
any concern at all that its products and processes should somehow enhance biological needs or preserve organic communities.

What happens when an economy is not embedded in a due
regard for the natural world, understanding and coping with the
full range of its consequences to species and their ecosystems, is
not only that it wreaks its harm throughout the biosphere in
indiscriminate and ultimately unsustainable ways, though that is
bad enough. It also loses its sense of the human as a species and
the individual as an animal, needing certain basic physical elements for successful survival, including land and air, decent food
and shelter, intact communities and nurturing families, without
which it will perish as miserably as a fish out of water, a wolf in a
trap. An economy without any kind of ecological grounding will
be as disregardful of the human members as of the nonhuman,
and its social as well as economic forms—factories, tenements,
cities, hierarchies—will reflect that.

Since technology is, by its very essence, artificial—that is
to say, not natural, a human construct not otherwise found
in nature, where there is no technology—it tends to distance
humans from their environment and set them in opposition to it,
and the larger and more powerful it becomes the greater is that
distance and more effective that opposition: "The artificial
world," says Jaques Ellul, the French philosopher, is "radically
different from the natural world," with "different imperatives,
different directives, and different laws" such that "it destroys,
eliminates, or subordinates the natural world." At a certain point,
one that we have reached in the 20th century, technology can
completely overwhelm so many other elements of that world as

to threaten its continued existence, and unless the technosphere re-establishes some connectedness to the biosphere it seems likely to carry out that threat.

4. The nation-state, synergistically intertwined with industrialism, will always come to its aid and defense, making revolt futile and reform ineffectual.

There is no sign of hurt or astonishment in any of the Luddite letters written in reaction to the government's decision to defend the new industrialism with some 14,000 troops—the tone is repeatedly one of defiance, of the "Above 40,000 Heroes are ready to break out" sort—but in fact it must have come as a surprising and frightening blow. Never before had the British government resorted to such a measure—so stark and clumsy and brutal, and accompanied by systems of spies and informers, zealous magistrates, illegal arrests, and rigged trials—to control its own populace. That response was a statement, all the more emphatic for being apparently unexpected, of the real meaning of laissez-faire: force would be used by the state to ensure that manufacturers would be free to do what they wished, especially with labor. By the time the Luddites were hanging "comfortably" on their two bars at Yorkshire castle, the power of the new industrialism was patent.

Since then, of course, the industrial regime has only gotten stronger, proving itself the most efficient and potent system for material aggrandizement the world has ever known, and all the while it has had the power of the dominant nation-states behind it, extending it to every corner of the earth and defending it once there. It doesn't matter that the states have quarreled and contended for these corners, or that in recent decades native states have wrested nominal political control from colonizing ones, for the industrial regime hardly cares which cadres run the state as long as they understand the kind of duties expected of them. It is remarkably protean in that way, for it can accommodate itself to almost any national system—Marxist Russia, capitalist Japan, China under a vicious dictator, Singapore under a benevolent one, messy and riven India, tidy and cohesive Norway, Jewish Israel, Moslem Egypt—and in return asks only that its priorities dominate, its markets rule, its values penetrate, and its interests be defended, with 14,000 troops if necessary, or even an entire Desert Storm.

Some among the Luddites might have entertained a dream that the British government could be overthrown—"shake off the hateful Yoke of a Silly Old Man, and his Son more silly and their Rogueish Ministers"—but it didn't take long to show the hollowness of that. Since then not one fully industrialized nation in the world has had a successful rebellion against it, which says something telling about the union of industrialism and the nation-state. In fact, the only places where rebellion has succeeded in the last two centuries have been where a version of a modern nation-state has emerged to pave the way for the introduction of industrialism, whether in the authoritarian (Russia, Cuba, etc.) or the nationalistic (India, Kenya, etc.) mold.

Some among the Luddites also entertained a dream that the British government could be reformed, either through new laws that would empower workers against their masters or by a broadening of Parliamentary representation. Immense effort was spent on this throughout the whole Luddite period and for decades afterward, absorbing the energy of tens of thousands of workers and siphoning off tens of thousands of pounds they could ill afford, but never once were the power alignments of British society significantly altered, never did the British government accede to any but the most meager demands. There is perhaps no figure of the Luddite era more pathetic than that of Gravener Henson after his long and arduous and quite costly work in organizing Nottingham stockingers, getting Parliament to consider a bill preventing "Frauds and Abuses" in the knitting trades, only to see his bill become so distorted in the Commons, as he said, that it ended up allowing manufacturers to "Cheat, Rob, Pilfer" as never before—and then finding that even that bill was rejected by the Lords.

5. But resistance to the industrial system, based on some grasp of moral principles and rooted in some sense of moral revulsion, is not only possible but necessary.

Probably no images emerge more clearly from the story of the Luddites than those that capture their boldness and bravery—the cropper at Cartwright's mill leaping up to shoot through the window in anger because a bullet had just been fired through his cap, the two sisters setting fire to the sofa and curtains in Emmanual Burton's mansion—and their willingness at considerable personal cost to express their opposition by hatchet, pike, gun, letter, march, or any other handy means. Yes, it is true that in a general sense the Luddites were not successful either in the short-run aim of halting the detestable machinery or the long-run task of stopping the Industrial Revolution and its multiple miseries; but that hardly matters in the retrospect of history, for what they are remembered for is that they *resisted*, not that they won. Some nowadays, honored with the haughtiness of hindsight, may call it foolish resistance ("blind" and "senseless" are the usual adjectives), but it was dramatic, forceful, honorable, and authentic enough to have put the Luddites' issues forever on the record and made the Luddites' name as indelibly a part of the language as the Puritans'.

What remains, then, after so may of the details fade, is the sense of Luddism as a moral challenge, "a sort of moral earthquake," as Charlotte Brontë saw it—the acting out of a genuinely felt perception of right and wrong that went down deep in the English soul. Such a challenge is mounted against large enemies and powerful forces not because there is any certainty of triumph but because somewhere in the blood, in the place inside where pain and fear and anger intersect, one is finally moved to refusal and defiance: "No more." "There is a time when the operation of the machine becomes so odious, makes you so sick at heart, that you can't take part," is the way that Mario Savio put it before another movement in 1964. "And you've got to put your bodies upon the levers, upon all the apparatus, and you've got to make it stop."

But although violence as a tactic—bodies on the levers—can be an extremely effective tactic for a while, as the Luddites discovered, it can also be extremely limited and no longer of much use at the point when it calls down the potent wrath of authority and turns away the allegiance of neighbors. Moreover, it is difficult to maintain such a tactic in a high-moral context, to argue for very long that the low means of destruction are justified by the high ends of principle, and when that context is shattered, when the disjunction between ends and means becomes too great within the ranks and without, then violence loses its utility except for the crudest purposes.

Besides, the ways of resisting the industrial monoculture can be as myriad as the machines against which they are aimed and as varied as the individuals carrying them out, as the many neo-Luddite manifestations around the world make clear. The "Great Refusal," in the words of Michel Foucault, is made up of "a plurality of resistances, each of them a special case: resistances that are possible, necessary, improbable, others that are spontaneous, savage, solitary, concerted, rampant, or violent." Lewis Mumford, at the end of his lengthy analysis of "the myth of the machine" a generation ago, argued that indeed anyone could "play a part in extricating himself from the power system" by "quiet acts of mental and physical withdrawal," and he thought he saw such resistance "in a hundred different places":

> Though no immediate and complete escape from the ongoing power system is possible, least of all through mass violence, the changes that will restore autonomy and initiative to the human person all lie within the province of each individual soul, once it is roused. Nothing could be more damaging to the myth of the machine, and to the dehumanized social order it has brought into

existence, than a steady withdrawal of interest, a slowing down of
tempo, a stoppage of senseless routines and mindless acts.

In the decades since, the power system has of course gone on to
increase its grip on the society as a whole, but in fact some degree
of withdrawal and detachment has also taken place, not alone
among neo-Luddites, and there is a substantial "counterculture"
of those who have taken to living simply, working in community,
going back to the land, developing alternative technologies, drop-
ping out, or in general trying to create a life that does not do violence to their ethical principles.

The most successful and evident models for withdrawal today,
however, are not individual but collective, most notably, at least
in the United States, the Old Order Amish communities from
Pennsylvania to Iowa and the traditional Indian communities
found on many reservations right across the country.

The Amish long ago worked out a way to exist within the
industrial monoculture, deciding that no technologies that tied
them to the outside world—combustion engines, radio and television, electric power, and telephones—would intrude into their
lives and make their communities beholden to institutions that had
no regard for the principle on which they ordered existence: "the
harmony of God, nature, family, and community." For more
than three centuries now they have withdrawn to islands mostly
impervious to the industrial culture, and very successfully, too, as
their lush fields, busy villages, neat farmsteads, fertile groves and
gardens, and general lack of crime, poverty, anomie, and alien-
ation attest.

In Indian country, too, where (despite the casino lure) the traditional customs and lifeways have remained more or less intact
for centuries, a majority have always chosen to turn their backs
on the industrial world and most of its attendant technologies,
and they have been joined by a younger generation reasserting
and in some cases revivifying those ancient tribal cultures. There
could hardly be two more antithetical systems—the Indian is,

among other things, stable, communal, spiritual, participatory, oral, slow, cooperative, decentralized, animistic, and biocentric—but the fact that such tribal societies have survived for so many eons, not just in North America but on every other continent as well, suggests that there is a cohesion and strength to them that is certainly more durable and likely more harmonious than anything industrialism has so far achieved.

It is not incidental that both Amish and Indian communities are morally based, guided by spiritual values that place primary emphasis on living in harmony with the earth and sustaining small-scale communities. That both should then be so careful and restrictive in their use of technology, explicitly refusing to adopt certain machines whose qualities they can ably judge, says not only that there is an ethical decision to be made about technologies but that some of them can be seen to fail this test. As the Irokwa Confederacy put it in their statement to the United Nations in 1977, "We must all consciously and continually challenge every model, every program, and every process that the West tries to force upon us." Rejecting always the "machinery hurtful to commonality."

6. Politically, resistance to industrialism must force not only "the machine question" but the viability of industrial society into public consciousness and debate.

If in the long run the primary success of the Luddite revolt was that it put what was called "the machine question" before the British public through the first half of the 19th century—and then by reputation kept it alive right into the 20th—it could also be said that its failure was that it did not spark a true debate on that issue or even put forth the terms in which such a debate might be waged. That was a failure for which the Luddites of course cannot be blamed, since it was never part of their perceived mission to make their grievance a matter of debate and indeed they chose machine breaking exactly to push the issue beyond debate. But because of that failure, and the inability of subsequent critics of technology to penetrate the complacency of its beneficiaries and their chosen theorists or successfully call its values into question, the principles and goals of industrialism, to say nothing of the machines that embody them, have pretty much gone unchallenged in the public arena. Industrial civilization is today the water we swim in, and we seem almost as incapable of imagining what an alternative might look like, or even realizing that an alternative could exist, as fish in the ocean.

The political task of resistance today, then—beyond the "quiet acts" of personal withdrawal Mumford urges—is to try to make the culture of industrialism and its assumptions less invisible and to put the issue of its technology on the political agenda, in industrial societies as well as their imitators. In the words of Neil Postman, a professor of communications at New York University and author of *Technopoly,* "it is necessary for a great debate" to take place in industrial society between "technology and everybody else" around all the issues of the "uncontrolled growth of technology" in recent decades. This means laying out as clearly and fully as possible the costs and consequences of our technologies, in the near term and long, so that even those overwhelmed by the ease/comfort/speed/power of high-tech gadgetry (what Mumford called technical "bribery") are forced to understand at what price it all comes and who is paying for it. What purpose does this machine serve? What problem has become so great that it needs this solution? Is this invention nothing but, as Thoreau put it, an improved means to an unimproved end? It also means forcing some awareness of who the principle beneficiaries of the new technology are—they tend to be the large, bureaucratic, complex, and secretive organizations of the industrial world—and trying to make public all the undemocratic ways they make the technological choices that so affect all the rest of us. Who are the winners, who the losers? Will this invention concentrate or disperse power, encourage or discourage self-worth? Can society at large afford it? Can the biosphere?

Ultimately this "great debate" of course has to open out into wider questions about industrial society itself, its values and purposes, its sustainability. It is no surprise that the Luddites were unable to accomplish this in the face of an immensely self-satisfied laissez-faire plutocracy whose access to means of forcing debates and framing issues was considerably greater than theirs. Today, though, that task ought not to be so difficult—in spite of the continued opposition of a plutocracy grown only more powerful and complacent—particularly because after two centuries it is now possible to see the nature of industrial civilization and its imperiling direction so much more clearly.

Certain home-truths are beginning to be understood, at least in most industrial societies, by increasing numbers of people: some of the fish at least not only seem to be seeing the water but realizing it is polluted. Industrialism, built upon machines designed to exploit and produce for human betterment alone, is on a collision course with the biosphere. Industrial societies, which have shown themselves capable of creating material abundance for a few and material improvement for many, are nonetheless shot through with inequality, injustice, instability, and incivility, deficiencies that seem to increase rather than decrease with technical advancement. Industrialism does not stand superior, on any level other than physical comfort and power and a problematic longevity of life, to many other societies in the long range of the human experiment, particularly those, morally based and earth-regarding, that did serve the kind of "apprenticeship to nature" that Herbert Read saw as the proper precondition to technology.

Say what you will about such tribal societies, the record shows that they were (and in some places still are) units of great cohesion and sodality, of harmony and regularity, devoid for the most part of crime or addiction or anomie or poverty or suicide, with comparatively few needs and those satisfied with a minimum of drudgery, putting in on average maybe four hours a day per person on tasks of hunting and gathering and cultivating, the rest of the time devoted to song and dance and ritual and sex and eating and stories and games. No, individuals did not necessarily live as long—one estimate has paleolithic longevity at 32.5, exactly the same as in the United States in 1900—nor did they produce so many progeny, but that is because, apprenticed to nature, they consciously restricted human numbers and accepted limited human duration so that other species around them could thrive, for the benefit of all. No, they did not have the power of five hundred servants at the flick of a switch or turn of a key, but then they did not have atomic bombs and death camps, toxic wastes, traffic jams, strip mining, organized crime, psychosurgery, advertising, unemployment, or genocide.

To propose, in the midst of the "great debate," that such societies are exemplary, instructive if not imitable, is not to make a romanticized "search for the primitive." It is rather to acknowledge that the tribal mode of existence, precisely because it is nature-based, is consonant with the true, underlying needs of the human creature, and that we denigrate that mode and deny those needs to our loss and disfigurement. It is to suggest that certain valuable things have been left behind as we have sped headlong down the tracks of industrial progress and that it behooves us, in a public and spirited way, to wonder about what we have gained from it all and reflect upon what we have lost. And it is, finally, to assert that some sort of ecological society, rooted in that ancient animistic, autochthonous tradition, must be put forth as the necessary, achievable goal for human survival and harmony on earth.

7. Philosophically, resistance to industrialism must be embedded in an analysis—an ideology, perhaps—that is morally informed, carefully articulated, and widely shared.

One of the failures of Luddism (if at first perhaps one of its strengths) was its formlessness, its unintentionality, its indistinctness about goals, desires, possibilities. Movements acting out of

rage and outrage are often that way, of course, and for a while
there is power and momentum in those alone. For durability,
however, they are not enough, they do not sustain a commitment
that lasts through the adversities of repression and trials, they do
not forge a solidarity that prevents the infiltration of spies and
stooges, they do not engender strategies and tactics that adapt to
shifting conditions and adversaries, and they do not develop
analyses that make clear the nature of the enemy and the alterna-
tives to put in its place.

Now it would be difficult to think that neo-Luddite resistance, whatever form it takes, would be able to overcome all those
difficulties, particularly on a national or international scale: commitment and solidarity are mostly products of face-to-face,
day-to-day interactions, unities of purpose that come from unities of place. But if it is to be anything more than sporadic and
martyristic, resistance could learn from the Luddite experience at
least how important it is to work out some common analysis that
is morally clear about the problematic present and the desirable
future, and the common strategies that stem from it.

All the elements of such an analysis, it seems to me, are in
existence, scattered and still needing refinement, perhaps, but
there: in Mumford and Schumacher and Wendell Berry and
Jerry Mander and the Chellis Glendinning manifesto; in the
writing of the Earth-Firsters and the bioregionalists and deep
ecologists; in the lessons and models of the Amish and the
Irokwa; in the wisdom of tribal elders and the legacy of tribal
experience everywhere; in the work of the long line of dis-
senters-from-progress and naysayers-to-technology. I think we
might even be able to identify some essentials of that analysis,
such as:

Industrialism, the ethos encapsulating the values and technologies of Western civilization, is seriously endangering stable
social and environmental existence on this planet, to which must
be opposed the values and techniques of an organic ethos that

seeks to preserve the integrity, stability, and harmony of the biotic community, and the human community within it.

Anthropocentrism, and its expression in both humanism and monotheism, is the ruling principle of that civilization, to which must be opposed the principle of biocentrism and the spiritual identification of the human with all living species and systems.

Globalism, and its economic and military expression, is the guiding strategy of that civilization, to which must be opposed the strategy of localism, based upon the empowerment of the coherent bioregion and the small community.

Industrial capitalism, as an economy built upon the exploitation and degradation of the earth, is the productive and distributive enterprise of that civilization, to which must be opposed the practices of an ecological and sustainable economy built upon accommodation and commitment to the earth and following principles of conservation, stability, self-sufficiency, and cooperation.

A movement of resistance starting with just those principles as the sinews of its analysis would at least have a firm and uncompromising ground on which to stand and a clear and inspirational vision of where to go. If nothing else, it would be able to live up to the task that George Grant, the Canadian philosopher, has set this way: "The darkness which envelops the Western world because of its long dedication to the overcoming of chance"— by which he means the triumph of the scientific mind and its industrial constructs—"is just a fact. . . . The job of thought in our time is to bring into the light that darkness as darkness." And at its best, it might bring into the light the dawn that is the alternative.

One last lesson of a slightly different kind stems not from the experiences of the Luddites, though they might have had such inklings in their more religious moments, but from the subsequent course of the industrialism of which they were the first victims.

8. If the edifice of industrial civilization does not eventually crumble as a result of a determined resistance within its very walls, it seems certain to crumble of its own accumulated excesses and instabilities within not more than a few decades, perhaps sooner, after which there may be space for alternative societies to arise.

The two chief strains pulling this edifice apart, environmental overload and social dislocation, are both the necessary and inescapable results of an industrial civilization. In some sense, to be sure, they are the results of *any* civilization: the record of the last five thousand years of history clearly suggests that every single preceding civilization has perished, no matter where or how long it has been able to flourish, as a result of its sustained assault on its environment, usually ending in soil loss, flooding, and starvation, and a successive distension of all social strata, usually ending in rebellion, warfare, and dissolution. Civilizations, and the empires that give them shape, may achieve much of use and merit—or so the subsequent civilizations' historians would have us believe—but they seem unable to appreciate scale or limits, and in their growth and turgidity cannot maintain balance and continuity within or without. Industrial civilization is different only in that it is now much larger and more powerful than any known before, by geometric differences in all dimensions, and its collapse will be far more extensive and thoroughgoing, far more calamitous.

It is possible that such a collapse will be attended by environmental and social dislocations so severe that they will threaten the continuation of life, at least human life, on the surface of the planet, and the question then would be whether sufficient numbers survive and the planet is sufficiently hospitable for scattered human communities to emerge from among the ashes. But it is also possible that it will come about more by decay and distension, the gradual erosion of nation-state arrangements made obsolete and unworkable, the disintegration of corporate behemoths unable to comprehend and respond, and thus with the slow resurrection and re-empowerment of small bioregions and coherent communities having control over their own political and economic destinies. In either case, it will be necessary for the survivors to have some body of lore, and some vision of human regeneration, that instructs them in how thereafter to live in harmony with nature and how and why to fashion their technologies with the restraints and obligations of nature intertwined, seeking not to conquer and dominate and control the species and systems of the natural world—for the failure of industrialism will have taught the folly of that—but rather to understand and obey and love and incorporate nature into their souls as well as their tools.

It is now the task of the neo-Luddites, armed with the past, to prepare, to preserve, and to provide that body of lore, that inspiration, for such future generations as may be.

Timeline

	Nottinghamshire	Lancashire/Cheshire	Yorkshire	United Kingdom
1811 NOVEMBER	c. 400 frames broken 1 Luddite killed 1,900 soldiers sent Luddites arrested			
DECEMBER	c. 400 frames broken 500+ soldiers sent Luddites arrested	Luddite meeting		
1812 JANUARY	300+ frames broken Luddites arrested 1,000+ soldiers sent		1 factory burned Machines broken	
FEBRUARY	c. 30 frames broken	1 warehouse burned 1 factory attacked	3 workshops attacked, machines broken	Bill introduced to make frame breaking capital offense; Byron's speech in opposition
MARCH	12 frames broken Assizes: 7 transported	1 factory attacked	c. 12 workshops attacked, machines broken 2 factories attacked	Dickens born Frame-breaking bill enacted into law *Childe Harold* published
APRIL	1 manufacturer shot	Exchange Hall riot 15+ food riots 10 factories attacked, 2 destroyed 10+ Luddites killed	4 houses, 2 workshops, 2 factories attacked 1 manufacturer killed 4 Luddites killed 1 manufacturer attacked	Malthus elected to King of Clubs

1812				
MAY	1 food riot 2,000 soldiers sent	1 manufacturer attacked Assizes: 10 hanged, 38 transported, 18 imprisoned 6,900 soldiers stationed	Arms raids, robberies 4,000 soldiers stationed	Prime Minister Perceval shot Turner show opens Edward Lear born
JUNE		38 arrested for oathing	Arms raids, robberies	Liverpool government installed; U.S. declares war on U.K.
JULY			Arms raids, robberies	House of Lords rejects Henson bill to aid stockingers
AUGUST		38 oathers acquitted	3+ food riots	
SEPTEMBER	1 food riot	1 factory burned	2 workshops attacked, machines broken Arms raids	Napoleon enters Moscow
OCTOBER			Luddites arrested	Napoleon retreats from Moscow
NOVEMBER	1 food riot 1 frame broken		Luddites arrested	
DECEMBER	c. 5 frames broken	Assizes: 14 hanged, 6 transported		Humphrey Davy knighted
1813				
JANUARY	c. 14 frames broken			Shelley starts fund for Luddite children

Acknowledgments

My deep thanks to Ben Apfelbaum, Knox Burger, Brian Carey, Muriel Cherly, Brian Donoghue, W. H. Ferry, Chellis Glendinning, Paul Gottlieb, Joy Harris, T. B. G. Hughes, Dave Kupfer, Jerry Mander, the New York Public Library Wertheim Study, John Paulits, Norman Rush, Dorothy and Roger Sale, Robert Silman, Charlene Spretnak, E. P. Thompson, Doug Tompkins, and Jay Walljasper.

As always, my special debt to Faith Sale.

Source Notes

E. P. Thompson, who has written more comprehensively than anyone else about the historical context of the Luddites, has called their history "opaque," and though that is an exaggeration it does suggest the problem of finding sources for the Luddite story. Organizing of any kind by working people was a criminal offense in early 19th-century Britain, and machine breaking was made a capital crime, so naturally those who organized to break the machinery of industrialism were not likely to leave a very satisfactory paper trail. Although anonymous letters sent in Ned Ludd's name to the newspapers, magistrates, and manufacturers are fairly numerous, private letters between individuals involved are almost nonexistent; nor are there any extant diaries or notebooks written by the participants or their families; nor did any of them apparently set down in later life, after England had grown calmer, any memoirs or recollections of their acts and rationales. (Some did presumably talk to a few local historians fifty years and more after the events took place, which has produced two interesting novels and a partial history—but these accounts, besides being secondhand, are somewhat romantic and contain all too much that one suspects was invented for the narrative.) A number of newspapers carried accounts of various Luddite raids and actions—the *Nottingham Journal,* the *Manchester Mercury,* and the *Leeds Mercury* are chief in the field here, supplemented by the sturdy *Annual Registers*—but these all suffer from the same inadequacies as current not-always-reliable journalism.

What we are most often thrust back upon, then, are the official accounts of Luddism: letters to the Home Office (whose job it was to monitor domestic unrest) by magistrates, city officials, and military officers giving reports of activities in their districts, which obviously are short on sympathy for the offenders; statements of the numerous spies and informers the government sent to infiltrate the Luddite ranks, which are subject to all the self-serving error one might expect in this line of work; and formal findings by Parliamentary committees, which were not normally very inquisitive and of course were always one-sided. These sources, though they must be used cautiously, can be serviceable.

To this can be added the work of a few contemporary historians, men like Peter Gaskell and Andrew Ure, who wrote of the new industrial economy, and

William Felkin and Edward Baines, who wrote of particular industries within it. And, for necessary spice, there is the occasional work of some of the great Romantic writers, most particularly Wordsworth and Carlyle.

The principle sources for this book are listed below and are referred to by author's last name and short title in the notes.

LUDDITES

Aspinall, A. *The Early English Trade Unions.* London: Batchworth, 1949.

Bailey, Thomas. *Annals of Nottinghamshire,* vol. 4. London: Simpkin, Marshall, n.d. (1853?).

Blackfaces of 1812. Letters of Robert Taylor, Ralph Fletcher, etc. Bolton: H. Bradbury, 1839. Originally published as *Letters on the Subject of the Lancashire Riots in the Year 1812;* Bolton: H. Bradbury, 1812.

Brontë, Charlotte. *Shirley* (novel). 1849. Reprint. Oxford: Oxford University Press, 1979.

Calhoun, Craig. *The Question of Class Struggle.* Chicago: University of Chicago Press, 1982.

Charlesworth, Andrew. *An Atlas of Rural Protest in Britain 1548–1900.* Philadelphia: University of Pennsylvania Press, 1983.

Darvall, F. O. *Popular Disturbances and Public Order in Regency England.* Oxford: Oxford University Press, 1934. Reprint. New York: Kelley, 1969.

Dinwiddy, John. "Luddism and Politics." *Social History,* vol. 6, no. 1 (1979), pp. 35–63.

Glen, Robert. *Urban Workers in the Early Industrial Revolution.* New York: St. Martin's Press, 1984.

Hammond, J. L., and Barbara Hammond. *The Town Labourer, 1760–1832.* London: Longmans, Green, 1917.

———. *The Skilled Labourer, 1760–1832.* London: Longmans, Green, 1920.

Historical Account of the Luddites. Huddersfield: John Cargill, 1812. Reprint, 1862.

Hobsbawm, E. J. "The Machine-Breakers." In Hobsbawm, *Labouring Man.* London: Weidenfeld & Nicholson, 1964.

Home Office Papers. Home Office 40 (1, 2); Home Office 42 (100–136); Home Office 43 (18–21).

Hughes, Glyn. *The Rape of the Rose* (novel). New York: Simon & Schuster, 1992.

Noble, David F. *Progress Without People: In Defense of Luddism.* Chicago: Charles H. Kerr, 1993.

Parliamentary Papers. *Reports of the Committees of Secrecy into "certain violent proceedings . . . in Northern Counties."* Commons, vol. 2, p. 309; Lords, vol. 53, p. 15, 1812. [Cited as Commons, Parliamentary Report, and Lords, Parliamentary Report.]

Peel, Frank. *The Risings of the Luddites, Chartists and Plug-drawers*. 1888. Reprint. London: Frank Cass, 1968. Introduction by E. P. Thompson.

Randall, Adrian. *Before the Luddites: Custom, Community, and Machinery in the English Woolen Industry, 1776–1809*. Cambridge: Cambridge University Press, 1991.

———. "The Philosophy of Luddism." *Technology and Culture*, vol. 27, no. 1 (1986) pp. 7–17.

Raynes, Francis. *An Appeal to the Public*. . . . London, 1817.

Records of the Borough of Nottingham, 1800–1832, Nottingham, 1952.

Rudé, George. *Protest and Punishment*. Oxford: Oxford University Press, 1978.

Russell, John. "The Luddites." *Transactions of the Thoroton Society*, vol. 10 (1906), pp. 57–61.

Stevenson, John. *Popular Disturbances in England 1700–1870*. London: Longmans, Green, 1979.

Sykes, D. F. E., and George Henry Walker. *Ben o' Bill's, the Luddite: A Yorkshire Tale* (novel). London and Huddersfield, n.d. (1898?).

Thomis, Malcolm I. *The Luddites: Machine-Breaking in Regency England*. 1970. Reprint. New York: Schocken, 1972.

———. *Luddism in Nottinghamshire*. London: Phillmore, 1972.

Thompson, E. P. *The Making of the English Working Class*. New York: Victor Gollancz, 1963. Reprint. Harmondsworth: Penguin Books, Pelican edition, 1982 (edition used here). [Cited as *MEWC*.]

Toller, Ernst. *The Machine-Wreckers* (play). Trans. Ashley Dukes. New York: Knopf, 1923.

LOCAL AND MANUFACTURING HISTORY

Baines, Edward. *History of the Cotton Manufacture in Great Britain*. 1835. Reprint. New York: Kelley, 1966.

Baines, Thomas. *Yorkshire, Past and Present*. 4 vols. London: Mackenzie, 1871.

Bamford, Samuel. *Life of a Radical* and *Early Days*. London: Fisher Unwin, 1893.

Belchem, John. *Industrialism and the Working Class*. Aldershot: Scolar, 1990.

Blythell, Duncan. *The Handloom Weavers*. Cambridge: Cambridge University Press, 1969.

Crump, W. B. *The Leeds Woollen Industry, 1780–1820*. Leeds: Thoresby Society, 1931.

Felkin, William. *History of the Machine-Wrought Hosiery and Lace Manufactures*. 1867. Reprint. Newton Abbot: David & Charles, 1967.

Foster, John. *Class Struggle and the Industrial Revolution*. London: Weidenfeld & Nicholson, 1974.

Gaskell, Peter. *The Manufacturing Population of England.* London: Baldwin & Craddock, 1833.

Gregory, Derek. *Regional Transformation and the Industrial Revolution.* Minneapolis: University of Minnesota Press, 1982.

Henson, Gravener. *History of the Framework Knitters.* 1831. Reprint. Newton Abbot: David & Charles, 1970.

Jenkins, D. T. *The West Riding Wool Textile Industry 1770–1835.* Edington: Pasold Research Fund, 1975.

Parliamentary Papers: *Cotton Weavers,* 1803 (114) III 4; *Clothworkers and Shearmen of York,* 1805 (105) III 127; *Woollen Manufacture in England,* 1806 (268) III 567; *Petitions of Several Weavers,* 1800–11 (232) II 389; *Framework Knitters' Petitions,* 1812 (247) II 204; *State of the Children Employed in the Manufactories,* 1816 (397) III 135; *Hosiers and Framework Knitters,* 1819 (193) V 401; *Manufacturing, Commerce, Shipping,* 1833 (690) VI 1; *Handloom Weavers' Petitions,* 1834 (556) X, 1835 (341) XIII.

Peel, Frank. *Spen Valley Past and Present.* Heckmondwicke, 1893.

Prentice, Archibald. *Historical Sketches and Personal Recollections of Manchester.* London: C. Gilpin, 1851.

Sykes, D. F. E. *The History of Huddersfield.* Huddersfield, 1898.

Ure, Andrew. *The Philosophy of Manufactures.* London: C. Wright, 1835.

THE FIRST INDUSTRIAL REVOLUTION

In addition to the standard sources and works on particular manufactures listed above, I found these most helpful:

Berg, Maxine. *The Machinery Question and the Making of Political Economy.* Cambridge: Cambridge University Press, 1980.

Braudel, Fernand. *The Perspective of the World.* Vol. 3 of *Civilization and Capitalism.* New York: Harper & Row, 1986. Chapter 6.

Brown, David, and Michael J. Harrison. *A Sociology of Industrialisation.* London: Macmillan, 1978.

Crafts, N. F. R. *British Economic Growth During the Industrial Revolution.* Oxford: Oxford University Press, 1985.

Ginswick, J., ed. *Labour and the Poor in England and Wales* (Letters to the *Morning Chronicle,* 1849–51). Reprint. London: Frank Cass, 1983.

Henderson, W. O. *Industrial Britain Under the Regency.* London: Frank Cass, 1968.

Hudson, Pat. *Industrial Revolution.* London: Edward Arnold, 1992.

Huggett, Frank E. *Factory Life and Work.* London: Harrap, 1983.

Inglis, Brian. *Poverty and the Industrial Revolution.* London: Hodder & Stoughton, 1971.

Kemp, Tom. *Historical Patterns of Industrialisation.* London: Longmans, 1978.

Mokyr, Joel, ed. *The Economics of the Industrial Revolution*. London: Allen & Unwin, 1985.

Perkin, Harold. *Origins of Modern English Society*. 1969. Reprint. London: ARK, 1985.

Rule, John. *The Labouring Classes in Early Industrial England 1750–1850*. London: Longmans, 1986.

Tames, Richard L., ed. *Documents of the Industrial Revolution 1750–1850*. London: Hutchinson, 1971.

MODERN TECHNOLOGY

There is an enormous body of literature on modern technology, much of it listed in the bibliographies to Lewis Mumford's two books here (updated by Jerry Mander in the bibliography to his book). I consider the most sensible to be the following:

Goldsmith, Edward. *The Great U-turn*. Hartland, Devon: Green Books, 1988.

———. *The Way: An Ecological Worldview*. London: Rider, 1992.

MacKensie, Donald, and Judy Wajcman, eds. *The Social Shaping of Technology*. Philadelphia: Open University Press, 1985.

Mander, Jerry. *In the Absence of the Sacred: The Failure of Technology and the Survival of the Indian Nations*. San Francisco: Sierra Club, 1992.

Mumford, Lewis. *The Pentagon of Power*. New York: Harcourt Brace, 1970.

———. *Technics and Civilization*. New York: Harcourt Brace, 1934.

Ponting, Clive. *A Green History of the World*. London: Sinclair-Stevenson, 1991. Paperback. New York: Penguin Books, 1993.

Postman, Neil. *Technopoly*. New York: Knopf, 1992.

Winner, Langdon. *The Whale and the Reactor*. Chicago: University of Chicago Press, 1986.

INTRODUCTION

Pp. 1–2—For Robin Hood, see John G. Bellamy, *Robin Hood: An Historical Enquiry* (Bloomington: Indiana University Press, 1985); James Clarke Holt, *Robin Hood* (London: Thames & Hudson, 1989); Percy V. Harris, *The Truth About Robin Hood* (Mansfield: Linneys, 1973); William Reginald Mitchell, *The Haunts of Robin Hood* (Clapham, England: Dalesman, 1970).

P. 3—Letters: Russell, "The Luddites," p. 59; Darvall, *Popular Disturbances*, p. 170.

P. 4—Song: Home Office 42/119; Thomis, *Luddism in Nottinghamshire*, p. 1. *Annual Register (1812)*, p. v.

P. 5—Sykes and Walker, *Ben o' Bill's*.

1. "WITH HATCHET, PIKE, AND GUN"

Pp. 7–16—For the Rawfolds raid in general, see Peel, *Risings of Luddites;* Sykes and Walker, *Ben o' Bill's; Annual Register (1812),* pp. 54–55, 60, 389; T. B. Howell, ed., *State Trials* (London: Longman, Hurst, 1823), vol. 31, pp. 959–1166; *Leeds Mercury,* April 18, 1812.

P. 8—For an important analysis of the croppers' reaction to industrialism, see Randall, *Before the Luddites* (Introduction, Chapters 2 and 3, and Conclusion); and Randall, "Philosophy of Luddism."

P. 9—Song: Peel, *Risings of Luddites,* pp. 47–48.

P. 10—*Leeds Mercury,* April 18, 1812; the full account is reproduced in John Lock, *A Man of Sorrow* (New York: Nelson, 1965), pp. 107–9.

P. 11—"You could hear": Sykes and Walker, *Ben o' Bill's.*

P. 12—Brook: Howell, *State Trials,* p. 1115.

Cartwright: Quoted in Hammond and Hammond, *Skilled Labourer,* p. 305.

Walker: Peel, *Risings of Luddites,* p. 92.

P. 14—Cartwright: Quoted in Hammond and Hammond, *Skilled Labourer,* p. 305.

P. 15—Patrick Brontë: Lock, *Man of Sorrow,* p. 114; Brontë, *Shirley,* pp. 30–31.

P. 16—"How gloomy": Peel, *Risings of Luddites,* p. 120.

P. 17—"Machines had": John Ellis, *Social History of the Machine Gun* (London: Croom Helm, 1975).

Lord Byron: Letter to Thomas Moore, Dec. 24, 1816, in Leslie A. Marchand, ed., *Byron's Letters and Journals* (London: J. Murray, 1973–82), vol. 5.

"These Temple destroyers": *The Yosemite* (New York: Century, 1912), pp. 261–62.

P. 18—France: F. R. Manuel, "The Luddite Movement in France," *Journal of Modern History,* vol. 10, no. 1 (1938), p. 180.

U.S. Luddism: John Zerzan, "Axis Point," *International Review of Social History,* vol. 31, no. 3 (1986); Gary Kulik, *Radical History Review,* no. 17 (1978).

P. 19—"Southern Agrarians": *I'll Take My Stand* (New York: Harper, 1930; reprint, Baton Rouge: Louisiana State University Press, 1980), pp. xliv, xlv, xlviii, 175.

P. 20—*Business Week,* March 28, 1983.

P. 22—David Noble, *Forces of Production* (New York: Knopf, 1984), p. 353.

P. 23—Yorkshire figures: See Randall, *Before the Luddites,* Chapter 2; Jenkins, *West Riding,* especially Chapter 1.

P. 24—William Wordsworth, *The Excursion,* Book 8, lines 151–56, 165–85.

2. THE FIRST INDUSTRIAL REVOLUTION

P. 25—"Their dwellings": Andrew Ure, *Cotton Manufacture of Great Britain,* vol. 1, p. 191, quoted in Hammond and Hammond, *Skilled Labourer,* p. 50.

Pp. 25–26—"There are": Henderson, *Industrial Britain*, p. 136.

P. 27—"wonder and astonishment": Patrick Colquhoun, *A Treatise on the Wealth, Power, and Resources of the British Empire* (London, 1815), p. 68.

Wordsworth: *The Excursion*, Book 8, lines 90–95.

E. P. Thompson, *Customs in Common* (New York: New Press, 1991), p. 15.

Patents: H. I. Dutton, *The Patent System and Inventive Activity During the Industrial Revolution* (Manchester: Manchester University Press), 1984, p. 2.

P. 28—Norbert Wiener, *The Human Use of Human Beings* (1950; reprint, New York: Avon Books, 1967), p. 193.

"iron monster": *New Moral World* (April, 1825).

Clark Kerr et al., *Industrialism and Industrial Man* (Cambridge: Harvard University Press, 1960), Chapter 2.

P. 29—Gaskell, *Manufacturing Population*, pp. 23, 52.

P. 30—Steam engines: John Langton and R. J. Morris, *Atlas of Industrializing Britain 1780–1914* (London: Methuen, 1986); Hammond and Hammond, *Skilled Labourer*, pp. 70ff.; *Oxford History of England* (Oxford: Oxford University Press, 1970), vol. 12, Chapter 20; Baines, *History of Cotton Manufacture*, pp. 227–43, 362ff.

"the most striking": Ibid., p. 243.

P. 31—"The modern miracles": Tames, *Documents*, p. 69.

"While the engine": C. Turner Thackrah, *The Effects of the Principal Arts, Trades, and Professions on Health and Longevity*, quoted in Edward Baines, *History of Cotton*, p. 458.

Ure, *Philosophy of Manufactures*, quoted in Thompson, *MEWC*, p. 395.

P. 32—"Any spinner": Cobbett, *Political Register*, Aug. 30, 1823, quoted in Hammond and Hammond, *Town Labourer*, pp. 19–20.

"kept on purpose": Parliamentary Paper, *Manufacturing*, 1833.

P. 33—1833 statistic: *Report of the Factory Commission*, 1834, quoted in Hammond and Hammond, *Town Labourer*, p. 23n.

Ure, *Philosophy of Manufactures*, p. 18.

P. 34—Enclosures: Phyllis Dean, *The First Industrial Revolution* (Cambridge: Cambridge University Press, 1967); Eric Hobsbawm and George Rudé, *Captain Swing* (1968; reprint, New York: Norton, 1975); W. G. Hoskins, *The Making of the English Landscape* (1955; reprint, Harmondsworth: Penguin Books, 1985); W. M. Howitt, *Rural Life of England* (London: 1838); Pat Hudson, *Industrial Revolution*, Chapter 3; J. M. Neeson, *Commoners: Common Right, Enclosure and Social Change in England, 1700–1820* (Cambridge: Cambridge University Press, 1993); K. D. M. Snell, *Annals of the Labouring Poor* (Cambridge: Cambridge University Press, 1985); M. E. Turner, *English Parliamentary Enclosure* (Hamden, Conn.: Archon Books, 1980) and *Enclosure in*

Britain, 1750–1830 (London: Macmillan, 1984); and Arthur Young, *Rural Economy* (1770) and *Observations* (1773).

Sinclair: Quoted in Elie Halévy, *England in 1815* (1913; reprint, London: Benn, 1961), p. 230.

P. 35—Sturt, *Change in the Village* (New York: G. H. Doran, 1912), pp. 77ff.

Pp. 35–36—For 18th-century cottage life: Thompson, *Customs in Common* (including his famous "Moral Economy" essay) and *MEWC*, Chapters 6 and 9; Randall, *Before the Luddites;* John Aikin, *Description of the Country . . . ,* (London: 1796); Samuel Bamford, *Walks in Southern Lancashire* (1844; reprint, Brighton, England: Harvester, 1972); Marjorie Filbee, *Cottage Industries* (Newton Abbot: David & Charles, 1982); Calhoun, *Question of Class Struggle,* especially pp. 130ff.

P. 36—Sturt, *Change in the Village,* pp. 77ff.

Gaskell, *Manufacturing Population,* Introduction.

Felkin, *Hosiery and Lace Manufactures,* p. 451.

P. 37—Doggerel: From a Wolverhampton traveler, 1811, in Pat Hudson and W. R. Lee, eds., *Women's Work and the Family Economy in Historical Perspective* (Manchester: Manchester University Press, 1990), p. 117.

Pp. 37–38—Oastler: Quoted in Randall, *Before the Luddites,* p. 46.

P. 38—Arkwright: Quoted in John and Paula Zerzan, "Industrialization and Domestication," in John Zerzan and Alice Carnes, eds., *Questioning Technology* (Philadelphia: New Society, 1991), p. 202.

Thompson, *Customs in Common,* p. 14.

P. 39—Sturt, *Change in the Village,* p. 78.

Carlyle, "Gospel of Mammonism," *Past and Present,* Book 3, Chapter 2.

Pp. 39–40—Population: See Dean, *First Industrial,* Chapter 2, especially pp. 32–33.

P. 40—Malthus: Quoted in Perkin, *Origins,* p. 91.

Green: Quoted in ibid., pp. 92–93.

P. 41—Brummel: R. J. White, *Life in Regency England* (New York: Putnam's, 1963); Hubert Cole, *Beau Brummel* (New York: Mason/Charter, 1977).

Knox: Quoted in Perkin, *Origins,* p. 94.

(Footnote): "All at once": Angus Bethune Reach on Cheshire, in Ginswick, *Labour and the Poor.*

P. 42—War costs: Paul Kennedy, *The Rise and Fall of Great Powers* (New York: Random House, 1987), p. 81.

"period of exertion": Prentice, *Sketches of Manchester,* p. 63.

Fernand Braudel, *The Wheels of Commerce,* vol. 2 of *Civilization and Capitalism* (New York: Harper & Row, 1982), p. 183.

P. 43—"general impoverishment": Ibid., pp. 614–16.

Poor Law: Chris Cook and John Stevenson, *British Historical Facts* (London: Macmillan, 1980), p. 194.

P. 44—Colquhoun, *A Treatise;* table in Perkin, *Origins,* pp. 20–21, with an update in Crafts, *British Economic Growth,* pp. 9–17.

Cotton workers: Baines, *Cotton Manufacture;* Blythell, *Handloom Weavers;* Tames, *Documents;* William Thom, *Rhymes and Recollections of a Handloom Weaver of Inverbury* (London: 1844); *The Beggar's Complaint . . . by One Who Pities the Oppressed* (Sheffield: J. Crome, 1812–13); Parliamentary Papers: *Weavers,* 1811; *Cotton Weavers,* 1803; *Artisans and Machinery,* 1824; *Emigration,* 1827; *Handloom Weavers' Petitions,* 1834 and 1835; Frances Colier, *The Family Economy of the Working Classes in the Cotton Industry 1784–1833* (Manchester: Chetham Society, 1965).

Estimates on numbers of weavers vary greatly. See Thompson, *MEWC,* p. 344; Blythell, *Handloom Weavers,* Chapter 3; B. R. Mitchell, *British Historical Statistics* (Cambridge: Cambridge University Press, 1988), pp. 376–77.

P. 45—"Oldham Weaver": This version is from Elizabeth Gaskell's *Mary Barton* (London: 1848).

"We are compelled": Quoted in Hammond and Hammond, *Skilled Labourer,* p. 203.

P. 46—"An English": Tames, *Documents,* p. 148–49.

Pp. 46–47—Factory workers: Of the vast literature here, the most interesting contemporary works are John Brown, *A Memoir of Robert Blincoe* (1832; reprint, Derbyshire Archaeological Society, 1966), vol. 36; James Phillips Kay, *The Moral and Physical Condition of the Working Classes Employed in the Cotton Manufactures in Manchester* (London: 1832); William Dodd, *The Factory System Illustrated* (1841–42; reprint, London: Frank Cass, 1968, ed. W. H. Chaloner); Friedrich Engels, *The Condition of the Working-Class in England* (1845; first English edn., 1892; reprint, Moscow: Progress, 1973, used here); and the various Parliamentary Papers, including *Labour of Children in the Mills,* 1832. See also Hammond and Hammond, *Town Labourer,* Chapters 2 and 8; Thompson, *MEWC,* Chapter 6, Sykes, *History of Huddersfield;* and Marjorie Cruickshank, *Children and Industry* (Manchester: Manchester University Press, 1981).

P. 47—"If they will": Thompson, *MEWC,* p. 340.

"mournful spectacle": Thackrah, *The Effects,* p. 27.

"that so many": Perkin, *Origins,* p. 131.

Health conditions: See Kay, Ginswick, Gaskell, Engels, Thackrah, and especially Edwin Chadwick, *Report on the Sanitary Condition of the Labouring Population of Great Britain* (1842; reprint, Edinburgh: Edinburgh University Press, 1965, ed. M. W. Flinn); also, Tames, *Documents,* pp. 131ff.; Rule, *Labouring Classes,* Chapter 1.

P. 48—Cobbett, Engels: Quoted in Rule, *Labouring Classes,* pp. 77, 88.

Owen: Quoted in Inglis, *Poverty and Industrial Revolution,* p. 124; this is Robert Dale Owen's description of his father's reaction.

"little blossoms": In Cruickshank, *Children,* p. 5.

Death figures: Chadwick, *Report on Sanitary Condition,* passim; Rule, *Labouring Classes,* pp. 89–90.

P. 49—"We have no": Dr. G. C. Holland, in Chadwick, *Report on Sanitary Condition.*

P. 50—British state: See Halévy, *England in 1815,* Part 1, Chapter 1, p. 7, Part 2, Chapter 3, p. 1.

P. 51—David Ricardo, *Principles of Political Economy,* 2nd ed. (London: 1821), Chapter 31, p. 466.

"No interference": Parliamentary Paper, *Petitions of Several Weavers,* 1800–1811; and see *Annual Register (1811),* pp. 291–92.

P. 52—"broke the neck": Alexander Gallway, Parliamentary Paper, *Artisans and Machinery,* 1824, p. 27.

Hammond and Hammond, *Town Labourer,* Chapter 7.

Free market: See especially William Reddy, *The Rise of Market Culture* (Cambridge: Cambridge University Press, 1984); Thompson, *Customs in Common,* Chapter 9, especially pp. 201–7; and Thompson, *MEWC,* pp. 309–10, 328–42.

P. 53—Oastler: Quoted in Thompson, *MEWC,* p. 329.

Macauley: Quoted in Hammond and Hammond, *Town Labourer,* p. 1.

P. 54—Environmental effects: See Engels, Ginswick, Thackrah, and especially Hoskins, and Terence McLaughlin, *Dirt: A Social History* (New York: Stein & Day, 1971); Keith Thomas, *Man in the Natural World* (New York: Pantheon, 1983); Michael Reed, *The Landscape of Britain* (London: Routledge & Kegan Paul, 1990); Roger Sale, *Closer to Home* (Cambridge: Harvard University Press, 1986).

Oliver Goldsmith: "Deserted Village."

John Clare: "Remembrances."

Wordsworth, *Excursion,* Book 8, lines 105–9, 128–30.

P. 55— John Stuart Mill: *Principles of Political Economy* (London: 1848), Book 4, Chapter 6, p. 2.

Thomas, *Natural World,* p. 276.

"It is impossible": Hammond and Hammond, *Town Labourer,* p. 45.

P. 56—"built back": McLaughlin, *Dirt,* p. 131.

Carlyle, "Gospel of Mammonism."

Dickens, *Hard Times,* Book 2, Chapter 2.

P. 57—"in Manchester": Henderson, *Industrial Britain,* p. 34–35.

"rainwater": Chadwick, *Report on Sanitary Condition.*

"The Aire": Quoted in Engels, *Condition,* pp. 79.

"At the bottom": Ibid., p. 89.

P. 58—Engels: Ibid., p. 313.

Braudel, *Perspective of World,* p. 592.

P. 59—von Neumann: Quoted in Mumford, *Pentagon of Power,* p. 186.

3. THE LUDDITES: NOVEMBER–DECEMBER 1811

P. 61—England in 1811: *Annual Register (1811);* Darvall, *Popular Disturbances,* Chapters 1 and 2.

P. 62—Weavers' petitions: Hammond and Hammond, *Skilled Labourer,* p. 83; Darvall, *Popular Disturbances,* p. 53; Home Office 42/115.

Parliamentary committee: *Annual Register (1811),* pp. 291–92.

Peel: Hammond and Hammond, *Town Labourer,* p. 101.

Social London and Prince Regent: See especially J. B. Priestley, *The Prince of Pleasure* (London: Heinemann, 1969); R. J. White, *Life in Regency.*

P. 63—Brummel: Cole, *Beau Brummel.*

"he was continually": Robert Huish, quoted in Priestley, *Prince of Pleasure,* p. 26.

P. 64—Nottingham: Thomis, *Luddism in Nottinghamshire;* Russell, "The Luddites"; Felkin, *Hosiery and Lace Manufactures;* Bailey, *Annals;* Henson, *Framework Knitters; Records of Nottingham;* M. I. Thomis, "Gravener Henson," *Transactions of the Thoroton Society,* vol. 75, 1971, pp. 91–97; A. Temple Patterson, *Radical Leicester, 1780–1850* (Leicester: University College, Leicester, 1954).

P. 66—Felkin, *Hosiery and Lace Manufactures,* p. 230.

"This is": Aspinall, *Early English Trade Unions,* p. 325.

Factories: Owen Ashmore, introduction to Brown, *A Memoir;* Felkin, *Hosiery and Lace Manufactures.*

P. 67—*Nottingham Review,* Dec. 6, 1811.

P. 68—Sound of wide frames: Parliamentary Paper, *Framework Knitters' Petition,* May 1812 (Thomas Large testimony).

(Footnote): Newcastle: Thomis, *Luddism in Nottinghamshire,* p. 2; Lords: *Annual Register (1812),* p. 385; Byron: see note for p. 96 below. Aspinall, *Early English Trade Unions,* p. 119; Thomis, *Luddites,* p. 50. It is worth noting that although Thomis argues against the importance of antimachine attitudes in his Luddites book, his article on Gravener Henson for the Thoroton Society (cited above) acknowledges (p. 92) that the 1812 attacks were "directed against . . . specific machinery," not specific employers.

Pp. 69–70—Machine breaking: Hobsbawm, "Machine-Breakers"; John Rule, *The*

Experience of Labour in 18th-Century Industry (London: Croom Helm, 1981); Cook and Stevenson, *British Historical Facts* (see note to p. 43), pp. 147–152.

"up to": Hammond and Hammond, *Skilled Labourer,* p. 225.

(Footnote): Hammond and Hammond, *Town Labourer,* p. 299.

P. 70—Yorkshire cropper: Ibid. p. 173.

Pp. 71–73— Raids reported in *Annual Register (1811),* pp. 93–94, 129–30; Bailey, *Annals,* pp. 246–58; Felkin, *Hosiery and Lace Manufactures,* pp. 231–34; Thomis, *The Luddites,* Appendix.

P. 72—"deranged": Felkin, *Hosiery and Lace Manufactures,* p. 232.

P. 73—Annalist: Bailey, *Annals,* p. 247.

P. 74—"many hundreds": Thomis, *Luddism in Nottinghamshire,* p. 10.

Letter: Russell, "The Luddites," p. 62.

P. 75—Thompson: *MEWC,* p. 601.

(Footnote): Felkin, *Hosiery and Lace Manufactures,* pp. 239–40.

P. 77—Origin of name: See also *Beggar's Complaint;* George Pellew, *Life and Correspondence of . . . Sidmouth* (London: John Murray, 1847), vol. 3, p. 80; Darvall, *Popular Disturbances,* pp. 1–2. Modern dictionary and encyclopedia definitions are all quite (unacknowledgedly) conjectural and unreliable, some of them even asserting that Ludd was a real figure, for which there is no support. See David Linton, *ETC.* Spring 1985, Winter 1981.

P. 78—Cornwall: *English Dialect Dictionary* (London: H. Frowde, 1898–1905).

King Ludeca: *Oxford History of England* (Oxford University Press, 1971), vol. 2, pp. 231–32.

Milton, *History of Britain* (London, 1670), Book 1.

P. 79—Threatening letters: E. P. Thompson, in Douglas Hays et al., *Albion's Fatal Tree* (New York: Pantheon, 1975), Chapter 6.

"There is": Felkin, *Hosiery and Lace Manufactures,* p. 233.

P. 80—Letter: Darvall, *Popular Disturbances,* p. 72.

Coldham: Thomis, *Luddism in Nottinghamshire,* p. 13.

Felkin, *Hosiery and Lace Manufactures,* p. 233, 234.

"within ten yards": Thomis, *Luddism in Nottinghamshire,* p. 5.

P. 81—"the screams": Bailey, *Annals,* p. 252.

"Chant no more": Home Office 42/119, in Thomis, *Luddism in Nottinghamshire,* p. 1.

P. 82—Magistrates: Felkin, *Hosiery and Lace Manufactures,* p. 233.

P. 83—Soldiers: *Annual Register (1811),* p. 130; Hammond and Hammond, *Skilled Labourer,* p. 262; Darvall, *Popular Disturbances,* pp. 73, 258–59; Felkin, *Hosiery and Lace Manufactures,* p. 231.

"a town": Bailey, *Annals,* p. 251.

Nottingham City Council: *Records of Nottingham,* p. 124.

Newcastle: Thomis, *Luddism in Nottinghamshire,* p. 17.

P. 84—"We find": in Aspinall, *Early English Trade Unions,* p. 116–17.

(Footnote): Russell, "The Luddites," p. 60; a similar version is in Thomis, *Luddism in Nottinghamshire,* p. 18.

P. 85—"Nothing could": Bailey, *Annals,* p. 254.

Lords: *Annual Register (1812),* p. 391.

P. 86—Calhoun, *Question of Class Struggle,* pp. 60–61.

Newcastle: Thomis, *Ludaism in Nottinghamshire,* p. 19.

P. 87—Lord Middleton: Ibid, pp. 14–15.

"You must": Russell, "The Luddites," pp. 59–60.

Nunn: Thomis, *Luddism in Nottinghamshire,* p. 10–11.

P. 88—Newcastle: Ibid., p. 19.

Becher: Ibid., p. 34.

Pp. 88–89—Byron: See note to p. 17 above; letters of Dec. 15, 1811, Jan. 16, 1812.

P. 89—Shelley: Quoted in Richard Holmes, *Shelley: The Pursuit* (London: Weidenfeld, 1974), p. 98.

4. THE LUDDITES: JANUARY–APRIL 1812

P. 91—Bailey, *Annals,* pp. 249–50.

P. 92—*Annual Register (1812),* pp. 11, 19.

Newcastle: Thomis, *Luddism in Nottinghamshire,* p. 26.

P. 93—"It is impossible": *Annual Register (1812),* p. 20.

"he was allowed": Bailey, *Annals,* p. 253.

"by about": Thomis, *Luddism in Nottinghamshire,* p. 22.

P. 94—Luddite letters: Russell, "The Luddites," facsimile B.

"well-known maniac": *Annual Register (1812),* p. 21.

P. 95—Perceval: Darvall, *Popular Disturbances,* p. 337.

Death-penalty bill: *Annual Register (General History),* pp. 35–38; Hammond and Hammond, *Skilled Labourer,* p. 267.

Pp. 96–98—Byron: Letters of Jan. 16, Feb. 5, and Feb. 25, 1812, in Marchand, *Byron's Letters* (see note to p. 17 above); the speech, usually abridged, is in standard reference works of collected speeches, e.g., Houston Peterson, ed., *A Treasury of the World's Great Speeches* (New York: Simon & Schuster, 1954), pp. 318ff.; and in Noble, *Progress Without People,* pp. 134–39, and Peel, *Risings of Luddites,* pp. 69–76.

P. 98—"I spoke": Byron letter, March 5, 1812, in Marchand, *Byron's Letters.*

Morning Chronicle: In Kelsall, *Byron's Politics,* pp. 48–50.

P. 99—"I have waited": Thomis, *Luddism in Nottinghamshire,* p.43; facsimile of letter in Thomis, *The Luddites,* p. 118.

"the framework knitters": David C. Douglas, ed., *English Historical Documents 1783–1832* (Oxford: Oxford University Press, 1959), vol. 11, p. 531.

P. 100—Felkin, *Hosiery and Lace Manufactures,* p. 439; Home Office 42/119 and Darvall, *Popular Disturbances,* p. 325.

Henson campaign: Henson, *History of Framework Knitters; Records of Notting-ham,* pp. 137–63; Hammond and Hammond, *Skilled Labourer,* pp. 228–29; Thompson, *MEWC,* pp. 585–590.

Henson: *Records of Nottingham,* p. 149.

P. 101—March assizes: Hammond and Hammond, *Skilled Labourer,* pp. 268–69; Bailey, *Annals,* p. 256.

Town clerk: Thomis, *Luddism in Nottinghamshire,* pp. 52–54.

P. 102—"By General Ludds": Ibid., p. 54.

Luddite individuals: Rudé, *Protest and Punishment,* pp. 125, 205.

Judge: Thomis, *Luddism in Nottinghamshire,* p. 53; Hammond and Hammond, *Skilled Labourer,* p. 269 fn.

P. 103—On the spread of Luddism: Aspinall, *Early English Trade Unions,* pp. 118–20; Thomis, *The Luddites,* pp. 121–26; Thompson, *MEWC,* pp. 643–45; Gregory, *Regional Transformation,* pp. 179–83; Glen, *Urban Workers,* p. 173–74.

"an *honest, industrious fellow*": Aspinall, *Early English Trade Unions,* p. 120.

Manchester Gazette, Jan. 4, 1812.

P. 104—"the remainder," "Never knew," "I have been": Gregory, *Regional Transformation,* pp. 150–51.

P. 105—Randall, *Before the Luddites,* p. 48.

P. 106—"already we": Aspinall, *Early English Trade Unions,* p. 120.

Newcastle: Thomis, *The Luddites,* p. 121.

"in imitation": Gregory, *Regional Transformation,* p. 182.

(Footnote): Thompson, *MEWC,* pp. 205, 943.

P. 107—"we have enjoyed": Thompson, *MEWC,* p. 643 fn.

Oaths: *Beggar's Complaint; Annual Register (1812),* p. 391; Raynes, *An Appeal,* pp. 11–12; Sykes, *History of Huddersfield,* p. 277; *English Documents,* p. 534; Peel, *Risings of Luddites,* p. 20. See also Hammond and Hammond, *Skilled Labourer,* pp. 336ff. and Thompson, *MEWC,* pp. 631ff.

P. 108—Thompson, *MEWC,* p. 557.

"You must raise": *English Documents,* p. 535.

P. 109—Lords, Parliamentary Report, and *Annual Register (1812),* p. 392.

(Footnote): Glen, *Urban Workers*, p. 172.

Pp. 109–112—Yorkshire violence: Hammond and Hammond, *Skilled Labourer*, Chapter 11; Peel, *Risings of Luddites*, pp. 36–38; Darvall, *Popular Disturbances*, pp. 108ff. Thomis, *The Luddites*, pp. 183–85.

P. 111—"First seizing": Peel, *Risings of Luddites*, p. 36.

"A large body": *Annual Register (1812)*, p. 51.

P. 112—Song: Peel, *Risings of Luddites*, p. 120.

Pamphlet: Thompson, *MEWC*, p. 654; Thomis, *The Luddites*, pp. 89–90; Dinwiddy, "Luddism and Politics," p. 53.

(Footnote): Clarkson, *Memories of Merry Wakefield* (Wakefield: Radcliffe, 1887).

P. 113–116—Lancashire: Hammond and Hammond, *Skilled Labourer*, Chapter 10; Darvall, *Popular Disturbances*, pp. 98ff.; Thomis, *The Luddites*, pp. 185–86; Glen, *Urban Workers*.

P. 113—"It is not": Quoted in Randall, *Before the Luddites*, p. 46.

P. 114—Stockport: See Glen, *Urban Workers*, pp. 175ff.

Letter: Thomis, *The Luddites*, p. 58.

P. 115—Manchester riot: Bamford, *Life of a Radical*, pp. 240ff.; *Annual Register (1812)*, pp. 49–51; Prentice, *Sketches of Manchester*, pp. 50ff.; Rogerson, in Crump, *Leeds Woollen Industry*, p. 136.

P. 116—"To all Croppers": Ibid., p. 229; Thompson, *MEWC*, pp. 609–10.

P. 117—"Sir. Information": Crump, *Leeds Woollen Industry*, pp. 229–30.

P. 119—On the question of how political (as opposed to merely industrial), or even revolutionary, the Luddites were much has been written, most of it merely speculative; Randall, *Before the Luddites*, pp. 266–83, has the most reasoned perspective, and Dinwiddy, "Luddism and Politics," and F. K. Donnelly, *Social History*, no. 3 (1975), and no. 2 (1976), are also interesting. See also Thompson, *MEWC*, pp. 629–59; Thomis, *The Luddites*, pp. 82–90; Darvall, *Popular Disturbances*, pp. 305–11; and Gregory, *Regional Transformation*, pp. 182ff.

P. 120—"Revolutionne sistom": Dinwiddy, "Luddism and Politics," p. 40.

"the army": Thomis, *The Luddites*, p. 87.

Home Office: Home Office 42/119–20, and Thomis, *Luddism in Nottinghamshire*, p. 82.

Lords: Lords, Parliamentary Report; and *Annual Register (1812)*, p. 391.

P. 121—Black Lamp: Thompson, *MEWC*, pp. 515–28; and for background, pp. 110ff. and 650–55; see also Randall, *Before the Luddites*, pp. 266–83.

P. 122—"What happens": Foster, *Class Struggle*, p. 65.

Baines: Quoted in Peel, *Risings of Luddites*, pp. 55–56.

P. 123—Charles C. Southey, *Southey: Life and Correspondence* (London: Longmans, 1849), vol. 3, p. 334.

5. THE LUDDITES: APRIL–MAY 1812

P. 125—Radcliffe: *Dictionary of National Biography;* Sykes, *History of Huddersfield,* pp. 288–90; Hammond and Hammond, *Skilled Labourer,* p. 316.

Leeds Mercury: Thomis, *The Luddites,* p. 147.

Grey: Quoted in Hammond and Hammond, *Skilled Labourer,* p. 303.

P. 126—"scouring the district": Sykes and Walker, *Ben o' Bill's.*

Booth: This version from ibid; other similar in Hammond and Hammond, *Skilled Labourer,* p. 307; and Peel, *Risings of Luddites,* p. 102.

"You Heroes": Ibid., p. xiv.

P. 127—"the people"; "the friends": Thompson, *MEWC,* pp. 641, 614.

P. 128—"A confidential": Home Office 42/122; Hammond and Hammond, *Skilled Labourer,* p. 309. Thompson has this from General Grey.

Peel, *Risings of Luddites,* p. 118.

"Vengeance": Home Office 42/122; Thomis, *The Luddites,* p. 80.

Peel, *Risings of Luddites,* p. 121–22.

Cartwright assassination attempt: Ibid., pp. 122–24.

P. 129—Letter: Thompson, *MEWC,* pp. 610–11.

"Justice Radcliffe": Sykes and Walker, *Ben o' Bill's.*

P. 130—Sheffield: *Annual Register* (1812), p. 56; Hammond and Hammond, *Skilled Labourer,* p. 309; F. K. Donnelly and John L. Baxter, "Sheffield and the English Revolutionary Tradition," in Sidney Pollard and Colin Holmes, eds., *Economic and Social History of Southern Yorkshire* (Sheffield: Southern Yorkshire County Council, 1976); M. I. Thomis and Jennifer Grimmett, *Women in Protest, 1800–50* (London: Croom Helm, 1982).

P. 131—Stockport: Glen, *Urban Workers,* pp. 176–77; *Annual Register (1812),* pp. 56–59.

(Footnote): Davis, *Society and Culture in Early Modern Europe,* (Stanford: Stanford University Press, 1975), pp. 147–48.

P. 132—(Footnote): Glen, *Urban Workers,* p. 164.

P. 133—Letter: Glen, *Urban Workers,* p. 178 (letter dated April 16); Thompson, *MEWC,* p. 620 (letter dated April 18).

"First Congress": Hammond and Hammond, *Skilled Labourer,* pp. 281–84; *Annual Register (1812),* pp. 58–59.

P. 134—Parnell: Hammond and Hammond, *Skilled Labourer,* p. 292.

Annual Register (1812), p. 58.

P. 134–35—Manchester: Hammond and Hammond, *Skilled Labourer*, pp. 287–88, 293–94; Prentice, *Sketches of Manchester*, p. 52.

P. 135—"I saw a": Glen, *Urban Workers*, p. 182.

Pp. 136–40—Middleton: Prentice, *Sketches of Manchester*, pp. 52–53; *Annual Register (1812)*, pp. 59–61; Hammond and Hammond, *Skilled Labourer*, pp. 288–89, 294–95; Foster, *Class Struggle*, p. 40; Thompson *MEWC*, p. 620; Bamford, *Life of a Radical*, pp. 245–50; Thomis and Grimmett, *Women in Protest*, pp. 47–48.

P. 137—*Leeds Mercury*, April 25, 1812.

P. 138—(Footnote): Hughes, *Rape*, p. 219.

P. 139—"Had some poor": In Hay et al., *Albion's Fatal Tree*, p. 323.

P. 140—*Leeds Intelligencer*, April 27, 1812; Thomis, *The Luddites*, pp. 78–79.

Letters, etc.: Home Office 42/122; Hammond and Hammond, *Skilled Labourer*, pp. 289–91; Thomis, *The Luddites*, pp. 82–83; Foster, *Class Struggle*, p. 40.

Fletcher: *Dictionary of National Biography; Blackfaces;* Darvall, *Popular Disturbances*, pp. 294–301.

Pp. 140–44—Westhoughton: Hammond and Hammond, *Skilled Labourer*, pp. 279–85, 295–96; *Annual Register (1812)*, pp. 61–62; Darvall, *Popular Disturbances*, Chapter 5.

P. 141—Deposition: Hammond and Hammond, *Skilled Labourer*, pp. 283–84.

P. 143—Taylor: In *Blackfaces*, p. 9.

P. 144—Fletcher: Hammond and Hammond, *Skilled Labourer*, p. 285.

Trentham: *Annual Register (1812)*, pp. 63–64; Bailey, *Annals*, p. 256; Thompson, *MEWC*, p. 589.

P. 145—"*No* intelligence": Thomis, *Luddism in Nottinghamshire*, p. 56.

Horsfall assassination: Peel, *Risings of Luddites*, Chapter 16; Sykes, *History of Huddersfield*, pp. 281–85; Sykes and Walker, *Ben o' Bill's.* Trial testimony: Howell, *State Trials*, pp. 1007–32.

P. 147—*Annual Register (1812)*, p. 64.

P. 148—Government force: Home Office 42/123; Darvall, *Popular Disturbances*, pp. 100–103, 260ff.; Gregory, *Regional Transformation*, pp. 167–68; Thompson, *MEWC*, p. 615; *Annual Register*, (1812), pp. 63–64.

(Footnote): Darvall, *Popular Disturbances*, p. 1; Thompson, *MEWC*, p. 617; John Belchem, *Industrialism*, p. 65; see also Charles Oman, *History of the Peninsular War* (Oxford: Oxford University Press, 1902), vol. 1, p. 230.

P. 149— "the scum": Quoted in Halévy, *England in 1815* (see note to p. 50 above), p. 83n.

Leeds Intelligencer: Darvall, *Popular Disturbances*, p. 263n.

Huddersfield: Harriet Martineau, *History of England* (London: G. Bell & Sons, 1878), pp. 398–99.

Spies and informers: Darvall, *Popular Disturbances,* pp. 292ff.; *Blackfaces;* John Clegg, *Annals of Bolton* (Bolton, 1888).

P. 150—"Merchants and": Sykes, *History of Huddersfield,* p. 285.

"regular associations": Foster, *Class Struggle,* p. 41.

Radcliffe: Hammond and Hammond, *Skilled Labourer,* pp. 316–17, 334.

P. 151—Letter: Hay et al., *Albion's Fatal Tree,* p. 322.

6. THE LUDDITES: MAY 1812–JANUARY 1813

P. 153—Verse: Home Office 42/123; Thomis, *Luddism in Nottinghamshire,* pp. 55–56.

P. 154—Perceval assassination: *Annual Register (1812),* pp. 74–75; Mollie Gillen, *Assassination of a Prime Minister* (London: Sedgwick & Jackson, 1972); Peel, *Risings of Luddites,* pp. 158–62.

Pp. 155–56—Reaction to assassination: Thompson, *MEWC,* p. 623; Cobbett, quoted in Gillen, *Assassination;* Prentice, *Sketches of Manchester,* p. 46; Hammond and Hammond, *Town Labourer,* pp. 103–4.

P. 156—Southey: *Southey: Life . . .* (see note to p. 123 above*),* vol. 3, pp. 337–38.

Darvall, *Popular Disturbances,* pp. 306, 310.

P. 157—Sir Francis Wood: Home Office 42/124, June 17, 1812.

General Maitland: Thomis, *The Luddites,* p. 95.

Commandant: Pellew, *Sidmouth,* (see note to p. 77 above), Chapter 30, p. 84.

Pp. 157–60—On whether Luddism was revolutionary, see notes for p. 119 above, and Lords, Parliamentary Report; *Annual Register (1812),* p. 390; Glen, *Urban Workers,* pp. 185–86; Peel, *Risings of Luddites,* p. 156; Thomis, *The Luddites,* pp. 92–95.

P. 162—Arms raids: *Annual Register (1812),* pp. 75–76, 83–84, 86, 88, 109.

Lloyd: Home Office 40/1, June 17, 1812; Thomis, *The Luddites,* p. 81.

"some hundreds": Dinwiddy, "Luddism and Politics," p. 53.

Parliamentary committee: Lords, Parliamentary Report, *Annual Register (1812),* p. 84.

P. 163—Fitzwilliam: *British Documents,* p. 376 (July 25, 1812).

Haigh: Howell, *State Trials,* pp. 1139–49; Peel, *Risings of Luddites,* pp. 174–76.

P. 165—"Every article": *Annual Register (1812),* pp. 84, 86.

Attacks on individuals: Lords, *Parliamentary Report (1812),* pp. 78, 389; Hammond and Hammond, *Skilled Labourer,* p. 320; Thomis, *The Luddites,* p. 80.

"the commotions": *Annual Register (1812),* pp. 85–86.

"the atrocious": Ibid, p. 84.

P. 166—Lancaster assizes: Hammond and Hammond, *Skilled Labourer,* pp. 293–97; *Annual Register (1812)*, pp. 84–85; *Blackfaces;* reports differ on the number of defendants, but fifty-eight is probably accurate.

P. 167—"was a boy": *Blackfaces*, p. 17.

Chester assizes: *Annual Register (1812)*, p. 78; Hammond and Hammond, *Skilled Labourer*, pp. 291–92; Glen, *Urban Workers*, pp. 183–84.

P. 168—Whittaker: Hammond and Hammond, *Skilled Labourer*, pp. 274, 291–92.

P. 169—(Footnote): Hammond and Hammond, *Skilled Labourer*, p. 274; Rudé, *Protest and Punishment*, p. 190.

Sidmouth: *Dictionary of National Biography;* Pellew, *Sidmouth;* Philip Ziegler, *Addington* (London: Collins, 1965).

P. 170—"Under his": Pellew, *Sidmouth*, p. 79.

"although the conduct": Ibid, pp. 86–87.

"Man cannot": Ibid, p. 90.

P. 171—Maitland: Hammond and Hammond, *Skilled Labourer*, pp. 312–17; Darvall, *Popular Disturbances*, pp. 259–65, 301–3.

"In pursuance": Raynes, *An Appeal*, pp. 40–41.

P. 172—James Starkey: Peel, *Risings of Luddites*, pp. 112–14.

P. 173— "The voluntary": Raynes, *An Appeal*, pp. 88–89.

P. 174—Clemency: Dinwiddy, "Luddism and Politics"; Hammond and Hammond, *Skilled Labourer*, pp. 337–39.

"It appears": Ibid., p. 338.

P. 175—Lady Ludd: Thomis and Grimmett (see note to p. 129 above), p. 139.

Maitland: Home Office 42/129; Hammond and Hammond, *Skilled Labourer*, p. 323.

P. 176—Reformism: G. S. Veitch, *The Genesis of Parliamentary Reform* (London: Constable, 1913).

Cartwright: In Thompson, *MEWC*, pp. 89–96, 666.

"It is the": Dinwiddy, "Luddism and Politics."

P. 177—Manchester thirty-eight: Hammond and Hammond, *Skilled Labourer*, pp. 297–300.

Henson: Thompson, *MEWC*, pp. 586–90; *Records of Nottingham*, pp. 137ff.

P. 178—"the breaking machinery": Hammond and Hammond, *Skilled Labourer*, p. 235.

"a particular": Hammond and Hammond, *Skilled Labourer*, p. 320.

P. 178–79—Radcliffe arrests: Peel, *Risings of Luddites*, pp. 177–79; Hammond and Hammond, *Skilled Labourer*, p. 322; *Leeds Mercury*, Oct. 24, 1812.

P. 180–83—York assizes: Howell, *State Trials;* Peel, *Risings of Luddites*, Chapters

23, 24, 26–30; Hammond and Hammond, *Skilled Labourer*, pp. 323–32; Thompson, *MEWC*, pp. 634–36; Thomis, *The Luddites*, pp. 146–47.

P. 181—"This may be": Howell, *State Trials*, p. 1063.

Annual Register (1813), p. 4, 5.

(Footnote): Thompson, Introduction to Peel, *Risings of Luddites*, p. xiii.

P. 182—"one of the greatest": Howell, *State Trials*, p. 1164.

P. 183—"No, sir": In Clarkson, *Memories* (see note to p. 112 above), p. 40, though he tells it about a Baron Wood, a relative of his wife's, and it was Thomson presiding; see also Hammond and Hammond, *Skilled Labourer*, p. 332.

Peel, *Risings of Luddites*, p. 264.

Prince Regent: Howell, *State Trials*, pp. 1167–70.

(Footnote): Shelley: Holmes, *Shelley* (see note to p. 89 above), p. 185.

P. 184—Nadin: *Dictionary of National Biography*.

Lloyd: Hammond and Hammond, *Skilled Labourer*, p. 333.

Radcliffe: Sykes, *History of Huddersfield*, pp. 288–89.

Cartwright: Hammond and Hammond, *Skilled Labourer*, p. 382; Peel, *Risings of Luddites*, pp. 281–82; *Leeds Mercury*, in Thompson, *MEWC*, p. 639; Fitzwilliam, *British Documents*, p. 532.

7. THE LUDDITES: 1813 . . .

P. 187—1814: Thomis, *The Luddites*, p. 181; Bailey, *Annals*, pp. 267, 271–273; Felkin, *Hosiery and Lace Manufactures*, p. 237.

P. 188—Loughborough: Bailey, *Annals*, pp. 283–85; Felkin, *Hosiery and Lace Manufactures*, pp. 237–42; *Records*, p. 230; Patterson, *Radical Leicester*, (see note to p. 64 above), pp. 105–7; Thomis, *The Luddites*, p. 182.

P. 189—Pentrich: John Stevens, *England's Last Revolution: Pentrich 1817* (Buxton, Derbyshire: Moorland, 1977); Joseph Arnould, *Memoir of . . . Lord Denman* (London: Longmans Green, 1873), pp. 108–16; Hammond and Hammond, *Skilled Labourer*, pp. 360–62, 368–71.

(Footnote): Byron, Dec. 24, 1816, in Marchand, ed., *Byron's Letters* (see note to p. 17 above); Kelsall, *Byron's Politics* (Sussex, England, and Totowa, N.J.: Harvester, 1987), pp. 50–51.

P. 192—Fletcher: Darvall, *Popular Disturbances*, pp. 299–301.

(Footnote 1): See Darvall, *Popular Disturbances*, pp. 209–11; Felkin, *Hosiery and Lace Manufactures*, p. 239; Thomis, *Luddism in Nottinghamshire*, p. 31; Thomis, *The Luddites*, pp. 77–86.

(Footnote 2): Colquhoun, in Perkin, *Origins*, p. 20.

P. 193—"thinking discretion": Clarkson, *Memories* (see note to p. 112 above).

P. 194—"machinery of": Randall, "Philosophy of Luddism."

"the fear of": W. Cooke Taylor, *Notes of a Tour of Lancashire* (London: 1842), pp. 167–69; see also Halévy, *England in 1815* (see note to p. 50 above), p. 289.

P. 196—Dawson: Thomis, *The Luddites,* p. 173.

On class consciousness, I side with Robert Glen, *Urban Workers,* in his Conclusions; see also Calhoun, *Class Struggle.*

P. 197—"good servants": Hammond and Hammond, *Skilled Labourer,* p. 377.

P. 198–201—On the "machinery question," see Berg, *Machinery Question;* Maxine Berg, *Technology and Toil in 19th-Century Britain* (London: CSE Books, 1979), especially pp. 73–96; Randall Jackson, *Speech . . . on the State of Woolen Manufactures* (London: 1806).

P. 198—Ure, *Philosophy of Manufactures,* p. 29.

P. 199—Ricardo, *Principles,* 2nd ed. (see note to p. 51), p. 466.

Thompson, *Customs* (see note to p. 27), pp. 200–207, 273–84.

P. 200—"a trade": Jackson, *State of Woolen Manufactures.*

"Unrestrained machinery": George Burges, in Berg, *Technology and Toil,* p. 77 (his italics).

P. 201—Baines, *History of Cotton Manufacture,* p. 243.

P. 202—Thompson, *MEWC,* p. 486. The debate on the standard of living of British workers in the Industrial Revolution has kept alive a considerable academic industry, especially in recent years, with "optimists" and "pessimists" both twiddling the same inadequate statistics. For anyone who still doubts Thompson's conclusion, however (or Braudel's), I can only recommend a careful study of Thompson's *The Making of the English Working Class,* Part 2, or the contemporary readings listed for pages 44 through 49 above, particularly the Parliamentary Papers.

Statistics: Cook and Stevenson, *British Historical Facts* (see note to p. 43), Chapter 14; Langton and Morris, *Atlas of Industrializing Britain 1780–1914* (see note to p. 30); Baines, *History of Cotton Manufacture;* Jenkins, *West Riding;* Felkin, *Hosiery and Lace Manufactures.*

Pp. 203—*Morning Chronicle:* Reports by Angus Bethune Reach on Lancaster, Cheshire, Yorkshire, and the Midlands, in Ginswick, *Labour and the Poor.*

Pp. 204—"Our homes": Hammond and Hammond, *Skilled Labourer,* p. 203.

8. THE SECOND INDUSTRIAL REVOLUTION

P. 205—*Annual Register (1956),* p. 23, on a May 8, 1956, debate.

C. P. Snow, *The Two Cultures and the Scientific Revolution* (Cambridge: Cambridge University Press, 1959), Lecture 2, "Intellectuals and Natural Luddites."

P. 206—"the benefits": Truman inaugural address, Jan. 20, 1949.

P. 207—Noble, *Progress Without People,* p. 1.

P. 208—Modern technology: see titles at beginning of Notes section.

P. 209—"Science explores": Mumford, *Pentagon,* p. 213.

P. 210—Oppenheimer: Quoted in George Grant, *Technology and Justice* (Toronto: Anansi, 1968), p. 24.

Grant, ibid.

P. 212—Herbert Read, *The Grass Roots of Art* (London: Faber & Faber, 1955), last page.

P. 214–16—Agricultural industrialization: Wayne D. Rasmussen, *Scientific American,* September 1982, p. 76; Wendell Berry, *The Unsettling of America* (New York: Avon Books, 1978); *Statistical Abstract of the United States* (Washington, D.C.: GPO, 1992), nos. 1073–82, 629–32; *New York Times,* Oct. 10, 1993, p. 23.

P. 215—(footnote): Rasmussen, *Scientific American,* p. 85.

P. 216—Manufacture of needs: See especially Alan Durning, *How Much Is Enough* (New York: Norton, 1992); *E Magazine,* November 1993.

Advertising: Durning, *How Much,* Chapter 9; *New York Times,* Dec. 7, 1993, p. D22.

P. 218—"the enlargement": Anthony Lake, *New York Times,* Sept. 22, 1993, p. A13.

Cities: *Time,* Jan. 11, 1993.

P. 219—Malls: *E Magazine,* January 1993.

New products: *New York Times,* Dec. 30, 1993, p. D16.

Worldwatch: Durning, *How Much,* p. 38.

On the role of the U.S. government funding, see Nobel, *Progress Without People,* Part 2.

P. 220—(Footnote): Rob van Tulder, "Subsidy Politics," *Comparative Political Studies,* vol. 20, no. 2 (1987).

P. 222—Multinationals: *New Internationalist,* August 1993; annual issues of *Fortune Global 500.* See also Richard Barnet and John Cavanagh, *Global Dreams: Imperial Corporations and the New World Order* (New York: Simon & Schuster, 1994).

P. 223—$185 billion: United Nations Center of Transnational Corporations, *World Investment Report* (New York: United Nations, 1992).

Roach: Quoted in *New York Times,* Sept. 5, 1993, Sec. 4, p. 4.

P. 225–27—U.S. job loss: Richard Barnet, *Harper's,* September 1993; Jeremy Rifkin, *The End of Work* (New York: Putnam's, Jeremy Tarcher, 1994); Kevin Phillips, *Boiling Point* (New York: Random House, 1993); *Fortune,* July 12, 1993; *Wall Street Journal,* Sept. 3, 1993, p. 1; *Wall Street Journal,* Feb. 24, 1994, p. 1; *Time,* Jan. 17, 1993; and *New York Times,* Dec. 26, 1992, p. 1; Feb. 14, 1993, p. 26; Feb. 24, 1993, (Op. Ed.); March 14, 1994, p. 1; March 22, 1994, p. 1.

P. 226—Leontief: Quoted in *New York Times,* Sept. 5, 1993, Sec. 4, p. 4.
"Automation roars": Ibid.

P. 227—Disposable jobs: *New York Times,* March 15, 1993, p. 1; *New York Times,* Dec. 26, 1992, p. 1; *Time,* Nov. 22, 1993.

P. 229—Moralia declaration: *New York Times,* Oct. 10, 1991, p. B10; a second declaration: *New York Times,* Feb. 25, 1994, p. A10.

P. 230—Environmental assaults are detailed relentlessly in *The State of the World,* issued annually since 1984 by the Worldwatch Institute and published by Norton; see also Ponting, *Green History.*

P. 232—1990 estimates of wealth: Durning, *How Much,* Chapter 2.

P. 234—Consumption: Ibid., p. 50.

P. 235—40,000 children: *Worldwatch,* November–December 1993, p. 37.

9. THE NEO-LUDDITES

P. 237—Glendinning: *Utne Reader,* March 1990, pp. 50–53.

P. 239—"what dangerous": Glendinning, *When Technology Wounds: The Human Consequences of Progress* (New York: William Morrow, 1990), p. 180.

P. 242—"What I learned": Ibid., p. 181.

P. 244–47—Non-Western resistance: *Third World Resurgence,* published in Penang, Malaysia, gives regular coverage; see no. 39, 1993. See also regular "campaigns" in *The Ecologist* (Dorset, U.K.), especially March–April 1993. Sabotage: Christopher Manes, *Green Rage* (Boston: Little Brown, 1991).

P. 245—Mali: Bill Rau, *From Feast to Famine* (London, New York: Zed Books, 1991), pp. 153ff.

P. 246—Piparwar: *The Ecologist,* March–April, 1993; *Financial Times* (London), Jan. 20, 1991, p. 8.

P. 247—Alvares: In Ashis Nandy, ed., *Science, Hegemony, and Violence* (Oxford: Oxford University Press, 1988), pp. 110–11.

Pp. 247–48—"against the whole": *New York Times,* Feb. 20, 1994, p. 3.

P. 248—For a complete and readable rundown on ecotage to 1990, see Manes, *Green Rage,* passim; also, the regular column "Monkey Wrenching" in *Earth First! Journal* (published quarterly from 1981 to 1991) and Dave Foreman, *Confessions of an Eco-Warrior* (New York: Crown/Harmony Books, 1991).

P. 249—Estimate: Manes, *Green Rage,* p. 9.

P. 250—U.S. labor: Stanley Aronowitz, *False Promises* (McGraw-Hill, 1973); Daniel Bell, *Work and Its Discontents* (Boston: Beacon Press, 1956); Noble, *Progress Without People.*

P. 251—HEW Task force: *Work in America* (Washington, D.C.: Government Printing Office, 1973).

P. 252—Sabotage: Noble, *Progress Without People,* pp. 20–48; Martin Sprouse,

Sabotage in the American Workplace (San Francisco: Pressure Drop Press, 1992); Laurie Taylor and Paul Walter, "Industrial Sabotage," in Stanley Cohen, ed., *Images of Deviance* (New York: Penguin Books, 1971).

P. 253—Kerr et al., *Industrialism,* (see note to p. 28), p. 7, Chapter 8.

P. 254—Foundation in Deep Ecology, 950 Lombard St., San Francisco, CA, 94133.

P. 255—Cobb, *Human Economy Newsletter,* September 1992.

P. 256—Jerry Mander, personal communication; see also Mander, *Absence of Sacred,* Chapter 2.

P. 257—Berry, *Utne Reader,* March 1990, p. 52.

(Footnote): See also Mander, *Absence of Sacred,* Chapter 4.

P. 258—Capra, personal communication.

Temple: *Catholic Worker,* January–February 1987.

Pynchon: *New York Times Book Review,* Oct. 28, 1984, p. 1.

Weisenbaum: Quoted in Temple, above.

P. 259—Felix Rizvanov, *The Alternator* (published by Slippery Rock University), November–December 1992, p. 1.

10. LESSONS FROM THE LUDDITES

P. 262—Ure, *Philosophy of Manufactures,* p. 368.

Automation, quoted in Noble, *Progress,* p. 161.

P. 263—Berry: *Harper's,* September 1988.

P. 264—Randall, *Before the Luddites,* p. 287.

P. 265—"structural change": See, for example, Edward Luttwak, "Why Fascism Is the Wave of the Future," *London Review of Books,* April 7, 1994.

"Only a people": Read, *Grass Roots* (see note to p. 212 above).

P. 266—Ellul: *The Technological Society* (New York: Knopf, 1964), p. 79.

P. 268—"shake off": See note to p. 116 above.

P. 270—Mario Savio: Quoted in Seymour Martin Lipset and Sheldon S. Wolin, *The Berkeley Student Revolt* (New York: Anchor Books, 1965), p. 163.

Mumford, *Pentagon of Power,* p. 433.

P. 272—Irokwa: Haudenosaunee, *A Basic Call to Consciousness: Akwesasne Notes,* 1977, quoted in Mander, *Absence of Sacred,* p. 192.

P. 273—Postman, *Technopoly,* Introduction.

Pp. 275—Longevity estimate: John E. Pfeiffer, *Emergence of Man* (New York: Harper & Row, 1972).

P. 277—Grant: in Abraham Rotstein, ed., *Beyond Industrial Growth* (Toronto: Toronto University Press, 1976), p. 125.

Index

Abbey, Edward, 240
Addington, Henry. *See* Sidmouth, Viscount
Africa, 41, 264
Agriculture: United Kingdom, 26, 34–35, 39, 43, 46, 51, 55, 125, 197; United States, 19, 214–16, 262–63
Algeria, 247
Alvares, Claude, 247
American Medical Association, 207
Amish, 271–72, 276
Annals of Nottinghamshire, 73, 81, 85, 91
Annual Register, 4, 68n, 92, 111, 130, 134, 137, 139, 143, 145, 147, 163, 165, 181, 205, 287
Anthropocentrism, 277
Archangel, 154
Archbishop of Canterbury, 64
Argentina, 41
Arkwright, Richard, 38, 70n
Armitage (magistrate), 144
Arms thefts, 79, 130, 162–65, 175, 283
Army (United Kingdom), 45, 61, 82, 83, 86, 92–94, 97, 115–16, 125–26, 132, 137–39, 147–49, 157, 171–72, 180–81, 190, 192n
Arnold, 71, 73, 76
Arson, 75, 105–6, 143; trials for, 166
Artisan, 57
Ashton: political agitations in, 121; population of, 48n; rioting in, 135
Ashton, Peter, 173
Asia, 41, 207, 226, 233, 244
Aspinall, A., 68n
Assizes, 282–83; Chester, 167–68; Lancaster, 166–69; Nottingham, 100–1, 166; York, 167, 174, 175, 179, 180–83, 184, 190, 267

Association for Relief of the Manufacturing and Labouring Poor, 193
Atkinson, Law, 127
Austen, Jane, 43, 63, 198
Australia, 41, 101–3, 166–69, 169–72, 190, 245, 246, 249–50, 252–53; transportation to, 79, 135, 166, 169, 190
Automation, 205, 223–28, 250–53, 262

Baines, Edward, 201, 288
Baines, John, 122, 182
Bamford, Samuel (Luddite), 187
Bamford, Samuel (weaver), 115, 136–38
Bamforth, Ben, 5–6, 11, 129, 150, 159, 173, 181
Band, James, 173, 174
Banford, 97
Bank of England, 43, 50
Barnes, William, 93–94
Barnsdale Forest, 1, 2
Barnsley, 184; food riots in, 175; machine breaking in, 162
Basford, 72; machine breaking in, 80, 92, 102
Bathurst, Lord, 149
Bavaria, 18
Bayley, Sir John, 101, 102, 103, 166
Becher, The Reverend John T., 88
Bedford, Grosvenor, 123
Bellingham, John, 154–55
Belloc, Hilaire, 17, 49
Ben o' Bill's, the Luddite, 5–6, 104, 110, 145, 146, 158, 159–60
Bentley, John, 131
Beornwulf, 78
Berkshire militia, 83, 93
Berry, Thomas, 240

Berry, Wendell, 240, 258, 263, 276
Betts (hosier), 72, 102
Bhopal, 21
Birmingham, 56
Blackburn, 70n; population of, 48n
Black Lamp, 121
Blackstone Edge, 2
Blackwell, John, 130
Blake, William, 17
Bolton, 56, 70n, 106, 135, 140, 142, 174,
    176; Luddites in, 141; machine breaking
    in, 162; political agitations in, 121; popu-
    lation of, 39, 48n; use of force in, 149
Booth, John, 12–14, 126, 159; burial of, 128
Bourbon Restoration, 18
Bradford, 118, 121n
Bradshaw, William, 131
Brandreth, Jeremiah, 189
Braudel, Fernand, 42–43, 58–59
Brazil, 245
Brodeur, Paul, 240
Brontë, Charlotte, 15–16, 126, 269
Brontë, The Reverend Patrick, 15
Brook, James, 12
Brook, Thomas, 11, 182
Brummel, Beau, 41, 43, 63
Buckley, John, 114–15
Bulwell, 71, 97; machine breaking in, 76,
    92, 144
Burton, Daniel, 136–38, 166, 193
Burton, Emmanuel, 136–40, 193, 269
Bury, political agitations in, 121
Business Week, 20
Butterfield, Mr., 163
Byron, Lord, 17, 43, 68n, 88–89, 98–99,
    155, 168, 177, 189n, 198, 258; speech to
    House of Lords of, 68n, 96–98, 282

Calhoun, Craig, 86
Canada, 41, 249
Capra, Fritjof, 255, 258
Captain Swing demonstrations, 18, 194
Cargill, 244–45
Carleton House, 64, 147
Carlisle, 106; food riots in, 147
Carlyle, Thomas, 17, 30, 39, 54, 56, 198,
    229, 288
Carnegie Institute, 226
Carnell, William, 102
Carson, Rachel, 240
Carter, Joseph, 163–64
Cartwright, Major John, 176, 195

Cartwright, William, 7–14, 23, 110, 127,
    144, 150, 172, 184–85, 269; assassination
    attempt on, 128–29. See also Rawfolds
    Mill
Castlereagh, Viscount, 43, 169
Census Bureau (U.S.), 228
Central America, 247
Ceylon, 244
Chambers English Dictionary, 205
Charles II, 99
Charlotte, Queen, 147
Charlson, Abraham, 167
Chernobyl, 21
Cheshire, 1, 103, 282–83; oathing in, 109n;
    rioting in, 135; valuation of damage in,
    192n
Chester: assizes in, 167, 169, 174, 183
Chesterton, G. K., 17
Childe Harold (Byron), 88, 99n, 282
Children: before Industrial Revolution,
    36; in Industrial Revolution, 32, 33, 47,
    48–49, 125, 202
China, 217, 234, 264, 268
Chorley, 70n
Chrysler Corporation, 210
Clare, John, 54
Clarkson, Henry, 112n
"Class", 196–97
Clemency for oathing, 173–74
Clifton, 163
Clinton, William, 20, 218, 221, 225
Clitheroe, 1
Cobb, Charles, 255
Cobbett, William, 4, 38, 48, 69, 155, 169,
    195, 198
Coldham, George (town clerk), 80, 84, 101,
    145
Colne, River, 110
Colombia, 245
Colonies, 41–42
Colquhoun, Patrick, 27, 44
Combination Acts, 32, 52, 121, 177, 187, 195
Computers, 20, 206–7, 238, 257–58
Constables, 4, 13, 73, 80, 83–84, 109, 114,
    144, 149, 192
Consumption, 38–42
Continental Blockade, 62
Cornwall, 78
Costa Rica, 245
Crompton, Samuel, 154
Cuba, 268
Cumberland militia, 10, 115, 137, 138

Cut-ups, 67, 68, 70, 75n, 87, 193
Cymbaline, 78

Darvall, F. O., 76, 148n, 156, 192n
Davis, John, 256
Davis, Natalie Zemon, 131n
Davy, Humphrey, 283
Dawson, William, 196
Dean, Jonathan, 12–13, 14, 182
Deansgate, 166
Death penalty, 95–100, 97, 109n
Death rates, 48–49
Deep ecology, 255
Deforestation, 54, 230
Denmark, 253
Derby, 121n, 176; machine breaking in, 79
Derbyshire, 1, 66, 67, 79, 92, 135, 189;
    machine breaking in, 76; rioting in, 135
Despard, Colonel Edmund, 113, 121
Devonshire, 188
Diamond, Stanley, 240
Dickens, Charles, 17, 43, 56–57, 113, 202,
    282
Dickinson, Carr, and Company, 111
Dictionary of National Biography, 170
Disraeli, Benjamin, 43, 169
Dragoons, 73–74, 76, 77, 80, 97, 148, 189
Dyott, General, 83

Earth First!, 248–49, 276
Economic conditions, 5, 23, 38; and cost of
    Luddism, 191–92; of Industrial Revolu-
    tion, 49–52, 198–99; and Napoleonic
    wars, 61–62
Ecotage, 248–49
Ecuador, 245
Edgeley, 132
Egypt, 34, 247, 268
Ehrenfeld, David, 240
Ellul, Jacques, 19, 240, 266
Emerson, Ralph Waldo, 17
Enclosure movement, 34–35, 54, 55; effects
    of, 39
Enfield Chase, 54
Engels, Friedrich, 43, 48, 57, 58
Environment: destruction of, 228–32; and
    Industrial Revolution, 23–24, 53–58,
    199
Epping Forest, 34
Europe, 17, 18, 26, 63, 207, 233, 243, 244,
    250, 255, 259, 264; forests of, 55; Neo-
    Luddism in, 252–53

Exchange Hall (Manchester), 115, 282;
    valuation of damage to, 192n
Exmoor Forest, 54
Exxon Valdez, 21

Factory system, 23, 25–26, 30–31, 104–5,
    202; labor conditions in, 46–49; in
    Nottingham, 66–68
Farrington, Joseph, 61
Fawkes, Guy, 157
Felkin, William, 36, 66, 80, 100, 188, 193,
    288
Ferry, W. H., 240
Finchley Common, 34
Fitzwilliam, Lord-Lieutenant Earl, 163,
    184, 185
Fletcher, Colonel Ralph, 121, 140, 142, 143,
    149, 174, 192
Food riots, 121, 130, 134–35, 136, 175, 192n,
    282–83; trial for, 166–67
Foreman, Dave, 240
Fortune, 207
Foster, Joseph, 111–12
Foster mill, 120
Foucault, Michel, 270
Foundation for Deep Ecology, 254
Foundation on Economic Trends, 254
France, 65, 117, 120, 157, 220, 244, 250;
    Luddism in, 18; war with, 4, 42, 50,
    61–63, 65, 91, 148
Frankenstein (Shelley), 16–17
Frankfurt School, 19
Friends of Parliamentary Reform, 176
Frome, 70n

Gaskell, Peter, 29, 36, 287
Gee Cross: rioting in, 135
Geiger, Henry, 240
General Agreement on Tariffs and Trade
    (GATT), 222, 244–45, 256
General Motors Corporation, 222, 250
Geoffrey of Monmouth, 78
George III, King, 63
George IV, Prince Regent, 43, 63–64, 83,
    86, 115, 116, 118, 147, 151, 159, 176, 177,
    183, 196
Germany, 86, 220, 250
Gibbons, Mary, 130
Glasgow, 106, 118, 157
Glendinning, Chellis, 237–39, 241, 242,
    255, 276
Global Environment Facility, 223

Globalism, 277
Gloucester, 70n
Goldsmith, Edward, 240
Goldsmith, Oliver, 54
Goodair, John, 114, 131–32, 168
Goodman, Paul, 19, 240
Gospel of Mammonism (Carlyle), 39
Grand National Consolidated Trades
    Union, 195
Grant, George Parkin, 210, 240, 277
Grass Roots of Art, The (Read), 212
Green, George, 102–3
Green, William, 40
Green movement, 254–55
Grenville, Lord William, 118
Grey, General Thomas, 125, 128, 148, 171
Grey, Lord Charles, 118
Griffin, Susan, 240
Guild movement, 18

Haigh, George, 163–64
Haigh, James, 14, 182
Haigh, Marshal and Company, 105–6
Hainault Forest, 54
Halifax, 118, 121n, 122, 127, 182, 184; popu-
    lation of, 48n
Hall, William, 178, 179, 181
Hammond, J. L. and Barbara, 52
Hancock, Benjamin, 102
Hanson, Colonel Joseph, 118n, 119
Hard Times (Dickens), 56–57
Hartley, Samuel, 13, 14, 127
Hawthorne, Nathaniel, 17
Heanor, 92
Heathcoat, John, 67, 75, 188–89
Heidegger, Martin, 19
Henson, Gravener, 100, 177–78, 187, 268,
    283
Hero of Alexandria, 29n
Hiroshima, 239
Hitchener, Elizabeth, 89
Hobart, 103
Hobhouse, Henry, 167, 168, 180, 181
Hobsbawm, Eric, 69
Holland, Lord, 96
Hollingsworth, 71, 144, 173
Hollinwood, 136
Home Office, 3, 68n, 81, 87, 88, 92, 100,
    103, 106, 112, 113, 120, 128, 134, 140, 147,
    150, 157, 162, 166, 167, 180, 287
Horbury, 113, 120

Horsfall, father of William, 185, 193
Horsfall, William: assassination of, 145–
    47, 150, 151, 161, 167, 175; trial of assas-
    sins of, 178–79, 180, 181–82
Hounslow Heath, 34
House of Lords, 68n, 85, 89, 120, 158, 283
House of Lords investigative committee,
    109–11
Hucknall Torkard, 94
Huddersfield, 6n, 7, 12, 117–18, 125, 127,
    131, 144, 145, 146, 151, 158, 165, 172, 185;
    Luddites in, 119; Machine breaking in,
    110–11, 162, 179; political agitations in,
    121; population of, 48n; use of force
    in, 149
Hughes, Glyn, 138n
Hussars, 94, 130
Huxley, Aldous, 19

IBM, 209, 227
Ilkeston, 76
Illich, Ivan, 240
India, 41, 42, 217, 240, 244, 246, 265, 268
Indians (U.S.), 20, 160, 271–72. *See also*
    Irokwa Confederacy
Indonesia, 245, 247
Industrialism, 18–19, 20, 21, 28–29, 33, 39,
    49, 55, 126, 157, 195, 228–29, 232, 236,
    267, 274, 276–77, 279
Industrialism and Industrial Man (Kerr
    et al.), 253
Industrial Revolution, 5, 20, 22, 23, 26,
    27–58, 45, 69, 160, 207, 208, 218, 225,
    230, 264, 266, 269; consumption and,
    38–42; effects of Luddism on, 198–201;
    environment and, 53–59; ideology of,
    49; and labor, 43–49; living conditions
    in, 47–49; as new culture, 58–59; social
    implications of, 29–30; technology
    of, 27–33. *See also* Second Industrial
    Revolution
International Monetary Fund, 222
Ireland, 47, 118, 119, 243
Irokwa Confederacy, 254, 263, 272, 276
Israel, 247, 268
Ivanhoe (Scott), 2

Jacobinism, 120, 140, 155, 159
Japan, 29, 220, 242, 247, 249, 268
Java, 245
Joan of Arc, 157

John, King, 3
Jones, W. O., 189–90
Jungk, Robert, 240

Kent, 61
Kenya, 268
Kerr, Clark, 28–29, 253
Kersal Moor, 132
Kimberley, 72, 93
Kirby: machine breaking in, 76
Knox, Vicesimus, 41
Korea, 244
Kvaloy, Sigmund, 254–55

Labor: before Industrial Revolution,
    35–36; and government, 51–52; during
    Industrial Revolution, 31–33, 43–49;
    and the new technology, 223–28;
    worker/master relationship, 197
Labor unions. See Unions
Lacy, Charles, 74–75
Ladakhi, 265
Laissez-faire, 49, 52, 95, 196, 204, 219, 259,
    263, 267, 274
Lamb, Caroline, 177
Lamb, William, 95
Lancashire, 1, 25–26, 44, 47, 50, 56, 70n,
    75, 110, 118n, 119, 121, 150, 171, 174, 193,
    282–83; assizes in, 166, 167, 169; condi-
    tions in, 62; force used in, 148, 157;
    Luddites in, 103; machine breaking in,
    162; oathing in, 109; valuation of dam-
    age in, 192
Lancaster: assizes in, 183; machine breaking
    in, 106
Latin America, 226, 248
Lear, Edward, 283
LeBlanc, Sir Simon, 166, 180, 181
Leeds, 9, 23, 31, 42, 48, 107, 116, 117, 144,
    157, 163; food riots in, 175; Luddites in,
    119; machine breaking in, 104, 105, 110,
    111; political agitations in, 121; violence
    in, 165
Leeds Intelligencer, 140, 149
Leeds Mercury, 10, 120, 125, 137, 179, 185,
    190, 287
Leicester, 65, 70n, 77, 121n; machine
    breaking in, 79
Leicestershire, 66, 79, 92
Leontief, Wassily, 226
Lessing, Doris, 240

Liverpool, Lord, 169, 172, 283
Lloyd, John, 134, 162, 168, 178, 184
London, 41, 43, 61, 70n, 78, 83, 86, 87,
    88, 120, 131, 134, 147, 155, 157, 176, 189;
    as government, 101, 148, 150, 154, 159,
    169, 175; population in, 39; society of,
    62–64, 66, 189
Loughborough, 67, 75, 84, 121n, 258;
    machine breaking in, 188–89
Ludd, Ned, 3–4, 9, 17, 74, 80, 81–82, 83,
    84n, 85, 94, 99, 102, 106n, 107, 110, 116,
    117–18, 126, 129, 131, 133, 135, 136, 141,
    144, 151, 153, 159, 164, 179, 189n, 241,
    258, 287; origin of personage, 77–78; as
    symbol of revolution, 138
Luddism: as movement, 75–76; begin-
    nings of, 3–6, 9, 74–75, 76–77, 79–
    80; decline of, 175, 187–91; effects of,
    191–201, 272, 277; failures of, 160, 272,
    275–76; financial toll of, 191–92; litera-
    ture reflecting, 16–17, 18–19, 240;
    philosophy of, 5, 16, 17, 18–19, 205;
    political effects of, 195–96; popular-
    ity of, 119; punishment of, 4, 82–83,
    100–1; relevance today of, 22; as revolu-
    tionary force, 5, 138, 157–62, 165, 170;
    sources for, 287; spreading of, 103; sym-
    pathy for, 88, 95. See also Luddites;
    Neo-Luddism; Oaths
Luddites: assassinations by, 128–29, 144–
    47; character, 101–3; communication
    among, 106–7; letters of, 74–75, 80, 83,
    94, 99, 117–19, 129, 139, 151, 159, 190,
    287; organization of, 4, 85–86; origin
    of name, 77–78; publications of, 113,
    116–17; secrecy of, 84–86; solicitations
    for support of, 79–80
Lytell Geste of Robyn Hode, 2

Maastricht Treaty, 243
Macauley, Thomas, 53
Macclesfield, 41n
Machine breaking, 5, 18, 68n, 78, 92–94,
    160–61; decline of, 175; in 1814, 187–88;
    first Luddite instance of, 79–89; previ-
    ous instances of, 69–70, 76; punish-
    ment for, 79, 95, 287; valuation of
    damages of, 4, 86–87. See also Indi-
    vidual cities
Machine gun, 17
McKibben, Bill, 240

Maitland, General Thomas, 148, 157, 171–72, 175, 177, 184
Malaysia, 244, 245
Mali, 245
Malta, 34
Malthus, Thomas, 40, 282
Manchester, 46, 47, 48, 56, 57, 58, 69n, 70n, 103, 106, 107, 109, 115, 118, 120, 132, 135, 136, 137, 140, 145, 165, 166, 171, 174, 193; conditions in, 25–26, 31; hangings in, 169; Luddites in, 141; machine breaking in, 105–6, 113, 114; political agitations in, 121; population in, 39; riots in, 121, 134–35; use of force in, 149–50; valuation of damage in, 192n
Manchester Gazette, 103–4
Manchester Mercury, 44, 134, 287
Mander, Jerry, 240, 254, 256, 276
Mansfield, 2, 73, 97; labor in, 87; machine breaking in, 76
Manufacturing Population in England, The (Gaskell), 29
Marcuse, Herbert, 19, 240
Marsden, 145, 146; use of force in, 149
Marsh: machine breaking in, 110
Marshall, Gervas, 102
Marsland, Peter, 114, 131
Marxists, 195
Melbourne, 92
Mellor, George, 7, 9–14, 12, 110, 128, 145–46, 158, 183; trial and execution of, 178–79, 181–82
Melville, Herman, 17
Merchant, Carolyn, 240
Mercia, 78
Mexico, 229, 243, 247–48, 264
Middleton, 139, 140, 166, 193; machine breaking in, 142, 144; rioting in, 136, 137
Middleton, Lord, 87
Militia, 4, 13, 50, 72–73, 73, 77, 83, 92–94, 130, 138, 139, 140, 142, 148, 149, 149–50, 157; effect of, 94. See also Army; Constables; Cumberland militia; Dragoons; Scots Greys
Mill, John Stuart, 55
Mills, Stephanie, 240
Milne, Nathaniel, 139
Milnsbridge House, 125, 127, 129, 150, 178
Milton, John, 78
Mitchell, Dr., 134
Mohawk, John, 254
Molyneux, Mary and Lydia, 143

Moore, Thomas, 189n
Morelia Declaration, 229
Morning Chronicle (London), 98, 203
Morocco, 247
Morris, William, 17
Mowat, Farley, 240
Muir, John, 17–18
Mumford, Lewis, 19, 21, 240, 270, 273, 276
Myth of the Machine (Mumford), 240

Nadin, Constable Joseph, 171, 174, 177, 184
Naess, Arne, 240
Napoleon, 4, 42, 44, 61–62, 64, 91, 118, 148, 173, 283
Nash, John, 63
National Society for Promoting the Education of Poor in the Principles of the Established Church, 64
National Science Foundation, 207
Nature. See Environment
Ned Ludd Books, 249
Neo-Luddism, 18–22, 205, 237–59, 270, 271, 279; definition of, 255; principles of, 237–38
Nepal, 247
Newcastle, Duke of, 66, 68n, 83, 84, 86, 88, 92, 95, 106, 155
New Lanark, 47
New Radford, 81
New Scientist, 205–6
New York Times, The, 226–27
Noble, David, 22, 207, 240
Noble (weaver), 81
Norberg-Hodge, Helena, 254, 265
North America, 207, 233, 248, 271
North American Free Trade Agreement (NAFTA), 243, 247
Norway, 255, 268
Nottingham, 4, 64, 64–65, 67, 78, 80, 81, 84, 86, 88, 89, 92, 93, 94, 95, 96, 97, 99, 101, 103, 104, 106, 107, 129, 131, 145, 151, 153, 155, 189, 193, 194; assize in, 166; conditions in, 66; food riots in, 175; force used in, 157; labor in, 87; machine breaking in, 79–88, 83, 144, 187; November–December, 1811, 64–68, 70; political agitations in, 121; raids in, 71–75; riots in, 121; use of force in, 148, 150; valuation of damage in, 192n
Nottingham Journal, 155, 287
Nottingham Review, 67, 77, 88
Nottinghamshire, 1–4, 61, 65, 65–68, 81,

100, 144, 177, 193, 282–83; effects of
Luddism in, 91; machine breaking in, 9,
71–81, 92–94, 100, 106, 175, 187,
191–92; oathing in, 109
Nunn, William, 87

Oastler, Richard, 37, 53
Oates, Woods, and Smithson Mill, 105
Oathing, 107–9, 113, 121, 134, 190, 283;
prosecution for, 168; punishment for,
173
Ogden, John, 182
Oldham, 56, 118, 135, 136, 140; arms thefts
in, 137; political agitations in, 121; popu-
lation of, 48n
Oliver (W. O. Jones), 189–90
Oppenheimer, Robert, 210
Orders in Council, 49, 62, 64, 154, 172, 196
Ottiwells, 193
Owen, Robert, 48, 195
Oxford English Dictionary, 205

Paine, Thomas, 113, 120, 122, 155
Pakistan, 247
Parker, Major John, 133
Parliament, 23, 32, 45, 46, 48, 50, 51, 56,
62, 69, 70, 95, 96, 99, 100, 115, 121, 123,
153–55, 154, 159, 162, 170, 177, 268, 287;
and Enclosure Movement, 34; and
industry, 50–51; and labor, 52–53, 62;
and new technology, 205; and reform,
176–78, 194–95. *See also* Combination
Acts; Orders in Council
Parnell, John, 134, 168
Peel, Frank, 122, 128, 146, 183
Peel, Sir Robert, 62
Pellew, George, 170
Pennine hills, 1, 2, 8, 30, 37, 57, 110, 113, 125
Pentrich, 79, 189
Perceval, Prime Minister Spencer, 95, 99,
118, 147, 283; assassination of, 153–56,
169
Perot, Ross, 243
Philippines, 247
Piparwar, 246
Place, Francis, 195
Poe, Edgar Allen, 17
Pollution, 24, 56–58, 230
Poor Law, 43–44, 48, 62, 66; effects of
Luddism on, 193
Population, 39–40, 232
Portugal, 4, 61, 148, 250

Postman, Neil, 273
Poverty, 23, 43–49, 61–62, 66, 91, 96,
103–4. *See also* Standard of living
Prescott, Charles, 134, 173–74
Preston, 48, 70n, 121
Prince Regent. *See* George IV, Prince
Regent
Pynchon, Thomas, 240, 258

Radcliffe, Joseph, 125, 127, 129, 146, 150,
151, 178–79, 181n, 184, 185; assassination
attempt upon, 165; threats against, 129
Radcliffe, William, 114, 131
Radford: machine breaking in, 93
Randall, Adrian, 105, 264
Ransom, John Crowe, 19
Rawfolds Mill, 7–16, 24, 110, 116, 126, 136,
137, 144, 151, 159, 167, 175, 176; prosecu-
tion of raid on, 125, 178–79, 182
Raynes, Captain Francis, 171–72, 174, 182
Read, Herbert, 212, 265, 274
Reform Bill of 1832: Chartist movement,
194
Reformism, 176–78, 268–69
Repression, 4, 51–52, 82–84, 92–95,
95–98, 115–16, 125–27, 132–34, 137,
139, 143–44, 147–50, 166–69, 169–72,
175, 178–83, 189–90, 190–91, 195–
98, 267–68. *See also* Army; Assizes;
Sidmouth
Revolution, 117–18, 119–21; Luddism as
symbol of, 138, 157–62, 165, 170; threat
of, 122, 268
Reykjavik, 249
Ricardo, David, 51, 199
Rifkin, Jeremy, 240, 254
Rights of Man, The (Paine), 120
Riots, 114–16, 130–39; forces used against,
137
Rizvanov, Dr. Felix, 259
Roach, Stephen, 223
Roberson, The Reverend Hammond, 14
Robertstown, 14
Robin Hood, 1–4, 6, 81–82, 87
Rochdale, 118; political agitations in, 121;
rioting in, 135
Romanticism, 17
Roszak, Theodore, 240
Rotherham, 175
Royal Dutch Shell, 222
Royal Horse Guards Blue, 83
Ruddington, 92

Rude, George, 148n
Ruskin, John, 17
Russia, 42, 173, 217, 259, 268
Rust, John and Mack, 215n
Ryder, Richard, 83, 84, 147–48

Sabotage, 18, 105–6; against the new tech-
    nology, 250. *See also* Ecotage; Machine
    breaking
Saddleworth, 136
St. Crispin Inn, 122, 182
Salford, 121n; use of force in, 149
Savio, Mario, 270
Scandinavia, 243, 250, 253, 254–55
Schofield, Mr., 116
Schumacher, E. F., 240, 276
Scientific American, 215n
Scotland, 118, 119, 171, 189; conditions in, 62
Scots Greys, 115, 132, 137, 139, 142
Scott, Sir Walter, 2, 63, 198
Sea Shepherd Conservation Society, 249
Second Industrial Revolution, 20–22,
    205–36, 237, 239, 250, 252, 261, 267–68
Sense and Sensibility (Austen), 63
Servile State, The (Belloc), 49
Sessions, George, 255
Shakespeare, 78
Sheffield, 49, 118, 121, 121n, 130–31, 157;
    food riots in, 147, 175
Shelley, Mary, 16–17
Shelley, Percy, 64, 89, 155, 183n, 198, 283
Shepard, Paul, 240–41
Shepshed, 79
Shepton Mallet, 70n
Sherwood Forest, 1–3, 2, 4, 97, 99, 103,
    129, 148, 193
Shirley (Charlotte Brontë), 15–16, 126
Shiva, Vandana, 254
Sidmouth, Viscount, 169–70, 172, 173, 175,
    178, 180, 183, 184, 189
Silesia, 18
Sinclair, Sir John, 34
Singapore, 268
Skircoats, 163
Smith, Adam, 38, 50, 51, 52
Smith, Hannah, 135
Smith, Mr. (of Hill End), 117, 158
Smith, Mr. (victim of Luddites), 110–11
Smith, Sir Sidney, 64
Smith, Thomas, 145; trial and execution of,
    178–79, 181–82
Snow, C. P., 205

Snyder, Gary, 240
Social conditions, 103–4; before Industrial
    Revolution, 35–37; during Industrial
    Revolution, 29, 31–33, 39–40; in
    Nottingham, 1811, 66
Society for a Human Economy, 255
Society for Obtaining Parliamentary
    Relief, 178
Society for Prosecuting Luddites, 150
Solomon Islands, 245
Somalia, 247
Somerset, 70n
South Africa, 41, 222
South America, 245
South Devon Militia, 92–93
Southern Agrarians, 19
Southey, Robert, 123, 155, 156
Southwell, 88
Soviet Union, 218, 240
Sowden, Joseph, 181
Spain, 250
Spengler, Oswald, 19
Spies, 4, 84, 106, 109n, 121, 144, 165, 170,
    171, 174, 177, 184, 189–90, 192, 287; in
    Westhoughton attack, 140–42
Spitafields, 69
Spretnak, Charlene, 255
Staffordshire, 155
Standard of living: in industrialized coun-
    tries, 223–28, 274–75; in United King-
    dom, 36–37, 43–49, 56–57, 61–62, 91,
    104, 201–4; in United States, 216, 224,
    225–28. *See also* Poverty
Starkey, James, 172
Starkey, Joseph, 182
Steam engine, 8, 23, 27–30, 33, 113, 114,
    201–3; and pollution, 56–57
Stockport, 103, 106, 132, 134, 144, 162, 167,
    173, 175; food riot in, 168; Luddite meet-
    ing in, 169n; machine breaking in, 113,
    114; oathing in, 109n; political agitations
    in, 121; riot in, 131–34
Stones, John, 141–43
Strasbourg, 244
Strategic Defense Initiative, 243
Sturt, George, 35, 36, 39
Sunday Times, 205
Sutton, 73, 92, 102; machine breaking in,
    76
Sydney, 169n
Sykes, Mrs., 132
Syndicalism, 18

Tasmania, 103
Tate, Allen, 19
Taylor, Dr. Robert, 143
Taylor, Enoch, 145
Technology: in early Industrial Revolution, 27–33; effects of Luddism on, 194, 198–201; imposition of, 208–13; intrinsic aspect of, 256–57
Technopoly (Postman), 273
Television, 217, 238
Temple, Katharine, 258
Temples, John, 168
Ten-Hours Movement, 194–95
Textile industry, 52, 62, 65, 65–69, 121–22; impact of technology on, 30, 194
Thailand, 246
Thames, 57–58
Thomas, Earl of Lancaster, 1
Thomas, Keith, 55
Thomis, Malcolm, 68n
Thompson, E. P., 27, 38, 75, 108, 121, 130, 148n, 158, 196, 199, 202, 287
Thompson, Joseph, 132, 168
Thompson, Justice Baron Alexander, 166, 180, 182, 183
Thompson, William, 104, 111
Thoreau, Henry David, 17, 273
Thorpe, William, 145; trial and execution of, 178–79, 181–82
Tillotson, 164
Time, 227, 251
Tintwhistle: rioting in, 135
Todmorden, 47
Towle, James, 188
Toynbee, Arnold, 27
Trade Union Acts, 194
Trentham, William, 144–45, 151
Tunbridge Wells, 61
Turner, J. M. W., 156n, 283
Turton, 47

Union for Parliamentary Reform, 176
Union of Concerned Scientists (U.S.), 229
Unions, 52, 187; effects of Luddism on, 192–93, 194–95; in Europe and Australia, 252; in the United States, 250–52
United Kingdom, 18, 55, 59, 61, 71, 282–83; conditions in, 32, 202; crime in, 144; economic conditions in, 5; and the European Union, 243; exports of, 41–42; forests in, 54; industrialism in, 16, 26, 27, 29, 33, 44, 50, 53, 126, 195; labor in, 52; militia in, 73, 83; Neo-Luddism in, 253; population of, 39, 43; revolution in, 156; setting for Luddism, 3; society of, 191; technology in, 225; textile industry, 2; trade with U.S., 62, 173; use of force in, 149; violence in, 194; and war, 63
United Nations, 272
United States, 18, 41, 206, 207, 218–19, 219–21, 224, 225, 226, 227, 228, 230, 234, 241, 242, 243, 244, 245, 259, 283; advertising in, 216–17; agriculture in, 19, 214–16, 262–63; industrialism in, 18, 29; longevity in, 275; Neo-Luddism in, 250–52, 253, 271; new technology in, 20; 1960s in, 161n; trade with United Kingdom, 62, 173; war with Britain, 91
Ure, Andrew, 31–32, 33, 198, 262, 287
Uruguay, 244

Vancouver, Charles, 54
Vandenberg Air Force Base, 242
Veblen, Thorstein, 19
Vietnam War, 218
Vonnegut, Kurt, 240
von Neumann, John, 59, 232

Wakefield, 1, 9, 112n, 118, 121n, 193; machine breaking in, 162
Wales, 48, 54
Walker, Benjamin, 145, 178–79, 181, 184
Walker, John, 12, 182
Walker, Mrs. (Benjamin's mother), 178
Walker, William, 135
Waplington, 94–95
Warfare, 50, 61–62, 93, 218–19, 220–21
Warminster, 70n
War of 1812, 91, 173
Warren, Robert Penn, 19
Warrington, 121n
Washington Post, The, 250–51
Watch-and-Ward battalions, 150
Watson, Paul, 249
Watt, James, 29
Watt and Boulton shop, 27–28
Weber, Max, 19
Weisenbaum, Joseph, 258
Wellington, Duke of, 4, 43, 148
West Country, 70n
Westgate, 112n

Westhoughton, 166–67, 194; machine breaking in, 140–44, 161

West Indies, 41

Westley, John, 71–72, 73, 83

Westminster, 158

West Riding, 23, 75–76, 110, 125, 130, 148, 151, 158, 165, 184, 193; arms thefts in, 162–63; conditions in, 202; Luddites in, 104; machine breaking in, 163, 175; use of force in, 149, 150; valuation of damage in, 192

When Technology Wounds (Glendinning), 238

Whittaker, Thomas, 168–69

Wiener, Norbert, 28

Wigan, 70n

Wild Earth, 256

Wiltshire, 70n

Windsor Forest, 54

Winner, Langdon, 240

Wired, 207

Wobblies, 18

Women: before Industrial Revolution, 36; in Industrial Revolution, 33, 47, 202; rioting of, 134–35

Wood, John, 145, 178

Wood, Sir Francis, 157

Wordsworth, William, 17, 24, 27, 40, 46, 54, 265, 288

World Bank, 218, 222–23, 245

World Trade Organization, 222

World War I, 17

World War II, 206, 215n, 220, 233, 234, 262

Worldwatch Institute, 219, 231

Wroe and Duncroft attack, 140–44

Xerox, 227

Yarmouth, 61

York, 121n, 125; assizes in, 167, 174, 175, 179, 180–83, 183, 184, 190, 267

York, the Duchess of, 86

Yorkshire, 1, 6n, 16, 21, 23, 37–38, 45, 49, 70, 104, 105, 106, 110, 112, 116, 121, 122, 127, 157, 163, 165, 171, 183, 189, 193, 282–83; machine breaking in, 7–15, 75, 162; oathing in, 109; valuation of damage in, 192n

Young, Arthur, 35

Young, Stark, 19

Zapatista rebellion, 247–48

Zerzan, John, 240